D1173843

ALSO BY ALICE SPARBERG ALEXIOU

Jane Jacobs: Urban Visionary

The FLATIRON

The New York Landmark
and the
Incomparable City
That Arose with It

ALICE SPARBERG ALEXIOU

THOMAS DUNNE BOOKS
St. Martin's Press
New York

THOMAS DUNNE BOOKS.
An imprint of St. Martin's Press.

THE FLATIRON. Copyright © 2010 by Alice Sparberg Alexiou. All rights reserved.
Printed in the United States of America. For information, address
St. Martin's Press, 175 Fifth Avenue, New York, N.Y. 10010.

www.thomasdunnebooks.com
www.stmartins.com

Book design by Phil Mazzone

Library of Congress Cataloging-in-Publication Data

Alexiou, Alice Sparberg, 1951–
    The Flatiron : the New York landmark and the incomparable city that arose with it /
Alice Sparberg Alexiou.
        p. cm.
    Includes bibliographical references and index.
    ISBN 978-0-312-38468-5 (alk. paper)
    1. Flatiron Building (New York, N.Y.)—History. 2. New York (N.Y.)—Buildings, struc-
tures, etc. 3. Office buildings—New York (State)—New York—Design and construction—
History—19th century. 4. Architecture—New York (State)—New York—History—19th
century. 5. Technological innovations—Social aspects—New York (State)—New York—
History—19th century. 6. New York (N.Y.)—History—1865–1898. 7. New York (N.Y.)—
Social life and customs—19th century. 8. City and town life—New York (State)—New
York—History—19th century. 9. New York (N.Y.)—Biography. I. Title.
    F128.8.F55A44 2010
    974.7'03—dc22

                                                                                2009045771

First Edition: June 2010

10 9 8 7 6 5 4 3 2 1

To my grandfather, Abraham Braun

CONTENTS

Contents

LIST OF ILLUSTRATIONS

List of Illustrations

List of Illustrations

ACKNOWLEDGMENTS

WRITING REQUIRES SOLITUDE, BUT no book comes together without the expertise and support of others. I am grateful to acknowledge the many people who helped me along the way.

First off, I thank Wendy Schmalz, my agent and friend, who is one of the finest people in the universe. I also thank Peter Joseph, my editor at Thomas Dunne Books, who was involved with every phase of this project. He was a joy to work with. So many times, his quick insights and eye for detail nudged me past those ruts that all writers get stuck in. Thank you as well to editorial assistant Margaret Smith.

Melanie James, librarian at the General Society of Mechanics and Tradesmen in New York; Janet Wells Greene, the library's former director; and Leonora Gidlund, director of the New York City Municipal Archives, helped me track down photos and documents. So did staff at the New York Public Library, the New York Historical Society, the Library of Congress, the Ryerson and Burnham Library of the Art Institute of Chicago, the Saratoga Historical Society, the Preservation Society of Newport County, and the Newport Historical Society. There are too many to name individually, but know that your work as librarians and archivists is much appreciated. Without you, history could not be written.

As *The Flatiron* took shape, questions of all sorts kept popping up. Gail Fenske, author of a recent book on the Woolworth Building, helped me locate evidence of Cass Gilbert's animus toward Harry Black. Historian and author Donald Miller, who knows more about Chicago than anybody on earth, helped me with research about that city. A special thank-you to fellow author Jim Rasenberger, who shared his sources on Sam Parks with me. Christopher Gray, who writes the "Streetscapes" column for *The New York Times,* confirmed that the original Flatiron blueprints are, alas, missing. Tony Robbins described for me the Flatiron Building from an architectural historian's perspective, and also clarified the meaning of that elusive term "Beaux-Arts." Carol Willis, director of the Skyscraper Museum in lower Manhattan, shared pages of Paul Starrett's notebooks with me, and also answered numerous skyscraper-related questions. She also ensures that new books on architecture and cities get maximum exposure at the museum's book and lecture series. She is the best friend an author can have, and I thank her for all her support, both for me and my fellow writers.

Dorothy Globus, curator at the Museum of Arts and Design in New York, has the world's best collection of Flatiron paraphernalia, and she graciously invited me into her home to view it. Miriam Berman, a graphic artist and grassroots restoration activist who has written the definitive book on Madison Square, helped me flesh out some of my Flatiron-related ideas. She is a colleague in the best sense of the word. Thanks, Miriam.

Charles Hobson, a documentary filmmaker, steered me to the source material on Louis Mitchell. Nancy Groce, a folklorist at the Smithsonian, helped me with the section on Tin Pan Alley. Long Island historian Robert Hughes helped me identify Harry Black's house.

My friend Chris Jensen, partner in the law firm Cowan, Liebowitz, and Latman, offered his expertise on copyright matters. Verna Shamblee, facilities director at Macmillan, who knows every nook and cranny of the Flatiron, answered some of my arcane building-related questions. Through her I learned that the staircase that had led downstairs to the Taverne Louis had been recently uncovered. Former and current Flatiron tenants sent me e-mails describing what it was like riding those old hydraulic elevators. Science-fiction writer David Kyle, who was born in 1919 and attended the Art Career School in the Flatiron penthouse during the 1930s, told me about the Chock full o'Nuts that used to be across the street from the building. Such details make a story come alive.

Jeffrey Gural and Jane Gural Senders, two of the Flatiron's current owners, made sure that I had access to the building. Sunny Atis, the building superintendent, gave me a guided tour. Engineer Steve Cohane, who worked on the building's recent exterior renovation, sat with me inside the Flatiron and answered my questions about bedrock, foundations, load, sub-basements, and wind shear. I also thank engineer Sazen Buell for helping me with the section on the Brooklyn Bridge.

To my great frustration, there were scant print sources for many of the characters in *The Flatiron*. In my quest to fill in their stories, I tracked down distant relatives of Isabelle May, Harry Black's second wife, and descendants of Corydon Purdy and Paul Starrett. All of them—Jacqueline Childs, Bill Ewing, Daniel Starrett, and Corydon Purdy III—were eager to share with me whatever they knew, and I appreciate their generosity. I particularly want to thank Corydon Purdy III, who sent me photos of his grandfather.

I often discussed my work-in-progress with a group of writers, all alumni of Samuel Freedman's book seminar at the Columbia University School of Journalism. Their input really helped, and I thank them, especially Harry Bruinius, who hosted our meetings at his writers space, the Village Quill. I miss those lively book discussions.

Every day, my friend and confidante, the writer Roberta Israeloff, helps me figure everything out.

Acknowledgments

I thank my mother, Esther Braun Sparberg, my sons, Alex and Joseph Alexiou, and my daughter-in-law Ayse Asatekin Alexiou, for all their love, and their enthusiasm over *The Flatiron*. This is, indeed, a family story. Special mention to Joseph for the photos he took. Also to Ayse, a chemical engineer, who explained to me all about steel, load, and stress.

My husband, Nicholas Alexiou, the smartest, most cosmopolitan person I've ever met, came to New York from Greece in 1967, when he was eighteen. From Nick, I have learned an immigrant's perspective of my native city. He loves New York for the same reason as did my grandfather, Abraham Braun, who arrived here in 1914 from Transylvania. New York gave both men opportunities that would have been unthinkable, had they stayed in their respective native lands. For Nick, the story of the Flatiron, and its associations with my grandfather, evokes strong emotions. He has lived this book project with me—offering feedback, love, encouragement, and solitude, in exactly the doses I've needed. He completely *gets* me, and puts up with me. I couldn't have written this book without him, and I mean it.

Finally, I thank my grandfather, Abraham Braun, whom I never met. He connected me and my family to the Flatiron Building, and I dedicate this book to him.

PROLOGUE

$\mathcal{O}$NCE UPON A TIME, the Flatiron Building was a member of my family. My maternal grandfather, Abraham Braun, along with three others, one of them a hungry young man named Harry Helmsley, purchased it from the Equitable Life Assurance Society in 1946. My grandfather died soon after, in January 1947, four and a half years before I was born. He was fifty-three. Those who knew him spoke of him with admiration. His two daughters adored him. He was a Hungarian Jew from Transylvania, who arrived in America when he was nineteen years old. Upon landing in New York, the young immigrant found opportunity everywhere. At various times, he built garages; bought and rented out two-family homes; manufactured buttons, dresser sets, and pocketbooks; and was in the wholesale grocery business. He married my grandmother, Sarah Kurnick, a Polish Jew, in 1921. During the Depression, he lost everything. But by the late Thirties, he was solvent again. He began buying real estate, a little at a time, in partnerships with friends, putting up whatever cash he could scrape together, and using his previously purchased and heavily mortgaged properties as collateral. By the early 1940s, his investments were making enough money to send each of his daughters to college. He insisted they attend universities outside of New York—my aunt attended the University of Wisconsin, my mother, the University of North Carolina at Chapel Hill—and study something practical. (My mother majored in chemistry, and became a professor.) All women, he told them, should have a career. They should not depend solely on their husbands. Hardly the typical advice a father gave his daughters in those days.

My grandfather, Helmsley, and their two additional partners paid $1,050,000 for the Flatiron Building. The four men together put $30,000 down on the purchase price. Equitable Life gave them a mortgage for the balance at a rate of 3 percent. The price was quite a bargain. The Flatiron had cost $2 million to build, in 1902. But in the aftermath of the Second World War, the economy was in recession, and real estate prices were depressed.

The central story of the Flatiron begins in the late nineteenth century, and concludes at the start of the Great Depression. In between, a lot of people in America got very, very rich. They parked their capital in New York, where everything was for sale, especially land—any piece of land—no matter how small.

When the Flatiron was erected—on what seemed an impossibly tiny, narrow triangle in the middle of an intersection—New York was in the midst of a huge construction boom. Speculators were tearing down the ubiquitous four- and five-story brownstones and wooden houses, replacing them with those newfangled structures called skyscrapers.

It is often claimed, incorrectly, that the Flatiron was the city's first skyscraper, or its first steel-frame building. But what is true is that even before this oddly shaped skyscraper was completed, people couldn't stop talking about it. And since its completion, artists famous and obscure have painted, sketched, and photographed the building, from all different angles. And from each angle, it looks different. Perhaps this is the reason people loved, and continue to love the Flatiron. Although when it was new, and the talk of the town, critics hated it.

By the time my grandfather and his partners acquired the Flatiron, it had long lost its glamour. Layers of soot marred its beautiful terra-cotta facade, and a Walgreens drugstore occupied the building's retail space at the northern corner. Across the street, once-glamorous Madison Square Park was the domain of bums. Cheap retail establishments lined the avenues. On the side streets, lofts still housed light manufacturing—my grandfather had a button factory at 26 West 17 Street.

But even in its shabby state, the image of the Flatiron remained familiar all over the world.

My grandfather's portion of the Flatiron remained in my family for fifty years. I love it so much. To me, this building embodies the very essence of our city. And for me it is something intensely personal. The Flatiron connects me to the grandfather I never knew, and yet passionately admired.

His was the quintessential New York story, of the immigrant who came from nothing, and made good. What little I know about his life I gleaned from archival tidbits, or heard from my mother. But she, as the children of struggling immigrants of her generation were wont to do, never dared to ask him the questions for which I, his granddaughter, now long to hear the answers. Abraham Braun landed at Ellis Island on January 1, 1914, along with his cousin, Andor Weisz. The two had crossed the Atlantic in the steerage of a ship that had left from Hamburg. The manifest indicates that Abe had paid for his ticket himself, and had perhaps $25—it is impossible to make out the exact amount—in his pocket.

He came from Nagyvárad, a city in Transylvania with a sizable Jewish population. Later, he would tell my mother that his own mother had smoked a pipe, and doted on him, the youngest of her four children. She died when Abraham was still a child. By the time he was a teenager, he was working in a celluloid plastics factory. One of his sisters was sent out to work as a maid when she was so young that she never went to school. She remained illiterate all of her life. Abraham could read—my mother says that he read voraciously, especially newspapers—but he couldn't write, except to scrawl his name on the bottom of a check, or to sign off on a letter. So perhaps he never went to school, either. But he taught himself things that he wanted to know. My mother remembers that when she was in high school, he used to help her with her physics homework. He had, she said, an instinctive knowledge of how machines worked. Thanks to his encouragement, my mother later became a chemistry professor.

The manufacture of celluloid plastics uses highly flammable and toxic chemicals. One day, an explosion rocked the factory where my grandfather, then fourteen, was working. He was seriously injured. As a result, one leg shriveled to several inches shorter than the other. For the rest of his life, he walked with a pronounced limp. Yet whoever filled out the ship's manifest had written "no" in the column headed "Deformed or crippled?" How I would love to know why! Had the official been too harried to notice my grandfather's handicap? Or did my grandfather somehow convince him to write that "no"? Whatever the reason, the "no" saved Abraham Braun from being sent back to Europe, along with others on board who showed signs of disease or mental feebleness, which disqualified them from entering the United States. Had he returned to Nagyvárad, he would almost certainly have been deported to Auschwitz along with the rest of the city's Jewish population, during the summer of 1944.

But he was lucky. He hunkered down in New York, worked hard, and had a family. His descendants—my mother, my brother and myself, his children and mine—are third- and fourth-generation New Yorkers. New York is filled with families like mine, the descendants of the millions of immigrants who arrived here in the late nineteenth and early twentieth centuries, and transformed the city into the New York we know today, a place that continues to thrive and grow, thanks to the immigrants who have never stopped coming here. Each new wave of foreigners reshapes the city a bit, in their own image, as they reinvent themselves, seeking a better life through hard work. For me, the Flatiron's story is my grandfather's story, but it is also something larger. It is the story of New York.

CHAPTER ONE

GEORGE ALLON FULLER

In 1876, TWENTY-FIVE-YEAR-OLD GEORGE Allon Fuller arrived in New York with his pregnant wife, Ellen, and their three-year-old-daughter Grace. He was tall and lean, with a high forehead, and a long, jutting jaw. His heavy black eyebrows, veering down over piercing dark eyes, gave his face a permanent scowl, indicating the intense nature of his character.

George Allon Fuller, undated.

After studying architecture at the Massachusetts Institute of Technology, he had joined the firm of Robert Swain Peabody and John G. Stearns soon after the pair had started it, in 1872. Peabody and Stearns designed and built palatial residences in Newport, Rhode Island, and other favorite locales of America's fabulously wealthy. Fuller worked as their chief draftsman, a task that Peabody, who had studied at the École des Beaux-Arts in Paris, considered crucial. "Sketch, sketch!" he often told Fuller. "And if you can't find anything else to sketch, sketch your boots!"

Fuller worked on everything from fussy Victorian interiors to designing building frames. It was the physical aspect of erecting buildings that fascinated him. After long days at his office spent standing over his drawing board, he went home at night and unwound by working on a two-story wooden apartment house that he was building himself. Occasionally he varied his routine by attending a Gilbert and Sullivan performance. He loved their music, and often sang bits from their operas to himself as he worked.

Fuller's work, and his work ethic, impressed his bosses immensely. Their firm was doing well, so well that they made him a partner. And now they were putting him in charge of their New York office. What a coup this was for the young man, to be practicing his profession in the world's fastest-growing city, where everybody, and everybody's money, was heading. Since the end of the Civil War, land values had been constantly escalating, and, most people believed, always would. However, the severe economic depression brought on by the panic of 1873 had lately caused the market to cool down considerably. Still, construction activity was continuing. And some of the new buildings rose nine or ten stories, heights never before imaginable, but now made possible by Elijah Otis's recent invention, the elevator.

Owners were willing to build high because land costs were so high; tall buildings would maximize the return on their investments. Down in the financial district at Manhattan's southern tip, and a short walk from Fuller's new office at 21 Cortlandt, stood the 230-foot-tall Western Union Telegraph Company's new headquarters, completed in 1875. The Western Union Building was at Broadway and Dey. Nearby, on Newspaper Row, next to City Hall Park, was Richard Morris Hunt's ten-story Tribune Building, which housed Horace Greeley's influential newspaper. The "Trib" Building, also completed in 1875, measured 260 feet high, almost as high as the city's tallest structure, which, appropriately enough, was a house of worship, the 284-foot Trinity Church. Built in 1846 by Richard Upjohn, Trinity Church would remain New York's tallest building until 1890, when it would cede its place to George B. Post's massive Pulitzer Building. With its dome, the Pulitzer Building would measure over 300 feet high.

The new, tall buildings threw shadows on the street, and dwarfed the neighboring structures, which at the most had four or five stories— as that is how many stair flights a person could be reasonably expected to climb. Architects hated the tall buildings, and the man on the street feared them. "Some structures have been run up to so great a height that the thoughtful passerby feels apprehensive of his security while in their vicinity," *The Phrenological Journal and Science of Health* reported in 1874.

But not Fuller. The tall buildings thrilled him. He loved the materials that held everything together: the brick and timber and, especially, the iron beams and columns. He also loved the machines used in constructing them. And he had no interest in what chiefly obsessed his colleagues—the aesthetics of exterior building design. For inspiration, they looked to the old world. Victorian Gothic, French Academic, and Queen Anne were just some of the styles that Peabody and Stearns were incorporating into their buildings. But why, Fuller thought, use the past as a basis for new structures? Especially here in America, where everything looked toward the future?

The problem of *load*—that is, what supports the weight of a structure's bricks, beams, walls, windows, roof (*dead load*), along with the people and objects inside it (*live load*)—especially intrigued Fuller. New York was the first city in the United States to have laws regulating how buildings could be constructed, altered, or demolished. Such laws were first passed in 1860. They were badly needed: the value of New York real estate was rising, but the only construction regulations on the books concerned preventing the building of wood-frame structures downtown, because of the fire hazard. The new laws created the city's first Buildings Department. Up to then, building inspections were carried out by local fire wardens, who had highly discretionary powers, and, therefore, were easily bribed.

New York's first building code included strict rules mandating the thickness of a structure's supporting walls. The taller the structure, the thicker the walls had to be. And now, in the 1870s, as buildings were rising higher, the walls had to be made so thick in order to conform to code that they were eating up nearly half of the ground-floor space, and much of the offices on the floors above, although less so as they were built higher, until, typically, by the top floor, the walls were fully one-half as thick as on the ground. All of which translated into a lot of wasted space, and therefore less rental income for the owner. The Tribune Building's walls at grade level, for example, were made of brick and measured more than five feet deep. Moreover, the wall requirement resulted in tall buildings that appeared clunky and awkward, without what architects today call *verticality*.

But brick or stone walls were not the only possible means to carry load. You could also incorporate iron as a supplement, something the Greeks were already doing thousands of years earlier, when they inserted wrought-iron bars inside the marble columns of their temples. But the use of structural iron did not significantly progress beyond what the ancient Greeks had done until the eighteenth century, when the English began experimenting with iron framing in industrial buildings.

In the United States, builders first began using iron in the form of columns and beams in the 1820s. By the 1840s, cast-iron fronts had become all the rage in New York's commercial buildings, such as the department stores located in an area called "Ladies' Mile," between Fourteenth and Twenty-third Streets along Broadway and Fifth Avenue.

Cast iron was light, strong, and durable. And it didn't burn, so it was thought to be ideal. That is, until Chicago's "Great Fire" of 1871 proved that cast iron melted under extreme heat, as described in the 1898 *History of Real Estate, Building, and Architecture in New York:* "Entire building fronts expanded and buckled and fell into the street from the effects of the intense heat radiating from burning buildings on the opposite side of the street, before their combustible interiors had taken fire." So during the 1870s, the cast-iron front fell out of favor. Architects were now making their commercial building fronts all-brick, except for the first story, where often they placed vertical cast-iron columns. Often they also placed such columns in a building's interiors, where they not only added visual interest, but functioned as additional load support. Architects also incorporated horizontal wrought-iron beams into building frames, to help support the floors.

As Fuller embarked on his architectural career in New York, he was probably wondering why even more iron wasn't being incorporated into building design. Perhaps you could rest a building's entire load on an iron frame; that way, you could eliminate the space-wasting masonry walls, and build high, even higher than Trinity Church. Obsessed with such engineering questions, Fuller fiddled around with calculations and built models.

He also forced himself to settle into the considerable work his Boston partners had given him immediately upon his arrival in New York. The firm had just received a plum assignment, and one that Fuller surely hated: to submit a design for the new Union League Club House, at the corner of Fifth Avenue and Thirty-ninth Street. Despite his antipathy, Fuller's drawing—a Queen Anne-style mansion of brick and Belleville stone—won out over eight other competitors. They included Richard Morris Hunt, who had designed the Tribune Building, and Charles McKim in collaboration with William Mead, both of whom later, with Stanford White, would found one of America's most influential architecture firms. At the same time Fuller worked on another commission that was somewhat of a consolation, the United Bank Building, at the northeast corner of Wall Street and Broadway. Fuller designed a nine-story building of brick and brownstone, with cast-iron columns on the bottom story. Perhaps he even suggested to his partners that they try substituting steel for some of the iron in the framing; that way, he would have argued, the building wouldn't need such thick walls. But they would have surely refused. They would have pointed out to Fuller that reducing the walls' breadth would have required special permission from the Buildings Department in the form of a variance. And besides, nobody at that time was using steel in building construction. Not only was steel far more expensive than iron, but it was also feared that steel was not safe, that it wasn't as strong as iron.

But Fuller thought such fears irrational. Steel was in fact stronger and more flexible than iron, so much so that steel was now replacing iron in the manufacture of T-rails for railroad ties. The results were so excellent that the old iron rails, always breaking and needing replacement, were becoming obsolete. So, Fuller no doubt was thinking, why not also use steel in buildings? And there was yet another reason to do this: steel manufacturing, up to now almost exclusive to England, was now booming in America, in part because Congress had imposed a heavy tariff on imports in 1870. So really, there was no reason not to use steel in building construction, save one: most people's tendency to instantly dismiss any new idea, and instead cling to what, no matter how bad, they know.

In fact, the so-called "East River bridge"—that would later be renamed the Brooklyn Bridge—was using steel, not iron, the usual material up to then for bridges, for its suspension cables. Fuller's office was located just a few short blocks from the riverbank. No doubt he walked down there often, to observe as the bridge's four huge, heavy cables were being spun right on the site. The newspaper *Brooklyn Eagle* likened the construction process to "a giant spinning machine." Into each cable went 600 one-eighth-inch-diameter threads of galvanized steel wire, so tightly bound that you couldn't fit a needle in between. The wire—3,400 miles worth, to be precise—had been manufactured to specification, and carefully tested before it left the factory to verify what the bridge engineers' careful calculations had showed: that the steel wire would support six times the bridge's actual load. The wire had been delivered from the factory in coils, each a few hundred feet long. When unrolled, it lay straight, with no kinks.

The spinning process started in a huge shed that sat on top of the Brooklyn anchorage. Inside, workers were dipping each coil into a vat of boiling linseed oil, which protected the steel wire from rusting. Then the coils were hung up on hooks. When the coils were dry, the process was repeated. Finally, each coil was straightened out into one long steel wire, to receive yet a third coat of oil that a worker rubbed in with his hands. He then spliced the wire with another already oiled wire by means of a special coupling machine, thereby forming one continuous length of wire that was next spooled onto a ten-foot-diameter wooden drum, from which, through a complicated process involving wheels, derricks, and castings, it was strung clear across the river. This process would be repeated 299 more times, before workmen, either standing atop one or another of the bridge's two massive granite towers, each measuring nearly 277 feet high, or inside "cradles"—narrow wooden platforms hanging at intervals on wires stretched above the river—gathered the 300 wires needed to form a single strand. The wires had to lie absolutely straight; any twisting would weaken them. Twenty strands were then gathered together to form each of the four cables, which then, by a special machine, was covered with wire wrapping. And now, a reporter for *Appleton's Journal* wrote in 1878, the cables "will be ready for a few centuries, let us hope, to take the responsibility of trans-fluvial communication between New York and Brooklyn."

Most of the bridge workers were sailors, used to working at sea and scaling terrifying heights. They gained access to the cradles via a temporary foot path made of wooden slats four feet wide that stretched from anchorage to anchorage, and in between angled steeply up to each of the towers. Soon after the paths were erected, people began to venture out on them, a pastime that became so popular that the bridge company had to give out permits. Even if you only made it up to one of the towers, you were rewarded with a spectacular and formerly unattainable view. Up to then, only birds could see New York from above. Now, from the Brooklyn side, you could see clear across the tip of Manhattan, all the way to New Jersey.

Fuller probably was among those who climbed the foot path up to the tower, and then clear across the river, along the way observing the bridge workers up close as they bound the thousands of individual wires, which together would be able to support a load of up to 49,200 tons.

In 1880, after spending four years in New York with Peabody and Stearns, Fuller decided that he had had enough of them and their antiquated ways. He left New York just as work on the United Bank Building was beginning. With his wife, Ellen, and their two daughters, Allon and Grace, ages three and seven, Fuller, now twenty-nine years old, boarded a train and went to Chicago. There, he entered into a partnership with another Boston architect, a man named C. Everett Clark.

Fifty years earlier Chicago had not even been a city, but just a stinking fur-trading post, its only structures log cabins and taverns. But now it was an industrial powerhouse, and growing faster than any city in the world, even faster than mighty, snooty New York. So if you were looking to make money, Chicago was the place to go. Especially if your business had anything to do with construction, because in 1871, nine years before Fuller's arrival, on a hot, windy October night, the entire city, then consisting mostly of low wooden buildings, had burned down. The Great Fire, as it came to be called, was one of the worst urban disasters ever. It had reduced Chicago to mud and ashes, and created all kinds of opportunities for architects.

William Le Baron Jenney, Louis Sullivan and Dankmar Adler, Daniel Burnham and John Root were some of the men remaking the city. Except for Jenney—who had served as an engineer in the Union army during the Civil War, and afterward gone to Chicago, where he opened an architectural office—all were young, at the most in their thirties. Sullivan, describing Chicago in 1873, the year of his arrival there, wrote: "The sense of ruin was . . . blended with ambition of recovery." Chicago was, Sullivan would later write in his *Autobiography of an Idea,* "magnificent and wild: A crude extravaganza: An intoxicating rawness: A sense of big things to be done. For 'Big' was the word. 'Biggest' was preferred, and the 'the biggest in the world' was the braggart phrase on every tongue. Chicago had the biggest conflagration 'in the world.' It was the biggest grain and lumber market 'in the world.' It slaughtered more hogs than any city 'in the world.' It was the greatest railroad center, the greatest this, the greatest that." No doubt about it, Fuller had come to the right place. Chicago needed rebuilding, and also *to be invented.* The city had virtually no past, architectural or otherwise. But now, the convergence of catastrophe, capitalism, and the talents of young Americans were encouraging new architecture styles and new ways of building, all distinctly American. And there was something else: Chicago had far fewer building regulations than New York. Here, the law didn't force you to use thick walls to support the weight of a high building. In Chicago, you could experiment.

Fuller's ambitions soon overwhelmed Clark. After two years, the men dissolved their partnership. Fuller then raised $50,000, equivalent to about $1 million in today's money—how exactly he got the money is not known—and set up his own company. The year was 1882, and Chicago was now filled with architecture firms. One of the first had been William Le Baron Jenney's, established in 1867. There Jenney had trained many of Chicago's brilliant young architects, who were now striking out on their own. Jenney's protégés included Louis Sullivan, now a partner in the firm of Dankmar Adler; Daniel Burnham, who had opened an office in 1873 with John Root; and the team of William Holabird and

Martin Roche, who had just started their architecture practice the previous year, in 1881.

But there was something different about Fuller's company. At that time, to be an architect meant that you were also de facto a builder and engineer. Architectural firms handled every aspect of building, from making the first sketches to supervising construction. But the new Fuller Company would handle only the construction aspect of buildings, designed by architects who came from elsewhere, because the firm would not employ any architects. Let somebody else, Fuller thought, do design. This was a radical idea.

And it was a brilliant one.

Fuller's timing was perfect. During 1882, the Fuller Company's first year of operation, the number of buildings constructed in Chicago reached a record high—3,113, to be exact. One of Fuller's first commissions was the Chicago Opera House, at the corner of Washington and Clark. He worked with architects Henry Ives Cobb and Charles S. Frost, who designed a gorgeous building, with floor-to-ceiling windows in the front. Along with the theater, the Opera House also contained a block of offices. Its load was carried in the traditional way, on masonry walls.

But Fuller did something daring: the floor beams were made of steel. This was the first time that anybody had used steel in buildings, even though its cost was dropping, due to the ever-increasing amounts being produced in the United States. Even in Chicago, a place known for taking risks, many architects were still afraid of steel.

Critics were now calling Fuller a capricious fool. He in turn called them Luddites, and began incorporating more and more steel in his buildings. He worked obsessively, juggling multiple projects that constantly overlapped. His workload would have killed some men. The pressure only made him thrive, and work harder. With each project, Fuller used more and more steel.

With Holabird & Roche, Fuller built the twelve-story Tacoma Building, which was completed in 1889; immediately afterward, the three also collaborated on the fourteen-story Pontiac Building, and a portion of the Monadnock Building. He constructed an earlier portion of the Monadnock with architect John Root. Fuller also built the ten-story Rand McNally Building with Root along with Root's partner, Daniel Burnham. Just how far Fuller was ahead of his time is evident by what *American Architect and Building News* had to say about the use of structural steel in 1889, as the Fuller Company was finishing construction on the Tacoma Building:

> Very little is really known today of the properties of steel and new facts are coming to light every day . . . and though events point strongly to steel becoming the metal of the near future, there exists among many reasonably conservative men, a wide and well-grounded distrust of its use in the higher engineer or architectural structures, on account of its mysterious behavior, and frequent erratic and inexplicable failures.

Monadnock Building, Chicago, undated.

The following year, 1890, the Fuller Company completed the Rand McNally Building, the first ever that was completely supported by an all-steel skeleton.

The Fuller Company was coordinating every aspect of building construction, from the choosing and purchasing of an appropriate site, to the buying and transporting of vast amounts of steel and brick and limestone, to hiring and overseeing the growing number of professionals and workers needed to build these tall structures. You needed architects and engineers, electricians and plumbers, stone carvers and brick masons, glaziers and iron and steel workers. You needed lawyers to draw up contracts. You needed to control costs, especially since most of these new structures were built on speculation, and financed by investors interested far more in their building's potential return on the dollar than the design. You had to deal with labor unions, which was becoming increasingly difficult. You had to wrestle down all these interests, many of them in direct conflict with each other, make them cooperate, and—perhaps the most difficult task of all—make them adhere to a timetable. Operating on such a huge scale, previously unimaginable, Fuller's firm by necessity delegated every task concerned with erecting a building to a smaller contractor. This, another of Fuller's revolutionary methods, later became standard in the building industry. It is called *general contracting.*

By 1891, the Fuller Company had contracts totaling over $8 million in Chicago alone, and was also building all over the United States. George Fuller was now a millionaire. The social activities of his wife and daughters were duly reported in the society pages.

Fuller then hired the architect Charles Frost, who had worked with him on the Opera House, to design a grand house commensurate with his social position. In 1882, Frost, along with architect Henry Ives Cobb, had literally created a castle on Lake Shore Drive for the real estate magnate Potter Palmer and his wife, Bertha—the doyenne of Chicago society. For Fuller, Frost designed a Queen Anne–style mansion. For his own new home, Fuller had chosen a lot along beautifully landscaped Drexel Boulevard, one of a system of thoroughfares designed by Frederick Law Olmsted. Drexel was on Chicago's South Side, where most of the millionaires lived.

Chicago's new, tall office buildings were all crowded into the "Loop," the city's half-square-mile downtown, so-called because it was encircled at first by streetcar tracks, and then the El. The buildings were like nothing anybody had seen before, and now the subject of so many conversations that calling them "tall office buildings" was beginning to feel awkward. Obviously a new word was needed. An unknown person one day hit upon the idea to describe them as "sky scrapers," a nautical term that signified the uppermost flag of a ship's mast. Some time in the 1880s, the words "sky scraper" began to appear in print to denote these buildings.

People gasped at the sight of the skyscrapers. They waited for them to collapse, but none did. Critics denounced what they considered the sheer ugliness of the new buildings. There was no possible way, they shouted, for skyscrapers to be made beautiful. Journalists decried these modern buildings that were now reaching up to the skies, like cathedrals, but for the worst possible reason: profit. Greed alone, the critics shouted, was the impetus behind them. Money had erected them, and their only purpose was to enable the men who had invested in them to make even more money.

"Nowhere is the naïf belief that a man may do as he likes with his own held more contentiously than in our astounding and repelling region of 'sky-scrapers,'" wrote journalist Henry W. Fuller (no relation to George) in *Atlantic Monthly* in 1897, "where the abuse of private initiative, the peculiar evil of the place and the time, has reached its most monumental development." But you couldn't go back to the old ways. "In a utilitarian age like ours, it is safe to assume that investors will continue to erect the class of buildings from which the greatest possible revenue can be obtained with the least possible outlay," wrote the great

Dankmar Adler in an 1892 essay entitled "Tall Buildings: Past and Future." Adler, along with Louis Sullivan, had designed Chicago's gargantuan Auditorium, a combination concert hall, office building, and hotel.

For the businesses that rented office space, skyscrapers were more practical than smaller buildings. What is more, people were beginning to *like them*. The surroundings were new, and comfortable; working in an office high up provided workers with amounts of light and ventilation that they had never before imagined. Adler noted in his essay that it was much easier to transact business in a Chicago skyscraper than in London, "where the average height of buildings is scarcely four stories . . . how much time is consumed going from place to place . . . by climbing the dark, steep and crooked stairs, that are almost sure to lead into dark, dingy, dusty and unwholesome quarters." New York, he adds, is "somewhat better, although even there . . . many of the offices are in small, dark, ill-ventilated, ill-smelling, antiquated buildings with a mere apology for elevator service . . . In Chicago the erection of many 'skyscrapers' has permitted the concentration of business in so small a space that it has become as easy to transact business with twenty different persons in twenty different offices in one day as it is in London with three, or New York with ten."

By the time Adler was writing his thoughtful essay, in 1892, about two dozen skyscrapers had been erected in the Loop, some as high as sixteen stories. The buildings had striking designs: sparse and original ornamentation, and very large, sometimes horizontal windows, now possible because steel skeletons, not thick brick walls, supported building load. Skyscrapers, a new kind of building, specifically American, and used solely for commerce, America's religion, had called for a new architectural style. And now one had come into being, which people were soon calling "Chicago style." Instead of cathedrals, America had skyscrapers, and they were rising higher and higher.

The pace of skyscraper construction in Chicago was growing increasingly frantic. During a single day in December 1891, the Buildings Department approved, and immediately issued permits for five new structures, each to measure sixteen stories—at that time, the world record for building height. Up to then Chicago had imposed no limit on how high you could build your skyscraper, a fact that had clearly suited George A. Fuller and all the architects and others in the construction business that had profited in one way or another from such regulatory freedom. But now, enough people were so vociferously objecting to the ever-loftier heights attained by Chicago's skyscrapers that city council members were forced to respond.

A mixture of fear and aesthetics were behind the call for height limits. So much about these new, monstrous structures was unknown, not just to laymen but experts. Many wondered if the steel, over time, would rust. "No one knows exactly how the metal in these structures is going to behave, for the reason that such combinations have never before been exposed in the same manner to the action of the elements," wrote *American Architect and Building News* in 1889. "Some day," said a Chicago alderman, "these tall buildings will topple over or a fire will cause a great loss of life." "With these high buildings the meridian sun of an August day fails to reach the pavement, and snow-drifts will not melt until July," said another alderman. And the fact that Chicago's furious building boom had resulted in a glut of office space added additional weight to the call to set limits.

So in 1891, Chicago's real estate board appointed an ad hoc committee, which over the next year and a half worked on drafting an ordinance to regulate skyscraper heights.

In the midst of Chicago's backlash against the unchecked growth of its own marvelous creation, New York, which had been lagging behind in skyscraper design, now for the first time inserted the words "skeleton construction" into its building code. The year was 1892. The revised code also mentioned "curtain walls," that is, outer walls that carried none of the building's load, but served only as covering. The code now allowed for a reduction in thickness for curtain walls, as adverse to "bearing" walls. But it also mandated, irrationally, that curtain walls had to be thicker on the bottom. Clearly, whoever had written New York's code revisions did not fully believe that a frame made out of steel could support a building's entire weight.

When Fuller heard about New York's finally updated building regulations, he knew the time had come to open a Fuller office in the city he had abandoned twelve years earlier. He would finally be able to build skyscrapers like Chicago's sleek, steel-framed beauties in New York. No more of the old clunky monstrosities with their medieval-like walls.

But he would have to wait a bit. For now, his firm was devoting most of its time to the upcoming World's Fair that Chicago would proudly host in 1893: the Columbian Exposition—so-called because it would commemorate the four-hundredth anniversary of Columbus's discovery of America. Under an impossibly short deadline, the Fuller Company, in collaboration with Daniel Burnham, the fair's chief of construction, was now building much of the "White City on the Lake": a fantasy-land of huge, faux-classical structures that represented a complete antithesis of the skyscraper, the new form that Fuller had helped create.

CHAPTER TWO

ENO'S FLATIRON

$\mathcal{D}$ANIEL BURNHAM, WHO HAD designed many of Chicago's first skyscrapers—the Montauk Block, the Rookery, the Monadnock Building, all pristine expressions of the new, completely American architecture style—nonetheless insisted on reverting to classical motifs for the 1893 Exposition. The reasoning behind his decision was purely pragmatic: grand buildings invoking Greco-Roman antiquity were currently all the rage in eastern cities, and above all, in New York. If this was the style that now appealed to big businesses, Burnham would give it to them. He was, above all else, a businessman.

American architects were learning about classicism from the French, at the renowned École des Beaux-Arts. The term *Beaux-Arts* would come to signify the architectural style associated with the school, which often blended renaissance elements with the classical. Richard Morris Hunt was the first American to study at Beaux-Arts. Many young architects then followed. They fell in love with Paris, and swooned over its beauty. How hideous New York, with its brownstones and tenements, now seemed in comparison. "So much of Paris is beautiful," wrote a reporter in the *Real Estate Record and Builders' Guide* in 1892. "The most striking feature of old continental cities is the great cathedral rising high above every surrounding structure; the striking feature of the modern city are the high office buildings, the factories, and the smoke stacks of 1,000 furnaces." As for New York, the reporter continued, "We have no palaces, no public buildings, no great structures of any kind to which we can point with pride, or which would, as mere works of architecture, induce a traveler to spend so much as a single night with us." For all New York's spectacular ascendancy in the world, the reporter continued, its most important architectural feature was its tenements, "an architectural spectacle, and an architectural problem, which is without parallel in the great cities in the world."

But New York's architecture was changing, as American architects, smitten with Paris after studying their craft at Beaux-Arts, returned home and began re-creating the French capital in their own city. Inspired by the courtyard apartment houses he had seen in Paris, Henry Hardenbergh built the palatial Dakota in 1882; ten years later he built the ten-story Waldorf Hotel, and in 1897, the neighboring Astoria, and afterward joined the two together into one 1,000-room hotel. Other grand hotels built at that time included the Savoy, New Netherland, and McKim, Mead, and White's Plaza—all clustered at Fifty-ninth Street and Fifth Avenue. These massive structures of classical, Renaissance, or Second Empire styles—some topped with turrets, others with mansard roofs, and decorated with heavy ornamentation—recalled a glorious European past that never existed in New York, or anywhere else in America.

Still, you could say that the buildings were worthy of New York's growing importance. It was then the third-largest city in the world, after London and Paris. Immigrants from all over the world were pouring in, to start a new life. In New York, you could find work, and become rich. The ships arriving daily at New York Harbor sailed past the Statue of Liberty, France's gift to the United States in 1876 to commemorate the centennial of the Declaration of Independence. The statue, by

Frederic-Auguste Bartholdi, rested on a classically inspired base designed in 1883 by Hunt, that was one of New York's earliest examples of Beaux-Arts style. And as the base, made of brick and stone, could not alone support the statue, it rested on an iron and steel frame constructed by a French engineer named Gustave Eiffel, who, in 1858, had designed the longest iron railroad bridge in the world, across the Garonne River, near Bordeaux, and the metal-and-glass Bon Marché department store in Paris. For the 1889 Paris Exposition, Eiffel constructed a 1,000-foot steel tower on the Champ de Mars. The Tour d'Eiffel, he said, would be a secular cathedral that would celebrate France, and the Industrial Revolution as well.

Beaux-Arts architecture represented the antithesis of Chicago's raw originality. But Burnham, one of the inventors of "Chicago style" architecture, now believed that Chicago had better pay homage to New York and its architects. This was despite the fact that Congress had awarded Chicago, not uppity New York, the bid for the Exposition in 1890. Chicagoans, always resentful of New Yorkers, had felt deliriously proud of this honor. And Burnham would make damn sure that his city, which easterners castigated as "a city of pork packers," and "a purposeless Hell" would prove itself worthy, by recreating ancient Athens on the shores of Lake Michigan.

To build the White City, Burnham had at first appointed only eastern architects: New York's Charles F. McKim, Richard M. Hunt, George B. Post, and Boston's Peabody and Stearns. Frederick Law Olmsted would design an extensive system of lagoons and gardens. Only after some powerful Chicagoans angrily objected to Burnham's exclusion of local talent did he assign one building to the team of Adler and Sullivan, and another to Jenney.

Sullivan, who had studied at Beaux-Arts and completely rejected its principals, thought Burnham a crass opportunist, more interested in architecture as a business than as a craft to be executed in the name of art. Sullivan considered Burnham's plans for the White City a betrayal of artistic principals. "The damage wrought by the World's Fair will last half a century from its date, if not longer," Sullivan would later write in his *Autobiography of an Idea,* published shortly before his death in 1924. Beaux-Arts style, he wrote, is an amalgam "of every known European style, period and accident . . . Thus we have now the abounding freedom of Eclecticism, the winning smile of taste, but no architecture. For Architecture, be it known, is dead."

Sullivan died, broke, in a Chicago hotel room in 1924, forgotten by the world, a tragic scenario unfortunately common to people like him: a difficult, visionary man who alienated people, and refused to compromise his principles in exchange for wealth. Only later would Sullivan's genius as an architect and thinker be acknowledged. And while his 1924 pronouncement that architecture was "dead" was absurd, his criticism of the White City—"a naked exhibitionism of charlatanry in the higher feudal and domineering culture, conjoined with expert salesmanship of the materials of decay"—had merit.

To be sure, the masses loved the fair's colossal buildings, shaped like Greek temples and Renaissance villas, some surrounded by lofty colonnades, and set among an elaborate design of canals and gardens. They admired the fair as an engineering marvel, a wholly artificial complex constructed with the latest technology. So why, Sullivan in effect was asking, did Burnham and his architect colleagues not employ modern images that celebrated that technology, that is, allow form to follow function? Instead, they were trying to cloak modernity with "materials of decay." Not just in artistic terms, but literally: although the original White City plans had called for the usual building materials—steel, iron, brick, and stone—cost concerns had led Burnham to use *staff*—that is, a combination of gypsum and cement cut into blocks, then painted and polished to resemble marble or granite. Wooden frames covered with wire netting then held the blocks. Nobody but experts, Burnham explained to the newspapers, would be able to tell the difference between staff and the most expensive building materials.

The White City, 1893.

The technique had been used in the 1889 Paris Exposition, with great success.

But the French traveling to Chicago to see the exposition were not impressed by the White City. A French critic for the *Gazette des Beaux-Arts* called it "a colossal *fumisterie*"—the word best translates as "cop-out"—"hatched in the brain of . . . certain Barnums who sought to attract the notice of the world to the phenomenal city." Instead, European visitors swooned over the steel-framed skyscrapers that had been constructed over the previous decade, which were like nothing they had ever seen before.

It was probably just around the time of the '93 Exposition when Fuller met a man twelve years his junior named Harry St. Francis Black, in Chicago. (Although by some accounts the two first met in New York.) Black was a stocky, short man, with a big voice and a round, clean-shaven, fleshy face. His chin had a deep cleft. His sparkling blue eyes conveyed both warmth and shrewdness, and bored right through you. His straight hair was smooth and black, parted on the right, and always carefully combed. He dressed nattily, and smelled of expensive shaving cologne. The corners of his wide mouth turned up in a faint smile. People who knew him described him as impossibly charming, and ruthless.

Harry St. Francis Black, circa 1902.

Black had been born poor, in 1863, in the small town of Coburg, Ontario, the son of Major Thomas Black, a Belfast-born British army officer, Sixty-sixth Regiment. His mother, Elizabeth Wickens Black, was born in Sherbourne, England. Black doubtless began learning how to conduct business when still a child, when he worked in the local general store. Probably every item there, even the most mundane—fabric, rope, tin dishes, soap, food items, washboards, candles—intrigued him, because they were all for sale. Harry Black must have discovered right then and there that he loved everything having to do with selling.

Besides the store, Coburg didn't have much to offer young Harry. School didn't interest him. In his late teens, he left Coburg and joined an expedition party to the Pacific Northwest. For the next three years, he roamed about, and traveled up and down the coast. He made a lot of contacts. On a tip from one of them, he went to Chicago, to check out a possible business opportunity. In 1882, he landed a job as a traveling salesman for a Chicago-based wholesale woolen manufacturer. He had been assigned the entire Pacific coast as his territory. There, Black sold woolen goods for ten years so successfully that he was able to start up two banks in Washington State. After that he established two stores, both called Black & Bell, one in Tekoa, Washington, the other in Menominee, Michigan.

Black returned to Chicago some time in the early 1890s. Maybe he combined business with a visit to the World's Fair. Whatever the circumstances, the next fact we know for sure about Harry Black is that in September 1894 the newspapers announced his engagement to Allon Fuller. The bride-to-be was, said the *Chicago Tribune,* "the daughter of the big contractor."

Harry and Allon married in Chicago the following month. He was thirty-two, she, seventeen. Their wedding took place in "the French drawing room," the *Chicago Tribune* duly reported, of the beautiful Fuller home on Drexel Boulevard. The wedding, however, was a modest affair, witnessed only by close friends and relatives. The couple was married by Black's brother-in-law, a pastor from Hamilton, Ontario; their sole attendant was a best man, a friend of Harry Black's named Burton Smith. The newlyweds left that same night for their honeymoon, which included a stop in New York before traveling down South.

In New York, the Blacks would likely have stayed at the Fifth Avenue Hotel, because it was the city's most deluxe, attracting local politicians and visiting dignitaries. Edith Wharton, writing in the 1870s, described the six-story white marble structure and its "densely lace-curtained and heavily chandeliered public parlor." The guest rooms were furnished with rosewood and silk, and all had a private bath.

And the hotel offered location, the most valuable asset of any piece of real estate. Situated on Fifth Avenue between Twenty-third and Twenty-fourth Streets, the Fifth Avenue was a short trip by cab or foot to all the places in New York where you could spend money and have fun: theaters, the department stores of Ladies' Mile, fancy restaurants like Delmonico's, and the huge Venetian-cum-Moorish-style pleasure palace Madison Square Garden that had been designed by Stanford White. There P. T. Barnum staged his annual circus show, which starred Jumbo, the huge African elephant that he had brought from the London Zoo.

Besides the Garden's amphitheater, which could accommodate

19,000 spectators, and during the summer was flooded so as to simulate Venice's Grand Canal, which visitors could traverse on gondolas, the new Garden had a concert hall, a swimming pool, and roof garden for the hot summer months, decorated with hundreds of electric lamps. The Garden also had a theater, topped with a 249-foot tower, on which perched an eighteen-foot bronze statue of the goddess Diana, by the American sculptor Augustus Saint-Gaudens. Diana, perching on an electrically illuminated crescent moon and carrying a bow, was naked, which caused great consternation in certain circles, in particular the Women's Temperance Union.

The Fifth Avenue Hotel belonged to old Amos Eno. Now in his eighties, Eno, born in Connecticut, had come to New York at age sixteen. He worked as a clerk in a dry-goods store and thereby learned about that particular business. Eventually he and a cousin founded their own dry-goods business, which made them a fortune. (It is worth noting the coincidence of both Black and Eno having cut their respective teeth working as lowly clerks, selling ordinary household goods.) Eno then began to invest in New York real estate, and did so well that he abandoned the dry-goods business. He built the Fifth Avenue Hotel in 1859 on the site of Franconi's Hippodrome, a gigantic canvas-and-wood-roofed structure which could seat 10,000 people. The Hippodrome had closed in 1856, after only three years in operation. For whatever reason, "the restoration of the FESTIVALS GAMES and AMUSEMENTS of the Ancient Greeks and Romans," as the newspaper ads had boasted, had failed to attract enough audiences.

In 1857, Eno's choice of location had seemed terrible. That at any rate was the view of New York's old landowning families, with names like Jones—this in fact was Edith Wharton's family, to whom we owe the expression "keeping up with the Joneses"—and Astor. Arrivistes, they thought smugly, of Eno and his ilk. Fifth Avenue was overwhelmingly residential in nature; the area near the Hippodrome consisted mostly of dull brownstone houses. People called the new hotel "Eno's

Amos Eno, 1897.

folly." Nobody, they thought, would want to stay in a hotel in such an unfashionable neighborhood.

But they were wrong. An upper middle class was thriving in New York, and starting to displace the old families, both in worth and presence. Eno knew exactly what he was doing. His new hotel, which boasted one of New York's first passenger elevators, became *the* place to stay. America's industrialists met and made their deals there. The Fifth Avenue also became a place where New York Republican party leaders informally convened in the part of the lobby that came to be called the "amen corner," because it was there that they made crucial moves such as nominating Teddy Roosevelt for governor of New York in 1898. Fifth Avenue now began to attract luxury hotels and retail shops. And Madison Park, right across the street, became the epicenter of New York. Wealthy families, including the grandparents of Edith Wharton and the Jeromes, whose daughter Jennie married Randolph

Churchill and gave birth to their son, Winston Churchill, had their mansions nearby. On Madison Square, reported *Harper's Magazine,* "the gaslights glittered brightest. . . . Hard by . . . the Patriarchs danced; thither came whoever was bent on dining most delectably and the folks who craved nourishment or refreshment in the liveliest company after the theatre. Rooms looking out on Madison Square were the ones most desired by visitors to the metropolis, and the benches in the square on spring days were esteemed by philosophers to be the best points from which to contemplate the passing life of a brilliant city."

Eno had an instinct for location. Rarely did his land purchases not increase in value, and most increased spectacularly. He had begun buying real estate in 1857. Now, in 1894, his investments were worth at least $20 million, which in today's money would calculate as at least twenty times as much. Only the Astors and the Goelets, New York's oldest and wealthiest families, owned more land than Eno.

Another of Eno's land purchases, which he also made in 1857, just before buying the Fifth Avenue Hotel site, was a tiny triangle of land—it measured 9,000 square feet—just south of Madison Square, at the intersection of Broadway and Fifth Avenue, and bordered on the south by Twenty-second Street. He paid $25,000, or possibly, as one source claimed, $32,500. People called the lot "the cowcatcher," perhaps because its shape recalled the metal piece attached to the front of locomotives to prevent derailment from livestock unwittingly crossing the tracks. Although some said that *cowcatcher* referred to the fact that cows from once-nearby farms often wandered into it to avoid the increasing traffic on the street.

The cowcatcher had another sobriquet: the flatiron, because its triangular shape recalled the common household tool used for pressing clothing and linens.

The flatiron contained one structure, the four-story St. Germaine Hotel, which dated from 1855, and occupied about one-third of the lot, on the southern end. Some time after 1880, Eno had the old St. Germaine torn down. In its place he built the Cumberland, a seven-story

Eno's flatiron, at the intersection of Broadway and Fifth Avenue, looking south, 1890.
Note the advertising screen on top of the retail stores. The Fifth Avenue
Hotel is in the foreground, to the right.

apartment house with a mansard roof and strangely curved edges. In
the meantime, he had filled up the rest of the lot with four three-story
commercial buildings. Tenants over the years included a dentist advertising "painless treatment," a hosiery shop, and a combination chiropo-
dist and manicurist shop called "The Fountain of Youth." At the tip of
the triangle was the Erie Railway ticket office.

Most of the Cumberland's north wall was exposed, which Eno
leased as advertising space, for a handsome sum. The companies that
leased the wall doubtless thought the expense worth it, because the location made their signs visible for blocks. Pedestrians walking south on
Broadway or Fifth Avenue could not avoid staring at the huge painted-on
signs facing them, encouraging them to buy Benson's Porous Plaster or
Spencer's Steel Pens, or Sapolio's Tonic ("Used Every Week Day Brings
Rest On Sunday"), or Brock's Fireworks, or to buy an apartment at
the Oriental Hotel in Manhattan Beach, Brooklyn, "Swept by Ocean

Breezes." The largest sign of all was *The New York Times,* which filled up the entire wall, and was not painted on but made of electric lights, and included its slogan: "All the News That's Fit to Print."

In addition to making money from the Cumberland's north wall, by the early 1870s Eno had figured out one more way to profit from his property. He set up a canvas screen on top of the Erie ticket office roof, and charged the enterprising owners of stereopticons or "magic lanterns"—these were the first slide projectors, invented about twenty years earlier and now extremely popular—to project advertisements upon the screen. Madison Square, just opposite, provided the perfect place for the spectators. To keep them interested, the operator alternated pictures with the ads, all in rapid succession. "Niagara Falls dissolves into a box of celebrated boot blacking, and the celebrated blacking is superseded by a jungle scene, which fades into an extraordinarily cheap suite of furniture," wrote a reporter in *Scribner's Magazine* in August 1880. Sometimes the Young Men's Christian Association paid to add their messages—"The blood of Christ cleanses all from sin," "Believe in the Lord Jesus Christ, and thou shall be saved"—to the mix. On balmy evenings, the slide displays lasted until as late as ten o'clock. Even in cold and nasty weather, the free shows drew crowds. *The New York Times* began using Eno's screen for their news bulletins. The experiment drew huge crowds. "All the important events of the day were rapidly displayed in large letters . . . so that the public was at once informed of the news. From 7 o'clock until midnight the bulletins appeared in quick succession . . . The latest move in Erie, the Tweed trial, the hotel inspections, the doings of Congress . . . the messages being transmitted by telegraph from the Times office, as soon as received," the *Times* reported on January 14, 1873. *The New York Tribune* now also began buying time on Eno's screen. On election nights, Eno's flatiron was now the nerve center of New York, as Democratic and Republican Party bigwigs held court across the street in the Fifth Avenue Hotel, and tens of thousands of New Yorkers filled Madison Square, where, staring at the screen, they waited eagerly for election returns.

In New York Eno was now famous. Everybody knew that all his properties were making him very, very rich, in particular the triangle at the intersection of Fifth, Twenty-third, and Broadway. People were now calling the lot not just "the flatiron," but "Eno's flatiron."

Over the years, many prospective buyers had made offers to Eno to buy his flatiron. He had refused them all. This lot, he often said, would be worth a million dollars in his lifetime. So he held on to it.

By 1894, the year Harry and Allon Black were enjoying their New York honeymoon, Madison Square was still a hopping place. But millionaires no longer built their mansions there, instead moving further uptown on Fifth Avenue. And theaters, which once concentrated around the Square, on the stretch of Broadway known as "the Rialto," between Fourteenth and Twenty-third Streets, were now increasingly moving uptown as well, to Longacre Square, at Forty-second Street. No doubt about it, the neighborhood was in transition. So who could say if the value of Eno's flatiron would continue to increase? In real estate, location is everything.

Some time after Black and Allon married, in 1894, Fuller began toying with the idea of taking Black into his company. He felt that it made absolutely no difference that Black knew nothing about architecture, or engineering, or steel, or anything at all about the building trade. Fuller would simply take Black under his wing, and teach him. Moreover, Fuller believed, his son-in-law's outsider status was actually an asset. Unlike architects or engineers, or anybody within the industry, Black would see the bigger picture. He was just what the company needed.

So, soon after the newlyweds returned to Chicago, Fuller asked Harry Black to join his company, as his vice president. Black threw himself into the business. In 1896, Fuller decided it was finally the right time to open a New York office. He asked a twenty-seven-year-old engineer named Corydon Purdy, with whom he had worked on many buildings in Chicago, to run this latest Fuller venture. Purdy, born in

Wisconsin, had studied structural and civil engineering at the University of Wisconsin, in Madison. He had worked in railroad construction, then steel bridges. Purdy, who in 1894 had come to New York and opened his own business with a partner, Lightner Henderson, agreed to head up the new Fuller office, but only for one year. He simply could not spare any more time. New York's real estate market, which had slowed down considerably after a severe economic depression that had begun in 1893, was finally recovering. Companies and speculators were now competing for architects and contractors to build new buildings. As consulting engineers, Henderson & Purdy had more contracts now than they could handle.

Fuller's move to New York could not have come at a better time, because investors wanted their buildings built tall. The taller the building, the more profit you would wrest from the plot that you had just purchased at outrageously high prices, which by the following week, only climbed higher. And now that New York's building code no longer forced you to rely on masonry walls, you could build as high as you wanted.

Black bid on, and won several projects for the Fuller Company in New York. Then he asked himself, why should we limit ourselves to New York? In 1897, after Corydon Purdy's stint with the Fuller Company was up, Black put a young man named Theodore Starrett in charge of the New York office, and went out on the road to feel out the market in other cities. Starrett, who had already been working at the Fuller Company for seven years, came from the Kansas prairie. He was the son of a preacher and a schoolteacher, who had moved their brood of five sons and two daughters to Chicago during the early 1880s. The five Starrett boys there entered various aspects of the construction business.

Black won contracts for the Fuller Company in Boston, Pittsburgh, St. Louis, and Baltimore. He put another Starrett brother, Paul, in charge of the Baltimore project. Black was feeling terrific. His father-in-law, however, was feeling anxious. Black, Fuller worried, was moving too fast.

Fuller, in addition, was ill.

Soon after Black and Allon had married, Fuller began to feel unnaturally exhausted, a state he attributed to his usual overloaded work schedule. Then he developed muscle spasms in his hands and feet. Sometimes, when he picked up objects, they dropped from his hands. For a while he tried to ignore his discomfort, but the people around him began to notice his symptoms. His family became alarmed. Finally, Fuller, at his wife Ellen's insistence, consulted a well-known neurologist in New York. The doctor told Fuller that he had "creeping paralysis," which is what we today call amyotrophic lateral sclerosis. There is, the doctor soberly told George and Ellen Fuller, no hope for recovery.

Amos Eno died in 1898, at age eighty-eight. He left an estate worth $20 million. Among his six surviving children was John C. Eno, who, upon his graduation from Yale in 1869 had received the wooden spoon, which signified that he was the most popular member of his class. In 1884, at age thirty-five, John was indicted for embezzling $4 million from his father's bank, Second National of New York, to make up for heavy losses that he had sustained in the stock market. Amos Eno had founded Second National in the early 1880s, and had made John its president. On May 24, 1884, when federal agents arrived at young Eno's home at 46 Park Avenue, which had been surrounded by police even before the indictment had been handed down, to arrest him, he was nowhere to be found. A few days later, he turned up in Canada, along with a Catholic priest, Father Ducey, apparently the young man's confidante, who had accompanied him in his flight across the border. It was said that Amos Eno, upon learning of his son's perfidy, had advised him to flee rather than face trial. Whether or not this was true we cannot know. In any case, after John had crossed the border, Amos repaid Second National the money his son had stolen. Even so, the scandal caused a run on the bank that lasted a day and a half. That, along with two other simultaneous bank failures, caused a general panic on Wall Street.

John Eno remained in Quebec with his wife, children, and Father Ducey. Newspapers reported that he engaged in various business ventures there, but did not specify of what sort. After successfully fighting extradition for nine years, he finally returned voluntarily to New York in 1893, where he was immediately arrested. His lawyers, after getting him freed on $20,000 bail, managed to have all the old indictments quashed. Since then, John Eno had been living quietly in New York.

And now John, along with his siblings, stood to inherit a great deal of money. Various cousins and institutions, among them Yale University, would also benefit. All this meant a lot of asset liquidation, and everybody was talking about old Eno's properties. For a while rumors circulated that the city of New York would buy Eno's flatiron and combine it with nearby Madison Square, thereby enlarging the already-existing park. In fact, in February 1899, soon after Eno's death, the New York State Assembly had passed a bill appropriating $3 million to the city specifically earmarked for this purchase. The Albany reporter for *The Sun,* noticing not only the egregiously inflated price that the city was to pay for the land, but also that the bill had passed the Assembly without any discussion, decided to do some investigating. He discovered that the brokers for the sale of the flatiron was the firm of Peter F. Meyer and Company, "Company" being Richard Croker, the boss of Tammany Hall.

After *The Sun* duly reported these facts, the city abandoned its plans to purchase the flatiron. It now ended up on the auction block along with the rest of Eno's properties, all to be liquidated in order to settle his estate among his many heirs. The flatiron sold quickly. The buyer was William, one of the Eno sons; he paid $690,000, $5,000 above "the last bid by an outsider," according to the *Real Estate Record and Builders' Guide* on May 6, 1899, and $2,310,000 less than the city would have paid, were it not for *The Sun's* Albany reporter.

William Eno held on to the lot for only three weeks, before flipping it over to Samuel Newhouse, whom people called the "Copper King," and his brother Mott. Born in New York to German Jewish immigrants, the two brothers had gone out west, first to Colorado and then Utah, where they were now making a fortune in copper mining. Their Utah Consolidated Gold Mines had just been acquired by Standard Oil for $12 million. Now the brothers were investing heavily in real estate. For the flatiron they paid $801,000.

The Newhouses announced to the newspapers that they intended to erect a new office building on the flatiron. Therefore, they said, they would not renew any of the building leases. The new structure, the Newhouses said, would be no higher than twelve stories, with retail on the street level, and bachelor apartments above. Not that they were opposed to building higher; but how could they, they said, given the limitations posed by the footprint? A skinny triangle in the middle of an intersection was more suitable for a pocket park than a skyscraper.

The flatiron block now became the talk of the town. People wondered what the new building would look like, and the tenants in the Cumberland apartment house waited anxiously for eviction notices. A year and a half went by. Land prices in New York kept rising; building activity was at an all-time high. But nothing was happening at the flatiron lot. It seemed the Newhouse brothers were in no hurry to build. Perhaps they were content to just watch their purchase appreciate.

Another six months went by. It was now December 1900, and George Fuller lay in a private sanitarium with a beautiful view of Long Island Sound in Mamaroneck, New York. He could hardly swallow or breathe, or move his limbs. And as if his terrible illness were not enough of a trial, Fuller was also now consumed by grief over the death of his older daughter, Grace. She had jumped from the fourth-story window of the Hotel Majestic in New York early one September morning in 1899, four months after the Newhouses had purchased the flatiron lot. Grace was instantly killed. She was twenty-six years old. Besides her husband, Horace Chenery, Grace left behind an infant son, whom she had named Fuller Chenery. Her physician afterward told the newspapers that during the previous six months she had been suffering from "an ordinary case of melancholia." Clearly, postpartum depression had driven Grace Fuller Chenery to suicide, although some said she first displayed signs of mental illness several years earlier, after her father became ill.

After Grace's death, Horace, a banker who came from a prominent Maine family, had approached Harry and Allon and asked them to adopt little Fuller Chenery. The Blacks, who after four years of marriage had no children, were taken aback. Why, Allon asked Horace, do you, a new father, ask such a thing of us? Horace Chenery told them that after his son was born, Grace, so despondent that she could not get out of bed, and showing no interest in her new baby, had made Horace promise that if anything should happen to her, her sister, Allon, and not he, must raise their son. The Blacks complied with Grace's request.

Now, fifteen months after Grace's suicide, George Fuller's wife, Ellen, and Allon, his surviving daughter, sat by his side and waited for the end to come. And yet, *The New York Times* claimed, despite his misery, he found the strength to put together one last construction project that netted his company $2 million.

George Allon Fuller died on December 14, 1900. He was forty-nine years old. His body was shipped by train to Chicago, in his private car, accompanied by his wife and daughter. The funeral took place at the family home on Drexel Boulevard. Besides Allon and Ellen, Fuller was survived by his brother, Eugene, his nephew, Frank, his parents, who lived in Massachusetts, and his year-old grandson, Fuller Chenery. He left an estate valued at $3 million, divided equally between his wife and Allon. He did not mention Harry Black in his will. Newspapers across the country carried Fuller's obituary, which described him as "the father of the skyscraper."

Immediately following his father-in-law's death, Harry Black assumed the presidency of the Fuller Company. And now there was nobody to stop Black from moving ahead as fast as he wanted.

On March 3, 1901, *The New York Times* reported that the Newhouses were planning to sell the flatiron, to a yet-unnamed corporation. Exactly two weeks later, the Cumberland Realty Company, consisting of a group of investors whom Harry Black had put together—Byron M. Fellows, Philip F. Barrington, David H. Lanman, William Greenough Jr., and Howard R. Cruse—was formed in New Jersey, capitalized at $700,000.

Three weeks later, Black merged the Fuller Company with the Central Realty, Bond, and Trust Company. Central had incorporated in 1899 with $3 million in capital; its backers had included sugar baron Henry Havermeyer, and other members of J. P. Morgan's U.S. Steel faction. The *Chicago Tribune* declared Central Realty the latest in the seemingly endless formation of trusts, and the first to involve real estate. The aim of "the skyscraper trust," the *Tribune* wrote on December 26, 1899, was to "control and regulate New York office building rents."

Black brought well-connected board members to the newly energized Fuller Company. Among them were the German Jewish patrician Henry Morgenthau, who had made a fortune in New York buying real estate (his son would serve as Treasury Secretary under Franklin D. Roosevelt, and grandson as New York's district attorney), former Mayor and Tammany man Hugh J. Grant, and National City Bank (the forerunner of Citibank) President James Stillman. The former Illinois judge Samuel McConnell, whom Black had known since his Chicago days, would serve as in-house counsel. "Ex-Judge," which is how everybody addressed him, had learned the law in the Springfield office of Abraham Lincoln, and been considered as a running mate to Democratic presidential candidate William Jennings Bryan in 1896. McConnell had left the bench to practice law, and the Fuller Company had been one of his biggest clients.

Black's deal resulted in an increase of the Fuller Company's capital to $20 million, thereby making it the largest construction company in the world to date. "Great Building Concern Organized," the *New York Times* headline trumpeted on March 30, 1901. "By operating on so large a scale and with practically unlimited capital, the George A. Fuller

Company will be in a position to purchase its materials—steel, brick, cement, fireproofing, elevators, &c—at figures so favorable that it will, according to present estimates, be able to produce a finished building at about ten per cent less than can any individual or combination of subcontractors," the *Times* wrote. Plus, the paper added, the merging of Fuller and Central Realty will "strip a building operation of much of its former complexity, and what is practically one corporation is now in a position to effect the purchase of a site, make a building loan, and then deliver the completed structure."

So the Fuller Company—which would soon inherit the sobriquet *skyscraper trust*—would control not only the rents of New York's office buildings, but everything having to do with construction.

The new Fuller Company had millions of dollars worth of contracts. It was currently working on a skyscraper for steel magnate Henry Frick in Pittsburgh, a new Willard Hotel in Washington, the Huntington Chambers in Boston, and the new Chicago Tribune Building. In New York, Fuller projects included the Jewelers' Building at Broadway and Maiden Lane, the Tontine Building at Wall and Water Streets, the Maritime Building at Pear and Bridge Streets, a new Union clubhouse, this one at Fifth Avenue and Fifty-first Street, and the Park Hotel at Madison and Sixty-third. And in partnership with the Alliance Realty Company, Fuller Construction was now finishing a massive, oddly shaped structure at the corner of Broad Street and Exchange Place. This new building, designed by the firm of Clinton and Russell, had twenty-one stories, and was to date the largest office building in the world. Even more impressive than its size was how quickly the Broad-Exchange building had gone up: Fuller Construction had broken ground in August 1900; by May 1901, it was ready for occupancy. Diagonally across the street, work was now starting on George B. Post's new Stock Exchange—not a Fuller project—which would be completed in 1903.

Harry Black was flying high. All of New York knew about him, the Canadian who had come out of nothing, married the boss's daughter, and was now, thanks to his talent for convincing New York's richest denizens to invest in his real estate deals, erecting the most massive, gorgeous buildings that New York had ever seen. He was living on a grand scale, and publicly, crashing through the gates of New York's high society, which, despite the efforts of Mrs. Caroline Astor to limit membership, was now increasingly accessible to parvenus like him. She couldn't stop them, because Black and his ilk had too much money, which in New York gave you power, clear and simple, no matter your family's name.

So Black had much to celebrate, but Allon wasn't there to share these latest successes with him. She had left for Europe in January 1901 soon after her father's death the previous month, to recuperate, and was remaining there, for the time being.

It wasn't just her grief that Allon was running away from. People whispered that Black had a roving eye. Moreover, temperamentally, the couple was badly mismatched. That Harry was fifteen years older exacerbated their differences.

George Fuller had sent his daughter Allon to exclusive boarding schools in Pennsylvania (Ogontz), and New York City (Miss Ely's). After she married Black, her main interest became raising show dogs. How she had felt about adopting her nephew after her sister's death is not known. Perhaps the baby filled a void in her privileged but increasingly empty life. Or perhaps she was indifferent. We don't know if she took the infant with her when she left for Europe in January 1901.

A photo of Allon taken around this time shows a dark-haired young woman with a long, pale face. She wears a large, floppy velvet hat topped with an ostrich plume. A gem-encrusted choker hugs her neck, and a long string of large pearls drapes her bosom. Her big, dark eyes have a sad expression. She does not smile. What a contrast the young woman's image makes with her husband's. When you look at a photo of Harry Black, you feel as if his sparkling eyes are boring right through yours. Everywhere he went, he spread feelings of excitement.

"My motto," Black was bragging to everybody in 1901, after reorganizing the Fuller Company, "is 'bigger and bigger.'" And he was right in step with the times: during the previous decade, the number of trusts in the United States had increased from about a dozen to 200. By 1904, there would be some 300 trusts, made up of 5,000 once-independent businesses. "This is the era of trusts. Almost everything we use, from the tin dinner-pail carried by the laboring man to the palace car in which the multi-millionaire travels, is made by a trust. Industrial consolidation is the order of the time," wrote a reporter in *Frank Leslie's Popular Monthly* in May 1901. There was John D. Rockefeller's Standard Oil, Swift and Armour's beef trust, and Duke's tobacco trust. The Havermeyers had their sugar trust. Other trusts controlled whiskey, cottonseed oil, lead, and rubber. And just one month prior to the Fuller Company's reorganization, J. P. Morgan and his associates had launched the biggest trust of all, U.S. Steel, which broke records with its capitalization of over $1 billion. Several members of U.S. Steel also sat on the new Fuller board, which de facto meant that fewer and fewer people controlled ever more of the building business.

The corporations were all based in New York, "the youngest of the world's great cities," in the words of journalist and social reformer Jacob Riis. Corporations badly needed space to house their exploding work forces, thereby further driving up an already heated-up real estate market. Many of the new skyscrapers were being built as company headquarters; others were syndicates, built on speculation encouraged by land values that were rising so rapidly that the existing structures on them were deemed worthless by their investors. "Gotham's Building Boom," a *New York Times* headline trumpeted on May 27, 1901, two months after the reorganization of the Fuller Company. "Ruins of what in many instances were modern buildings are to be seen on every side," the *Times* reported. "In their place will go up structures costing many millions, which will be utilized for a variety of purposes."

And besides skyscraper mania, there was another force driving up the cost of New York's land: tenement house construction on the Lower East Side, now literally the most densely populated area on earth. Tenements had proven a gold mine to their owners, as they packed their

properties to capacity with the increasing number of immigrants landing daily at nearby Ellis Island. Most of the East Side's population now
consisted of Russian and Polish Jews, refugees of the pogroms staged
by czarist Russia starting in the 1880s. Thus the neighborhood's sobriquet: "the Ghetto." The claustrophobic tenements functioned both as
places for living and working. It was not uncommon, Riis wrote in his
famous book *How the Other Half Lives,* to find an entire family of twelve
people crowded into a single room, where in between cooking, wash-
ing their clothing, and sleeping, they made their miserable living doing
needle work.

Riis's book, which had come out in 1890—using words, and, most
of all, photographs to spectacularly document the filthy hell of tenement life—outraged people's consciences. A reform movement ensued;
and now, in 1901, lot owners were rushing to build tenements on their
properties before a recently passed law, due in part to Riis's activism,
would curtail their profits.

The new law, which would take effect on June 1, only partially
grandfathered existing tenements; they would now require alterations
ranging from fireproofing to inserting airshafts. The old tenements
were firetraps that occupied virtually every foot of their lots in order
for landlords to squeeze out every last drop of profit. Individual apartments had no running water; families shared a single toilet in the hall-
way or basement, or in the worst cases, an outdoor privy. Only the
rooms that faced the street had windows; back rooms had only airshafts for ventilation, if you even could call it that. In such fetid conditions, typhus and smallpox outbreaks flourished. The new law required
tenements to be built only with fireproof materials, and have at least
twelve feet of open space in the back. In addition, each tenement apartment now would have running water, a toilet, and exterior windows.
Owners vocally opposed the new law, which would, they complained,
limit the profits they could extract from their properties. Tenements,
however, would continue to be profitable.

In May 1901, the Newhouses sold the flatiron to the Cumberland

Realty Company for nearly $2,000,000, thereby reaping the handsome profit of $1,000,100 on their initial investment. The papers claimed that the flatiron was the most expensive piece of property in the world. Whether or not this assertion was literally true, enough people, because they had read it in the newspaper, believed it as to make it as good as true. So now the world believed that Harry Black had purchased the most valuable piece of land on earth, which made him feel as proud as he'd ever felt in his life.

Perhaps Black had been coveting the flatiron ever since old man Eno had died in 1898, and it went on the auction block. But Black at that time did not bid on it, perhaps because George Fuller was dying by then, and Black may have decided it was the wrong time to ask his father-in-law for the purchase money.

But now Fuller was dead, and Black could do what he wanted. And Black wanted the flatiron for a new company headquarters, because, he believed, it was absolutely the perfect spot, the crossroads of Broadway and Fifth, the two greatest thoroughfares of the city that was the center of the world. Black loved the neighborhood, and was convinced it would remain New York's commercial center.

But, already on the wane for several years, the district was rapidly changing.

The theaters by now were gone, and the ubiquitous brownstone houses were more and more giving way to commercial buildings, but not of the luxurious sort. Instead, the area was turning into a wholesale manufacturing district, as clothing manufacturers and sweatshops began to occupy the hundreds of loft buildings now being built on the side streets. Expensive stores and restaurants were moving uptown, among them Delmonico's, once at Fifth and Twenty-sixth, which had relocated in 1899 to Forty-fourth Street. Eno's Fifth Avenue Hotel still stood on Fifth between Twenty-third and Twenty-fourth Streets. But the elegant hotel now felt like an anomaly in a neighborhood that was beginning to have seedy pockets.

Even so, Madison Square Garden still attracted crowds. And while more and more bums were choosing Madison Square as their home when the weather was fine, it still attracted the prosperous classes, especially on Sunday afternoons, as *the* place to stroll if you wanted to see and be seen. Shoppers still frequented Ladies' Mile, which started with Stern's Department Store at Twenty-third Street, and traveled down Fifth and Sixth Avenues all the way to Stewart's department store, at Ninth Street.

By erecting the new Fuller headquarters on the flatiron, Harry Black hoped to boost the neighborhood back to its former splendor.

Black would not build a puny twelve-story affair such as the Newhouses had envisaged, but a skyscraper, the first to be built north of Union Square. He didn't consider the tiny footprint or its peculiar shape a detriment. One would just, he thought, have to design a very skinny skyscraper. Not that Black, even after all the years he had worked with George Fuller, knew anything about construction, or architecture. But no matter. Working out the specifics wasn't Black's problem, but the architect's. And he already had an architect. Two months earlier, in February 1901, as Black was putting together the Cumberland Realty deal, and simultaneously transforming the George A. Fuller Company from a family-owned firm into a conglomerate, Black had hired Daniel H. Burnham.

CHAPTER THREE

CHICAGO'S GIFT

*T*HE '93 CHICAGO EXPOSITION had made Daniel Burnham, who had presided over the construction of this gigantic project, an international celebrity. He now traveled constantly about the country by train, overseeing his architecture firm's many commissions. When Black asked him in 1901 to design the Fuller Company's new building in New York, Burnham was running back and forth between ongoing projects in Chicago, Cincinnati, Fort Wayne, Philadelphia, Pittsburgh—he was working there with Black and the Fuller Company on a skyscraper for railroad magnate Henry Frick—New Jersey, and New York. In addition Burnham had just been appointed chairman of a three-member U.S. Senate commission—the other two were the architect Charles McKim and the landscape designer Frederick Law Olmsted Jr.—to devise a renewal plan for Washington, D.C. Burnham would, in effect, complete what Pierre L'Enfant had started in 1791, when the French engineer gave the capital the shape we know today: avenues radiating from the Capitol and the White House, cutting diagonally across the grid-pattern streets. L'Enfant's plan had included parks and abundant fountains to

Daniel Hudson Burnham, circa 1910.

relieve the discomfort of Washington's torrid summers. The avenues were to be bordered with gardens. Such aesthetic improvements had yet to happen. For example, the area L'Enfant had envisioned as a grand thoroughfare connecting the White House and the Capitol was still a muddy wasteland, where cows were let out to pasture, with lumber-yards here and there, crisscrossed by railroad tracks.

What a disgrace, people were saying, that the capital of the United States, which now rightfully felt itself no longer merely a nation, but an empire, after its recent victory in the Spanish-American War, should have such a shabby appearance. Eight years earlier, Americans, visiting the Chicago Exhibition, for the first time realized that cities could be beautiful. The image of the glistening, classical-inspired White City had stuck in their minds. Returning home, they noticed how ugly their cities were, with their low wooden-and-brick buildings, and narrow, muddy streets.

And now, Burnham would make Washington, D.C., and other American cities beautiful too. Just as Pericles, at the height of Athens' empire in the fifth century BC, had done for that city. These days Burnham was thinking often about Pericles, and frequently mentioned the great states-man in his speeches. In his address to the commission in Washington,

D.C., Burnham had noted that by turning Athens into a city of great monuments, Pericles had thereby helped increase Athens' prosperity. Burnham imagined that Pericles, like himself, recognized the commercial value of beauty. For inspiration, he would look to the past. He would create public spaces and buildings that recalled Greek and Roman temples and Renaissance palazzi, because, based on the popular reaction to the '93 Exposition, images from the past were what the public craved.

Burnham, fired up by his mission, had a schedule that would have killed a lesser man. Sometimes he arrived by train in Chicago in the morning from whatever city he had been in the day before, after sleeping all night in a Pullman car, and he went directly to his office in the Loop. In his letters to his wife he complains about how hard he worked, but at the same time, he loved it. "Business rolls up ever higher and higher," he would write to his wife in April 1901. "But, dear, I am a better man for you and the children when I am full of work."

Daniel Burnham was a huge man, over six feet tall, with a deep voice, a full head of thick brown hair and a bushy mustache. As a young bachelor in Chicago he was rumored to have been quite the rake. But once he married Margaret Sherman, the daughter of a stockyards magnate, everything we know about him indicates that he became a model husband, and the devoted but strict father of five children.

Group photos of the Burnham family exude prosperous respectability. The Burnhams loved to socialize, both as a couple and with the entire family. Their beautiful home was always filled with their and their children's friends. During Burnham's travels, he wrote constantly to Margaret, telling her how much he missed her, and depended on her. In his letters he frequently mentioned their children, and offered specific guidelines on what they must or must not do. His two daughters were to dress in a ladylike fashion; he was going to hear his son John recite all his lessons to him when he returned home; he demanded progress reports from his son Hubert while the latter was at college, and told him before embarking on a cruise not to incur even a penny's worth of debt or drink any alcohol.

Burnham had worked with Black's father-in-law, George Fuller, on many buildings in Chicago. The two men had liked and respected one another. At Fuller's funeral the previous year, Burnham had served as a pallbearer. But Burnham did not like Harry Black.

The feeling was mutual.

Black had an ego as vast as Burnham's, but the two men's personalities were very different. Black, justifiably, thought Burnham pompous and controlling. Whereas Burnham found Black ostentatious and crude. He disapproved of the younger man's excessive love of luxury. Not that Burnham spurned luxury; indeed, he lived in a manner commensurate with the status that he had achieved through his talents both as an architect and businessman. His mansion in suburban Evanston was set in the woods, with tennis courts and landscaped gardens. When the weather was good, he and Margaret entertained guests on a huge terrace that overlooked Lake Michigan. Burnham loved rich food and expensive cigars. He played golf at a country club. He had his suits specially tailored in London. Once, he paid $1,800 for five pearls at Spaulding and Company in Chicago, to add to his wife's necklace.

But compared to Harry Black's life, Burnham's seemed modest. Black had multiple houses, a stable of French cars, and threw famously lavish parties, which received frequent notice in the society pages. ("In Palm Beach," the Chicago Tribune wrote, "Harry Black furnished food for talk by the select set at the beach.")

Besides the nature of their respective personalities, there was an additional source of tension between Burnham and Black: the construction of the Frick skyscraper that they were currently working on was going badly. During 1901 they were often running back and forth to Pittsburgh, where the Fuller Company was constantly behind schedule, and Frick was driving everybody concerned insane with his nonstop complaints about shoddy workmanship and construction delays. Black was sanguine about the Frick project. For one, he had too much now that he was dealing with to devote to it the kind of attention that Frick was demanding. In the end, Black believed, it would all turn out fine, and anyway, there was no point trying to please Frick, who was just impossible, always sniffing around the site, interfering with technical matters that he knew nothing about. When Frick wrote Black a letter, complaining about the Fuller Company's performance on the Frick project, Black apparently ignored it. Frick then notified Burnham, who, furious, wrote to Black on May 29, 1901: "Think it your duty to this large commission on which you are earning so great a sum, to respond. You should go to Pittsburgh not later than Saturday morning."

Still, for all his animus toward Black, Burnham had eagerly accepted the flatiron commission when Black had offered it to him in February 1901. The offer was impossible to resist. It was unheard of for a Chicago architect to receive a commission in New York. Even if the architect was Daniel Burnham, whose New York colleagues—Richard Morris Hunt, Charles F. McKim, George B. Post, all of whom he had invited to design the White City—had, to show their gratitude, thrown a huge gala for him in 1893 at Madison Square Garden. Three hundred of New York's most prominent citizens had convened at the Square's banquet hall, which had been festooned with evergreens, potted palms, and scarlet banners, for a two-hour-long dinner, accompanied by the music of a Hungarian gypsy band. Afterward, Hunt, the master of ceremonies, presented Burnham with a foot-high, solid silver loving cup filled with sparkling wine, which was "sent from lip to lip around the room, each distinguished man being warmly cheered as he drank."

Burnham believed that whatever difficulties would come with the flatiron project would be worth it, because he would now, finally, have a building in New York. Not just a building, but a skyscraper, to serve as an advertisement for not just the Fuller Company but himself, too.

By now Burnham no longer personally worked on the individual projects he took on, instead delegating them to architects who worked for him. They, upon completing their plans, presented them to Burnham for his final approval. The resulting buildings were credited solely to D. H. Burnham & Co., without any mention of the individuals who had done the actual designing. This was the accepted practice at all architecture firms of the time.

Nevertheless, we know that Burnham assigned the Fuller project to Frederick Dinkelberg, an architect in his early forties whom Burnham mentions in his correspondence. Dinkelberg had started his career as an architect in New York, in 1881, and practiced there for ten years. During this time he met the brilliant but opium-addicted Charles Atwood. In 1892, Burnham, after the sudden death of his beloved partner, John Root, the previous year, chose Atwood as design chief for the Chicago Exposition. Atwood, who in 1895 would die a drug-related death at age forty-six, then introduced Dinkelberg to Burnham. Burnham hired Dinkelberg to work on the Exposition. Afterward, Burnham invited Atwood and Dinkelberg to join his newly organized firm, formerly Burnham & Root, now D. H. Burnham & Co.

Dinkelberg, a tall, skinny man with a long face and large, dark eyes, had led a privileged childhood in Lancaster, Pennsylvania, where he was born in 1859 to an Italian countess and a wealthy contractor. He studied architecture at the prestigious Pennsylvania Academy of Fine Arts in Philadelphia. By the time he received the flatiron assignment in 1901, Dinkelberg was well known among his peers. He had already designed at least one skyscraper, a twenty-six story building in the early 1890s, now long gone, at the southern tip of Manhattan, on Broadway, between Battery Place and Morris Street. In the mid-1890s, he built a block of classically inspired limestone row houses in the upper-class white Harlem neighborhood that later, with the influx of black haute-bourgeoisie after World War I, came to be called "Sugar Hill." These houses, now designated New York landmarks, still stand. One of them, the St. Nick's Pub at 773 St. Nicholas Avenue, has been operating as a jazz club since the 1930s.

Dinkelberg believed wholly in the design philosophy of D. H. Burnham & Co., that is, creating modern buildings in the image of ancient architecture. "In regard to the development of a so-called new American style of architecture, it is most probable that the law of gradual evolution it has obtained so far will continue," he wrote in an essay that appeared in the May 1908 issue of *Inland Architecture*. "It is very doubtful, to my mind, whether we can create a new style by an abrupt breaking off or ignoring of traditional architectural forms."

But how was one to integrate elements from ancient Athens or Renaissance Florence into the new species of structure invented in America, as much machine as shelter from the elements, that rose as high as 300 feet, its weight supported not by huge blocks of marble or granite, but riveted steel beams? As New York built more and more skyscrapers, journalists were asking this and the larger question of whether a skyscraper could in fact be beautiful. In newspapers and magazines such as *Scribner's* and *Architectural Record* debates now were raging over the so-called "problem of the skyscraper." But this was not a new story. Five years earlier, the visionary Louis Sullivan, by then marginalized by the architectural establishment because of his prickly personality and unwillingness to compromise his artistic ideals, had already addressed the problem in an essay published in *Lippincott's*.

"How shall we impart to this sterile pile, this crude, harsh, brutal agglomeration, this stark, staring exclamation of eternal strife, the graciousness of those higher forms of sensibility and culture that rest on the lower and fiercer passions?" Sullivan wrote in an essay entitled "The Tall Office Building Artistically Considered." The solution, he wrote, lay in nature: "It is the pervading law of all things . . . that form follows function. This is the law. Shall we, then, daily violate this law in our art? . . . the shape, form, outward expression, design or whatever we may choose, of the tall office building should in the very nature of things follow the functions of this building . . . and thus . . . take its place with all other architectural types made when architecture, as has happened once in many years, was a living art. Witness the Greek temple, the Gothic cathedral, the medieval fortress."

The function of a skyscraper was not worship, or defense, but economic profit, both for its builders, and the companies who leased space in it. Its form, above all, Sullivan wrote, must be lofty. "It must be every inch a proud and soaring thing, rising in sheer exultation that from bottom to top it is a unit without a single dissenting line . . . the man who designs in this spirit and with the sense of responsibility to the generation he lives in must be no coward, no denier, no bookworm, no dilettante. . . . He must realize . . . that the problem of the tall office building is one of the most stupendous, one of the most magnificent opportunities that the Lord of Nature in His beneficence has ever offered to the proud spirit of man."

How ironic that Sullivan, who died broke and embittered, but holding fast to his principles, offered such a wonderfully articulated and insightful solution to the "problem of the skyscraper."

Since signing him in February 1901, Black was continuously pressuring Burnham to work faster on the plans for the Fuller project. What with New York's now furious pace of building activity, Black kept saying, the price of materials was climbing constantly, which meant that every day of delay translated into dollars lost. There was no time to lose. Construction must begin, he said, by the summer. And it will, Burnham told him. That Black's officious manner irritated him was no wonder, especially in view of the seemingly impossible task that Burnham had accomplished ten years earlier, namely, the building of the White City in only sixteen months. During that time, problem after problem popped up—windstorms that knocked down half-completed structures, labor unrest, and the individual architects' egos that kept banging up against the others'—and threatened to prevent the fair's completion. But the fair had nonetheless opened right on schedule, in May 1893. During the frantic months when construction was going on, Burnham had spent most nights in a shanty right on the fairgrounds, in order not to lose precious time traveling back and forth to his home in Evanston. For it was his nature to take full control of whatever he considered his responsibility, that is, both of his family, or the practice of his profession.

Among the aspects of Burnham's personality that made him a good administrator, one in particular stood out: his careful attention to details. For years he kept a daybook, in which he carefully recorded where he went, with whom he met, and when. In an entry that he made on March 5, 1901, just one month after receiving the Fuller assignment, Burnham noted that he arrived in New York from Chicago at about seven in the morning. After stopping briefly at his hotel to freshen up and eat breakfast, he hurried downtown to Harry Black's office. Burnham spent the rest of the day with Black. The following morning, after the two had breakfast together at Burnham's hotel, they went back to Black's office. There, Burnham writes, "Black accepted Burnham's gridiron [sic] design."

Besides these few facts, we know nothing more of what transpired between the two men during these two days. So we are left only to imagine Black's reaction when he, presumably for the first time, saw sketches of a strange, wafer-thin skyscraper in the shape of a right triangle, topped with a heavy, ornate cornice. In keeping with the architectural fashion of the day, the building had three horizontal divisions, each corresponding, respectively, to a classical column's base, shaft, and capital. The building's two main elevations each soared straight up to the sky like giant screens, and were punctured continuously with rows of rectangular windows. The otherwise-monotonous fenestration was broken up by three vertical rows of eight gently protruding bay windows traveling up the middle section of the building. Bays, Burnham perhaps would have reminded Black, were often used in Chicago skyscrapers, because they helped break the force of the fierce winds that blew off Lake Michigan, and would perform a similar function for the new Fuller building, which, standing in the middle of an intersection, would be especially vulnerable to the elements.

Burnham would have explained to Black that the building's bottom section would be of limestone, but the rest would be brick and, mostly, terra-cotta, now a popular material, and especially for skyscrapers.

The sketch showed the skyscraper with twenty stories, which filled up the entire lot, except for the tip at Twenty-third Street. And that was because Dinkelberg had designed each side of the triangle to meet the other in a soft curve, rather than a sharp angle, a novel idea for a New York building. But this design detail was typical of Chicago architecture.

Black would not have liked that even a tiny piece of a parcel that had cost $155.03 a square foot would sit empty. He doubtless reminded Burnham that in Manhattan, any unused space, even the slightest bit, and in the most inconvenient configuration—the amount under discussion here measured a mere ninety-three square feet, all crammed into a narrow little right triangle—translated into significant amounts of lost rental income. And, in the same vein, Black probably complained as well about the new building's proposed height. By now, at least fifteen New York office buildings measured at least 250 feet high. The highest, the twin-towered Park Row Building, which still exists, stood 391 feet tall. But the new Fuller building, according to the design that Black was now studying, would stand at only about 285 feet.

Burnham perhaps pointed out to Black that the flatiron location made for unprecedented wind exposure, on all three sides of the building. And the taller the building, the more vulnerable it would be. So Black should not worry about making his new company headquarters the tallest building in New York and therefore the world, because its unique location would make the Fuller Building stand out on its own merits. Not just because of its unusual design, but because there were, so far, no other high buildings nearby to compete with it.

We can imagine Burnham saying to Black: "The Fuller Building will look like nothing that anybody has ever seen before. It will be Chicago's gift to New York."

Theodore Starrett, whom Black had put in charge of the Fuller Company's New York office back in 1897, had soon realized that he did not like working for anybody other than himself, and especially not for

Harry Black. The two men constantly fought. More than once, Starrett had resigned from the Fuller Company. Finally, in 1901, he resigned for the last time, and immediately joined with another builder, Henry S. Thompson, to form a new company to rival Black's. Theodore then brought his three younger brothers into Thompson-Starrett, which had been capitalized at the respectable but not especially impressive sum of $1 million. Starrett told himself that he would show that son-of-a-bitch Harry Black that his wasn't the only real estate game in town.

And in fact it wasn't. During the last year or so, as property values kept appreciating, the number of realty companies was rapidly multiplying. By now New York was home to over fifty real estate companies, with capitalizations ranging from a few thousand to millions of dollars. But some were tiny operations, consisting of a few men who owned tenements or small flats, who had scraped together just enough money to allow them to incorporate their businesses. And even the larger ones were no match for the Fuller Company, by far the largest. According to the *Real Estate Record and Builders' Guide*, the company was worth $20 million.

Black, who surely dismissed Theodore Starrett's attempt to compete with him as laughable, promptly replaced him with his brother Paul, the eldest of the five Starrett boys. Black knew Paul well, having first hired him in Chicago to work for the Fuller Company some time during the late 1890s. Paul had first begun learning about the building business from Daniel Burnham, who hired him in 1887 as a $7.50-per-week stenographer at Burnham & Root. Burnham liked the young man, who was serious and hardworking, and fascinated with everything that had to do with building. Burnham made Paul the superintendent over two huge structures—Machinery Hall and the Mines and Mining Building—during the construction of the '93 Exposition.

At some point during his time with Burnham, Paul Starrett told his mentor that he wanted to study engineering. Burnham told him not to waste his time. The thing to do, he told Paul, is to go into business for yourself.

"You can hire any number of engineers who will be content spending their whole lives doing routine," Burnham said. "You Starrett boys are different. You have a genius for organization and leadership."

For now, though, Paul Starrett was doing very well by Harry Black, whom he could not help but like. Black made Starrett head of Fuller's New York operation in 1901 as a reward for the excellent job Starrett had just done in Washington, D.C., overseeing the construction of the architect Henry Hardenburgh's elegant new Willard Hotel within the incredibly short deadline of one year. Thanks to Starrett's careful budgeting, the Willard commission had even yielded a nice profit.

Starrett rushed to New York to begin work on his new building assignment. Assisting him was Corydon Purdy, the brilliant young engineer who had worked in Chicago with Fuller during the 1880s, and whom Black had just contracted for this latest job. Starrett and Purdy decided what, and how much of individual materials were needed: concrete, timber, bricks, and tar for the foundation and basement, and the cast-iron columns to be placed under the Fifth Avenue sidewalk; boilers and pipes, sinks and flush toilets; wooden doors, window frames and glass; elevators, and iron grilles for the elevator shafts; limestone quarried in Indiana for the base, bricks, and terra-cotta, manufactured to order in New York, which would clad the building's steel skeleton. Starrett invited electricians, plumbers, glazers, terra-cotta manufacturers, and elevator companies to submit bids. Those asked rushed to compete, even though winning the job meant keeping your prices low. But even if you ended up not making a lot on the job you'd won, you were still grateful to get picked, because the Fuller Company now controlled so much of New York's building industry.

Starrett put in an order to the American Bridge Company, one of the dozens of formerly independent steel companies that now belonged to U.S. Steel, for 3,680 tons of structural steel, based on Corydon Purdy's calculations. He calculated that costs for the new building, including labor, would total at least $1 million. Now the weather

Corydon Purdy, circa 1930.

was turning warm, and it was time to prepare the flatiron site for construction.

One morning in early May 1901, the men of the Northwestern Salvage and Wrecking Company arrived at the site with their heavy equipment to begin demolition of the existing properties. By now most of the leases in the buildings had expired. To the few tenants whose leases still had some time left, the new landlord had offered monetary compensation. Among them were four recent college graduates, who had celebrated the Cumberland Realty's gift to them of one month's free rent, plus $145, with a dinner at the Waldorf-Astoria. So now the buildings stood empty, except for one tenant, Colonel Winfield Scott Proskey, of the National Guard's Seventy-first Regiment. He lived on the sixth floor of the Cumberland, and had refused all offers of money. And now, he was refusing to budge. He would remain in his apartment, he said, until his lease ran out, in October.

Cumberland Realty dispatched two men to try to reason with Proskey. They told him that the George A. Fuller Construction Company was the force behind Cumberland. "They're pretty big people," the men told Proskey. They told him not to be a fool.

"You don't scare me," Proskey said. The men then warned him that with all the construction going on, Broadway would be all torn up during the coming summer months, and Proskey was in danger of contracting malaria. Proskey, a native of Florida, told them that he didn't mind.

Workmen began tearing down the other buildings on the flatiron. Within a few days, only the Cumberland was still standing. Thomas Shanley, head of one of Northwestern Wrecking Company's crews, now knocked on Proskey's door. Proskey opened it. He was a big man, more than six feet tall. Behind him, Shanley noticed, a Colt revolver lay on a table.

Shanley told Proskey that he had orders from Cumberland Realty to begin dismantling the building that very day. "Go ahead," Proskey told him. "I'm not leaving."

Shanley had the water and gas shut off. He took the building elevator out of service. Proskey promptly set up a bucket hoist to bring water through his window. He brought in a small tank of gas, to which he attached a burner, and a portable oil stove. The next day, the wreckers tore all the doors off their frames, and all the windows from all the apartments, except for Proskey's. They removed the glass from the skylight above the staircase, and demolished the staircase, too. Proskey promptly went out and got a ladder, which he placed where the staircase had been.

By now it was mid-May. Every day of delay was costing Cumberland Realty thousands of dollars. Proskey went to court, where he was represented by his brother Samuel, an attorney, who obtained an injunction against the Cumberland Realty to immediately cease any demolition that would make Colonel Proskey's apartment dangerous and uninhabitable. The judge also ordered Cumberland to reinstate water, gas, and elevator service to the lone tenant until his lease ran out. But Strong & Cadwalader, representing the opposing side, stated that the terms of the injunction meant that Fuller could lawfully proceed with the demolition. The only condition to be met, they said, was that Proskey be able to continue living in his apartment. "We merely have to run an elevator for him," they said. Cumberland Realty immediately installed an elevator, which, like most at that time, was hydraulically powered. It ran only when the water pressure was unusually good. In the meantime the wreckers continued to demolish everything in the building that didn't touch Proskey's apartment. The five floors below him were torn up, and huge cracks began to spread across Proskey's walls and floors.

By now people all over the country were following a newspaper story about the lone tenant holding up a $2 million building project in New York. *The New York Times* remarked that if Gilbert and Sullivan were still alive, they would surely use Colonel Proskey, "the plucky soldier," as a subject for one of their comic operas. Cumberland Realty in desperation now offered Proskey $5,000 to vacate. Proskey refused. On May 19, he told the *Chicago Tribune* that he was not interested in money, but whether a landlord had the right to break a tenant's lease, adding, in his Florida drawl, "This is a question of personal *honah*." Although on the same day, according to an affidavit later given by a Fuller Company official, Proskey countered Cumberland's offer with a demand for a rent-free apartment in the Fifth Avenue Hotel, with a window facing Madison Square Park for the duration of his lease, and $10,000.

Proskey returned to his apartment. Ten days later, Cumberland's attorneys told the newspapers of a new discovery: Proskey had filed for bankruptcy three months earlier. According to court papers that Strong & Cadwalader had unearthed, he owed creditors nearly $20,000. His sole assets consisted of two suits, a military uniform, and his apartment lease.

Within a few weeks Cumberland Realty had purchased Proskey's lease from a court-appointed trustee for an undisclosed sum. Some time in mid-June, he left the Cumberland Hotel for the last time. His name disappeared from the newspapers. But Proskey would resurface again in 1910, when he, then living in California, and another man, a Nevadan named George Wendell, would pay nearly a quarter of a million dollars in cash for California's Plumas-Eureka gold mine, one of the West's largest. The newspapers claimed that the mine had yielded $40 million.

The half-demolished Cumberland now stood empty, an ugly ruin that would soon be razed to the ground, to make way for a new skyscraper.

CHAPTER FOUR

PREPARING TO BUILD

$\mathcal{A}$ DRAWING OF THE NEW building that would soon arise at the intersection of Twenty-third Street, Broadway, and Fifth Avenue appeared on the front page of the *New York Herald* on June 2, 1901, with the caption: FLATIRON BUILDING.

The image really did resemble a monster version of the cast-iron object found in everybody's kitchen. And what a strange location—a little triangular lot in the middle of an intersection!—for this strangely shaped new skyscraper. People were talking about the Flatiron Building—the name had entered the popular lexicon—even though it hadn't yet been built. It didn't yet exist, but it was already famous. As thousands every day rushed by the rubble-strewn Cumberland site, doubtless many were trying to picture the Flatiron Building in their respective minds. An editorial in *Life* magazine that appeared on June 20 stated:

> In this partly civilized age and city, it is proposed to erect on the
> flatiron at Twenty-third Street, where Fifth Avenue and Broadway

converge, an office building more than twenty stories high. The land has been bought at a great price, and the buyers propose to make their purchase profitable at any cost of damage to the sightlines of Madison Square. New York has no law that restricts the height of buildings, and there is nothing to hinder the consummation of this appalling purpose. Moreover, Madison Square is not a bad-looking place as it is, and ought to be one of the beauty spots of the city. It is grievous to think that its fair proportions are to be marred by this outlandish structure. In Boston they sometimes contrive to avoid such calamities, but here in New York the price of land determines the height of the building, and we have to take what comes. All we can do is to hope that it won't be as bad as we fear, and if it is, to look the other way.

But it is a pity.

The Flatiron would be the first skyscraper north of Union Square. Inevitably, it seemed, many more would follow, as Manhattan property values continued to soar. At the minimum investors were building fifteen stories, if they wanted any return on their money. A building's first five stories paid the taxes, the second five, the other building expenses. But only above the tenth floor did the profits begin to roll in. So you wanted your new building as high as possible. Fifteen years would pass before New York would finally impose height restrictions and setback requirements for skyscrapers. It would be the first zoning law in the nation, but for now, a builder was limited only by his ability to attract investors. Speculators were busy buying up whatever old buildings they could. After quickly demolishing them, they combined the now-empty lots, and on them erected fifteen- and twenty-story apartment houses, hotels, and office buildings.

Nowhere was construction activity more frenzied than along Broadway. "The spirit of change is making the familiar street unrecogniz-

Excavation for the Flatiron Building, fall 1901.

able," wrote a reporter for *The Brooklyn Eagle,* during the summer of 1901. "Probably not more than a hundred old buildings can now feel safe." Reporters that summer took to riding the trolley up Broadway to keep track of the pace of progress. Standing at the dingy windows, they enjoyed terrific views of block after block of buildings being torn down, alternating with the skeletons of just-started new structures, and piles of building debris—broken bricks, chunks of stone, pieces of timber— and ugly plywood boards walling off entire blocks.

And the noise! It was enough to drive you out of your mind. Wrote one trolley-hopping reporter: "Above the harsh clang of the bells and the roar of the overhead railroads, you hear the teeth of the drill biting into the rock on which New York is built. A thunder clap of dynamite blows loose a boulder, and looking over the side of the car, which tears without nervousness over a ramshackle, propped and wedged temporary way, you see . . . New York, the greatest mining camp on earth."*

Workmen digging out foundations resorted to dynamite when their pickaxes and pneumatic drills hit Manhattan's famously hard bedrock—schist, a variety of granite. The Interboro Rapid Transit Company was also using dynamite to blast out tunnels for the new subway that would begin at Bowling Green and travel up Broadway until Twenty-third Street, where it would veer east to Fourth Avenue, and continue north, cross the river, and reach all the way to the Bronx. Construction was moving along rapidly, and causing much disruption for whatever lay in its path. Dynamite blasts caused windows to crack and buildings to shake. Streets were ripped up and traffic diverted. Passersby glancing down into the pits saw the suddenly exposed guts of the city—electric lines, steam, water, and gas pipes, and sewers and water mains—suspended by chains attached to heavy cross timbers. Underneath, to depths of sometimes one hundred feet, workmen—Irish, Italians (brought over from Italy, many of whom would return home after the job was done), and "negroes," as people then called African Americans, toiled. The new subway was helping to push New York's frantic real estate activity northward, to Thirty-fourth Street and beyond.

At Herald Square, a reporter for the socialist *World's Work* wrote, Thirty-fourth Street "stood up like a ridge out of a great hole of excavations." Here was the construction site of the new Macy's department store, another Fuller Company project. Black had acquired the contract

---

* John Foster Fraser, a British journalist then covering American business for the *Yorkshire Post*. Fraser then returned to England, where he published a book, *America at Work* (London, Cassel & Company, 1903), containing some of his newspaper articles. America both fascinated and repelled him. In the prologue, he writes: "Personally I would not care to live in America, because there is such a lack of repose, because the general conversation among men is always on one subject—money-making."

through his relationship with Henry Morgenthau, a member of Black's board and a friend of the Straus family, who owned Macy's. At ten stories high, and occupying the entire block between Thirty-fourth and Thirty-fifth Streets, the new Macy's, the newspapers exclaimed, would be "mammoth," in fact, the largest store in the world.

As soon as the news of the store's impending move to Thirty-fourth Street from Fourteenth broke—the spring of 1901—Saks, another department store, announced that it, too, would move uptown. Morgenthau and ex-Mayor Grant, another board member of Harry Black's new skyscraper trust, immediately purchased the entire block front on the west side of Broadway between Thirty-third and Thirty-fourth Streets—just south of the Macy's site—for $1,650,000. They then sold it to another syndicate for $2 million. All the tenants on the block—James Corbett's saloon, Childs' restaurant, and the theatrical landmark Wilson's drugstore—had just been ordered to vacate their stores, which were going to be leveled. Rumor had it that in their place, another huge department store would be built. And the northwest corner of Thirty-fourth and Fifth was now an empty lot, where, until recently, had stood the white marble, mansard-roofed mansion that department store magnate A. T. Stewart had built for himself just after the Civil War. "Beautiful it was, and costly, but it had to yield," wrote a reporter in the *New York Tribune* on January 30, 1902. "Piece by piece, the sculptured marble, the fluted columns, were taken down and relegated to the oblivion of the second-hand building material yard." In its place, the Knickerbocker Trust Company would erect a bank building, now being designed by McKim, Mead, and White. To the west, on Seventh Avenue, the Pennsylvania Railroad Company had just purchased land to build a new railroad station—yet another Fuller project. Speculators were also buying up properties in the theater district around Longacre Square, on Forty-second Street.

Harry Black continued to insist that even with the steady movement of the city uptown, and Madison Square's nearby cross streets growing decidedly grittier, the neighborhood would continue to hold

A. T. Stewart's mansion, Thirty-fourth Street and Fifth Avenue, 1879.

its own. And in fact property values were doing just fine. One reason was that New York, with its availability of capital and lacking the class system still in place in the European capitals, was now becoming an intellectual capital. Writers, publishers, artists, photographers, musicians: all were coming to New York, needing cheap space. So as luxury retail tenants headed north, many practitioners of these arts, as well as other businesses in some way connected to the arts, were moving into the vacated spaces.

Between Union and Madison Squares, most of the ten-cent weekly magazines that the growing middle class was now gobbling up—*Munsey's, Frank Leslie's, McClure's,* filled with stories and reportage by such greats as Theodore Dreiser and Ida Tarbell—had their offices. Publishers of popular music—another specifically New York-centered endeavor that fed the average person's soul in the form of mass-produced sheet music, to be played at home on a piano—now filled the shabby brownstones lining Twenty-eighth Street between Broadway and Fifth.

There, passersby heard daily the tinny sounds of tunes being played by composer-hopefuls on the cheap pianos provided for auditions. (And therefore, we believe, arose the expression "Tin Pan Alley."*)

And besides these various publishing concerns, all of which depended on human intellect in order to make profits, wholesale clothing businesses were also proliferating in the area between Fifth and Sixth Avenues, stretching from Fourteenth all the way up to Thirty-fourth Streets. The growth of this industry was due in large part to Jewish immigrants who, having worked in sweatshops when they first arrived in America, were now making the leap to owning their own *schmatte* (clothing) businesses. Jewish entrepreneurs were rapidly buying and selling existing loft buildings, and constructing new ones, to house their clothing factories and showrooms. Most were twelve stories high, made of brick. "This is one of the most interesting and wholesome current movements in real estate," the *Real Estate Record and Builders' Guide,* a weekly must-read for everybody connected to the business, noted on October 12, 1901. Most of the new lofts had twelve stories, and some had entrances on two streets, "and are thus peculiarly adapted to a wholesale business."

At lunchtime, the Italian and Jewish immigrants who worked in the loft buildings poured into the streets, to the displeasure of the merchants along nearby Ladies' Mile. These girls, the merchants complained, stood in front of shop windows, gawking at merchandise that they couldn't afford to buy. There were so many of them that they blocked shoppers from entering the stores. Some area merchants banded together to form an association with the express aim of protecting the area from what they considered its ongoing deterioration. But these merchants were confusing value with aesthetics. In New York, making money trumped all, to such a degree that grittiness, if its existence proved

---

* But there are many explanations for how this term first arose. See Irving Lewis Allen, *The City in Slang* (New York: Oxford, 1993).

financially lucrative, equaled glamour. This was how New York differed from European capitals, most of all Paris, and nobody understood this better than Harry Black.

Of course the trade-off for all the opportunity that New York offered was its lack of charm and beauty. Everybody knew this, most of all industrialists like Frick and Morgan who, craving beautiful cities, debarked for Europe, and returning, commissioned Beaux-Arts-trained architects to re-create Paris in New York—in the form of grand public buildings and apartment houses. The neighborhood around Eno's flatiron was particularly devoid of charm, but now the new Fuller Building, with its distinctive shape and Beaux-Arts detailing, would change that.

At the end of June, a heat wave suddenly erupted in New York. Temperatures, accompanied by unbearable humidity, shot up into the nineties. Wealthy New Yorkers closed up their houses along Fifth and Madison Avenues and departed for their country homes, leaving uptown Manhattan so quiet and deserted that a stranger might think a plague had visited the city. Joining the exodus were Harry Black, who left his Madison Avenue apartment for the summer and headed for a resort in Atlantic City, as Allon was still in Europe.

Great suffering afflicted all the unfortunate souls who had no means of escape from the sweltering city. Inside the crowded tenement houses, where half of New York's population lived, some apartments had no windows, only airshafts. Entire families slept on roofs and fire escapes, or even their front stoops. People rode the streetcar across the Brooklyn Bridge to Coney Island, where they spent the night on the beach, lying on blankets. Hospitals were packed with patients suffering from heat-related illnesses, who, *The New York Times* wrote, had been "hauled through the streets by exhausted ambulance horses." Most of the streetcars by now ran on electricity, but just about every other kind of vehicle in the city still relied on horses. The poor animals, too, were collapsing from the heat in such great numbers that everybody was scrambling to find replacements to draw the patrol wagons, ambulances, cabs, and ice wagons. As a result ice deliveries came late, or not at all. Those unlucky enough not to get their ice had to buy it at the nearest butcher or corner saloon, if indeed it could be spared. And the water being drawn from the river used in the making of ice was now so warm that it slowed down the process, thereby adding to the city-wide ice shortage.

Every day, newspapers printed the names of people who had died from the heat. Horses were dying, too. Their stinking carcasses laid in the streets for days before the city's overwhelmed health department could finally collect and dispose of them. On July 1, as thermometers about the city were registering over 100 degrees, fourteen horses collapsed in the streets around Madison Square Park alone. Perhaps some were hauling away debris from the flatiron lot, where the Cumberland Hotel had finally been reduced to rubble.

The park was crowded with people seeking relief from the heat. Most were standing about, rather than sitting, because during the past week, the benches that up to now had lined the park's shady paths had been moved into the direct sun. In their place now stood lovely cane-bottomed, green-cushioned rocking chairs. But if you wanted to plop down on one, it would cost you five cents. The benches remained free. To offer two classes of seating in New York's parks was, until now, unheard of. A man named Oscar Spate had arrived from his native London in April expressly to introduce this idea, which, he believed, would make him rich. He approached New York's park commissioner, George Clausen. "I represent," Spate said, "the Comfort Chair Company of London." He made Clausen a proposition: He would purchase 200 chairs for New York's parks, and rent them at a nickel apiece. For this privilege, Spate said, he would pay the city $500 a year. Pay chairs, Spate told Clausen, were a long-established custom in both London and Paris.

Not only did they offer comfort, but also protected decent people from having to share a bench with bums. Would not New Yorkers as well, Spate said, appreciate this opportunity?

Clausen loved Spate's idea. The chairs, he thought, would help clean up New York's parks, in particular Madison and Union Squares, which New Yorkers were now increasingly avoiding, due to the large numbers of men who, as *The Brooklyn Eagle* on July 10, 1901, put it, "did not work or wash," and were congregating there every afternoon. Their presence was more than just a nuisance. A physician whom Clausen knew, who lived in one of the fine residences along the Madison Avenue side of the park, had recently complained to him that Madison Square was a breeding ground for all manner of diseases. In the past year, the physician told Clausen, he had seen men coughing up tuberculous sputum onto the ground; others wandering about with contagious scalp diseases, such as barber's itch and ringworm; and children with pustulous eruptions. Why, one day he'd even seen a man with smallpox stretched out comfortably on one of the benches.

Clausen gave Spate a five-year contract, which took effect immediately, in mid-April. The spring weather had been unusually cool, so nobody had paid much attention to the chairs, which, besides Madison Square, had also been placed in Union Square and Central Park. But then the heat wave began. And now, on the hottest July 1 on record, an eighteen-year-old student at the College for Dentistry named Abraham Cohen plopped himself down in one of Spate's chairs in Madison Square Park, removed his collar, and wiped the sweat off his face.

All of a sudden, a tired-looking man in a gray uniform was standing over him, asking him for five cents.

For what? Cohen asked, whereupon the man explained to him that he worked for the Comfort Chair Company, which owned the new chairs. If Cohen wanted to sit on a Spate chair, the guard said, it would cost him five cents. The guard added that he worked for Spate, not the city.

Cohen did not budge. Soon a police officer named Louis Lues appeared. "Come on, young feller, pay the man or move along," he told Cohen.

Cohen replied that he had every right to sit on the chair.

"You've got a right to go sit on a bench," Lues said. He pointed to the row of benches that were baking in the sun. By now a crowd had gathered around the two men.

Cohen replied: "If you bring me a bench under the shade of this tree, where they have always been, I'll sit on it." The crowd applauded.

"Say, don't you get fresh, young fellow," Lues retorted.

"Well, I'll sit on the walk, then," Cohen said. "I'm not particular about a seat, but I want to stay here because it's shady." His response further delighted the onlookers, one of whom shouted: "Dat's right, kid. De park's free."

Lues, by now understandably furious, told Cohen to go to hell and arrested him. As Lues led his prisoner away, the crowd followed, jeering at the policeman and cheering Cohen. When one man began laughing hysterically, Lues arrested him, too. "When I think of the officer telling him to go to a warmer place than this—as if there could be any warmer place than New York is now—why, I just can't help laughing," the onlooker later explained to the judge, who released both him and Cohen, but ordered that the latter had to pay if he wanted to sit in one of the lovely green chairs.

The newspapers pounced on the Cohen story, which New Yorkers in turn eagerly gobbled up. In the meantime, a series of furious storms on July 3 broke the heat. Clerks in sweltering skyscraper offices, upon hearing the rumble of thunder, had rushed up to the rooftops, where they stood, hatless and in their shirtsleeves, watching the black clouds and breathing in the gusts of wind, as the first drops of rain splashed on their upturned faces. The rain started pouring down, hard. Horses down on the street stood, or kept walking, enjoying the feel of the water streaming from their sides. By evening, temperatures had dropped by 20 degrees. The heat wave had lasted an entire week and killed more than 200 people and 150 horses.

But the rain did nothing to cool off the Spate controversy, which by now was front-page news, and the subject of indignant editorials in defense of the common man, not just in the populist press. "No, the parks are for the public, undistinguished by their bank accounts," the staid *The Sun* solemnly wrote. William Randolph Hearst's notoriously sensational *Evening Journal* turned the Spate chairs into screaming headlines and the subject of cartoons. In the meantime, the *Journal* filed a suit enjoining Clausen from carrying out his contract with Spate.

Then young Abraham Cohen sued Clausen on the charge of false arrest. The policeman who had arrested Cohen was also named as a defendant.

People were now deliberately heading for Madison Park, just so they could sit in the Spate chairs, and then refuse to pay, or to move. "What? Ain't this a free country? This is a public park, ain't it? You don't get no five cents from me. See?" was a typical response to one of the poor attendants whose job it was to ask chair occupants for payment. On one afternoon, "Terrible" Terry McGovern, a featherweight boxer known for his lightning-quick knockout punches, sat in a Spate chair and dared one of the attendants to "come and collect." The attendant declined. Crowds—"benchers," the papers now called them—were gathering daily at Madison Square expressly to jeer at the humiliation suffered by Spate attendants, who sometimes in their desperation would run off to find policemen to arrest their harassers. Except that the police were refusing, because their commissioner, Michael Murphy, had ordered his men not to arrest any Spate chair scofflaws. The rumor was that Murphy had it in for Clausen because Tammany hadn't gotten a cut from the Spate contract. Sometimes the benchers also harassed those who, when asked to pay for the privilege of sitting in a Spate chair, willingly handed over a nickel.

Finally, one afternoon, a mob totaling 1,000 men and boys—according to *The New York Times*—chased an attendant clear across Fifth Avenue, into the Fifth Avenue Hotel, with some shouting "Lynch him! Kill him!" Others overturned chairs or benches or picked up chairs and threw them in the street, where a brewery wagon crushed one "into kindling wood." The riot overwhelmed the few policemen assigned to the park. More policemen had to be called in, who, upon arriving, dispersed the mob and made several arrests. Rioting in the park continued over the next several days.

Clausen had had enough. The park commissioner called a press conference at the Plaza Hotel on July 11, where he told reporters that he had granted Oscar Spate the privilege of renting chairs to the city because he believed it would benefit the public. Especially, Clausen said, the women and children whose means did not permit them to leave the city during the summer. But, he continued, "the great public of New York, so far as may be picked from the majority of great organs of public opinion, seems to condemn the innovation. And I hold it to be the first duty of a public servant to bow to the public will." Therefore, he said, he was annulling the contract he had made with Spate. As for the chairs, the city would purchase them, and confine their use to women and children.

That evening, some 10,000 people gathered at Madison Square to celebrate Clausen's decision. One hundred and twenty-five policemen were deployed for crowd control, but their presence, it turned out, was not needed. According to *The New York Times*, officials declared it one of the best-natured demonstrations ever held in the city. Bands played and fireworks went off, courtesy of Hearst's *Journal*. Among the orators who spoke was Tammany leader Dr. W. J. O'Sullivan, who attacked Clausen for "introducing into our democratic city a European idea which inclined to a class distinction. He was antagonizing a fundamental proposition upon which our free institutions rest."

But with the riots, a line had been crossed. The non-Hearst papers, up to now championing what was thought a popular cause, now pulled back. "There will be no paid park chairs . . . Whether that is wise or not, it is unmistakably the will of the majority rules. At the same time there ought to be some way of providing seats in the smaller parks for women and children . . . Anybody who has tried to find a park seat along the Battery wall, or in Union or Madison Squares in the afternoon knows that the benches are infested with a class of men whose presence would drive clean women and children to move on," wrote *The Brooklyn Eagle.* The voices of those who had liked Clausen's idea just fine were making news. "If the Spate chairs must go, why should not hansom cabs go, parlor cars go, orchestra and all reserved seats go—indeed, everything go that the disgruntled don't like?" wrote "W. P." to *The New York Times.*

As for Oscar Spate, he was livid. He, like so many others, had been lured to America by the promise of free enterprise. Now he felt betrayed. That same evening he went to court, where he obtained a preliminary injunction against Clausen's voiding of their contract. As for Spate's chairs, the judge ruled that for the time being, the public could use them without charge. So the matter remained unsettled.

Hearst's *Evening Journal* now sued for an injunction against the use of pay chairs in city parks. At three in the afternoon on July 11, the injunction was granted. Spate conceded defeat. He ordered his attendants to gather up his chairs. His fifteen-year-old son, Garner Spate, whom Spate had put in charge of Madison Square, told the attendants: "Men, it is all up for the present. We must hustle these chairs out of here." Many people were sitting on the chairs when the attendants began their work. All vacated when asked to do so, except for one, a Philadelphia businessman, who refused to move, even when asked to do so by several policemen. "If I had my way," one of the officers said, "I'd hang you from the nearest tree."

Oscar Spate sold his chairs to Wanamaker's, which in turn advertised "A Sale of Historic Chairs! The Climax of the Spate Park Chair Incident." The chairs were, according to the ad, "large and comfortable, made of the best materials ever put into chairs of this sort."

Spate left New York. Six years later, he turned up in Pittsburgh, a city where many people had great wealth on account of the steel industry. There he took the name Reginald Spaulding, and set up a "business," as it were, charging money in exchange for introducing wealthy Pittsburghers to members of the English nobility. He even claimed that he would have them presented at the Court of St. James. The operation was a fraud, and the law eventually caught up with Spate. He was convicted and sentenced to thirty days in the Allegheny County jail, where he peeled potatoes all day.

The news of his incarceration reached his aged, three-times married, and very wealthy now-widowed mother in London, who was in ill health. Reginald Seymour—this was Oscar Spate's real name—was his mother's favorite son, but his shenanigans had been a constant source of sorrow to her. Within a day or two of hearing of this latest fracas she died, leaving him a millionaire. Still, despite efforts by a London barrister representing his mother's estate to free him, he had to serve the eighteen days remaining on his jail term. "To think that with all this money I should be here peeling blasted potatoes," he told a *New York Times* reporter. "My word! But when I get out I shall hasten to London and claim what belongs to me." America had disappointed Reginald Seymour.

On August 1, as the Spate chair fracas was winding down, Corydon Purdy filed a permit application with the city to erect a steel-framed structure measuring 286 feet tall. It would have twenty stories, plus an attic. Besides steel, it would consist almost entirely of terra-cotta, a material much used by the ancients for their tiles and drainpipes, and now being reinvented as a state-of-the-art product for skyscrapers.

The 1871 Chicago fire had proven that "burnt earth" did not burn, and New York's new building code required skyscrapers to be fireproof. The terra-cotta business was now booming, an ideal material from inside to out. Manufacturers used it to coat and therefore fireproof cast-iron columns, turned it into blocks and tiles, or fashioned it into slabs of "lumber," to be used in a variety of ways. The Flatiron's elevator shafts would have terra-cotta partitions and iron grilles. The roof would consist of terra-cotta arches, concrete, and flat tiles, with terra-cotta coping on the edges. The floor partitions, to be supported on horizontal steel beams, would be made of hollow terra-cotta blocks, now standard in skyscraper construction because of their fireproof quality.

And save for the first four floors, which would be entirely of buff limestone, the Flatiron exterior would consist of terra-cotta, which was the perfect skin for steel skeleton buildings and currently all the rage. It weighed one-third of equivalent masonry walls. Purchasing, cutting, and sculpting a chunk of stone into a building adornment cost ten times more than creating a piece of, as people now called it, architectural terra-cotta. This terra-cotta was beautiful, designed by architects who looked to classical and Beaux-Arts motifs for their inspiration, and executed en masse by skilled workers in factories, many in New Jersey, which had an abundance of clay pits.

And there was another, the Atlantic Terra Cotta Company, just across the channel called Arthur Kill, in Tottenville, a village on the extreme southern point of Staten Island. Tottenville had eight shipyards, from where two freight boats left daily for Manhattan. Atlantic had won the bid for the Flatiron commission, and there, some time during the second week in August, Frederick Dinkelberg, who had sketched designs for the Flatiron's thousands of terra-cotta pieces, arrived from Chicago to inspect the plaster molds. He had been sent by his boss, Daniel Burnham, who, overwhelmed with commissions that kept him constantly on the road, reacted with his characteristic micromanaging. The Proskey-caused delays had made Burnham, always impatient, desperate for the Flatiron project to finally get under way. Before Dinkelberg's departure, Burnham had fired off a testy note to one of the Flatiron project managers, a man named Macruber. "Models of exterior ornament of Flatiron should be made by the very best man in New York. Subject to inspection before being executed. Will you see to this?" A few days later, Burnham wrote to Macruber again, this time indulging in his idiosyncratic habit of referring to himself in the third person: "You understand of course that we expect to have semi-glazed terra cotta and not the ordinary stuff. This was agreed upon between you and our Mr. Burnham when in New York."

In Chicago, Dinkelberg had sketched square and rectangular bricks and tiles of Romanesque and geometric designs, and oriels—slightly projecting windows—that would ascend from the seventh to fifteenth floors, on each of the two long sides of the building: jambs, sills, lintels, spandrels and moldings decorated with sunbursts and flowers, oval medallions of acanthus leaves, lion's heads and gargoyles, rondels of women's faces, a tooth-edged cornice, pilasters, and columns with Corinthian capitals. Here and there, he placed a fleur-de-lis. A terra-cotta balustrade would wrap around the roof, where, right at the point, a pair of terra-cotta cherubs would perch, looking out over Manhattan. They were the *genii loci,* guardian spirits of the Flatiron.

Atlantic would produce tens of thousands of terra-cotta pieces for the Flatiron. Dinkelberg perhaps remained in Tottenville for a week or so to supervise the manufacture of plaster molds, and no doubt enjoying himself after hours as the company guest at one of that town's lovely resort hotels. In the meantime the workers began production of his terra-cotta. They mixed fresh clay with grog—used terra-cotta ground into powder—in carefully measured proportions, packed the resulting clay by hand into the molds, which they then tied up with wire cords, and left all to dry. Then the pieces would be removed from the molds and left to dry for two more weeks, before being sprayed with glaze to produce a matte finish, just as Burnham had so vehemently specified.

Finally, the pieces would be slowly fired in Atlantic's three gigantic cone-shaped kilns—each one measured forty-eight feet high, with twenty-four-feet diameters—over a period of ten to twelve days, at temperatures that gradually climbed to over 2,000 degrees Fahrenheit before cooling down. Every finished piece, after being marked with a number to allow for easy assemblage on the construction site, would be packed into a wooden crate, along with straw to prevent breakage, to be loaded onto wagons that workhorses would then haul the short distance to the docks. Freight ships would then carry the cargo to Manhattan, where it would be unloaded onto wagons that horses dragged up Broadway, to be delivered at the construction site.

In mid-August, as terra-cotta production was beginning, the Buildings Department rejected the Flatiron Building application, instead presenting Purdy with a list of additional conditions that would have to be met if he wanted approval. Specifically, he would have to provide detailed information about the girders and beams to be used for the floor framing, and fireproofing. And, most important, the department wanted sketches of Purdy's wind bracing system, because the force of the wind could cause a skinny, tall, triangular structure, standing alone in the middle of an intersection, to twist about on its axis if not properly braced.

Harry Black was no doubt rankled by this latest construction delay, another among the countless headaches that piled up in proportion to the many ongoing Fuller projects. He didn't, however, waste his time trying to find solutions. No, that job belonged to the people who worked for him, like his man Paul Starrett, who was also having to confront the mess that the new Macy's, now in the excavation stage, had turned into. Black had won the contract by bidding ridiculously low, and now the Fuller Company was committed to building the "largest store in the world" for the Nathan Straus family for no more than twenty cents a cubic foot, a completely unrealistic price. Black had thereby created a nightmare for Starrett, who, besides the Flatiron, was now in charge of all of the Fuller Company's work above Fourteenth Street. Black, though, was confident that Starrett could pull it off, since wasn't that precisely why he was paying Starrett? Black's job was to make the deals, and that in his mind was enough to keep a man busy. And nobody could deny that he was doing a good job. He had already created the biggest real estate company in New York—newspapers were now calling it "the skyscraper trust," much to his delight. But he wanted more: more capital, and a bigger company. And, naturally, he wanted his own skyscraper, like any proper trust, such as Standard Oil and U.S. Steel—both of which had built lofty headquarters worthy of their respective names one short block apart on Broadway's southern tip.

So it was high time to get started on the new Fuller Building, which people were already talking about. Except that they were calling it the "Flatiron" Building, which probably displeased Black, since the whole idea of a corporation having its own building was to advertise. Perhaps Black consoled himself by believing that once the Fuller Building actually existed in reality, rather than just as an idea in the public's consciousness, its correct name would naturally displace the homely sobriquet.

Black, at this point, pressured Corydon Purdy to get moving on redoing the Flatiron application. How hard, Black surely thought, could it be to sketch out a few drawings, and do a few calculations? Besides, Black was sailing to Europe in mid-September, and he wanted badly to see the excavation under way before leaving. It would be a business trip, mostly, to start expanding the Fuller Company business to London, Paris, and Germany. In Paris, he would join Allon, whom he hadn't seen in seven months. She had been abroad since January, following her father's death.

Purdy obliged. Twelve days later, the hardworking young engineer submitted an amendment to the original application. His responses to each of the Buildings Department's objections—they numbered ten in all—were typewritten, and accompanied by various tables and detailed ink illustrations. One table listed the dimensions of each support column. Another showed the measurements for each steel configuration—knee-braces, spandrel plate girders, gusset-plates—that would be riveted to the angles of the steel beams, to protect the building from twisting in the wind. More drawings showed how each floor would be framed. A table listed the thickness of the walls for each floor. In addition, Purdy noted that the fire apparatus as required by the 1899 building code—four-inch diameter standpipes, to run from the cellar all the way up to the roof, with outlets for fire hoses—would be provided.

But the last item on the Buildings Department's list of objections was proving a sticking point. It read: "Proper fire escapes must be installed." The new code specifically required skyscrapers to be fireproof, that is, they must be built of brick, stone, terra-cotta, Portland cement, iron, steel, and have no combustible material—specifically wood. And they were also to have a certain number of enclosed interior fire stairs, based on the building's height and square footage. But the code made no mention of exterior fire escapes, which in fact were better suited to the ubiquitous tenement houses than skyscrapers. Interior fire stairs usually precluded the need for outdoor fire escapes in skyscrapers. The Buildings Department imposed the latter on skyscrapers only on a case by case basis. And who knows why whoever examined the Flatiron application decided thus. Perhaps it had to do with assuaging the public, who, always terrified of fire, would be reassured by the sight of a fire escape attached to the outside of the Flatiron Building. Even though experts kept insisting that skyscrapers were safe, in fact, far safer than the old, highly combustible brick-and-wood-frame buildings, people were not convinced. The thought of being trapped on, say, the fifteenth floor, in a burning building that held, as the Flatiron would, 1,500 occupants, terrified them.

In its advertisements, Fuller Company proudly and specifically proclaimed itself as the builder of fireproof buildings. And nobody knew more than Purdy about fireproofing. He had delivered several papers on the subject. No record exists of how he, Dinkelberg, Burnham, Black, and everybody else who was working on the Flatiron reacted to the Buildings Department's demand for exterior fire escapes. But surely they were dismayed. Because of the Flatiron's shape and location, all of its sides would be visible, from every angle. So any fire escape attached to it, even if fashioned of the most ornate iron grille work, would also have to be visible, and therefore cause incalculable aesthetic damage to the skyscraper.

In Purdy's response to the Buildings Department, he tried to convince them to let him off the fire escapes requirement. "All of the exterior walls are façade," he dictated to his secretary, who then typed these words onto a separate form, along with the rest of Purdy's responses to the department's various objections to his Flatiron plans. The form, which survives in New York's municipal archives—one snippet of the paper trail that adds up to the Flatiron story—was then sent over to the Buildings Department. Hopefully, the department would reconsider.

The Buildings Department's response, which somebody there wrote by hand right onto the form, next to Purdy's typewritten objection, was: "Fire escapes will be put on as required by the Department of Buildings." But through those words appears a large slash—presumably made by somebody else. So no fire escape would mar the Flatiron's exterior, after all. And why this turnabout happened, we do not know. However, just about this time—the end of August 1901—the Tammany members of the city's Board of Aldermen, the equivalent of today's City Council, tried to rush through an ordinance nullifying Section 105 of the fire code. Section 105 required all material in skyscrapers to be of metal, fireproof wood, or metal-coated wood. Section 105 at the very least doubled the cost of windows in skyscrapers, because frames had to be made of metal, or special fireproof wood, with metal-coating, whereas ordinary buildings had simple wooden frames around their windowpanes.

But the non-Tammany aldermen blocked the amendment, which, if passed, would obviously have resulted in huge construction-related savings for skyscraper builders. The press soon got wind of the story. "There is a deal somewhere in this matter," Alderman McInness, the Republican minority leader, told the *Times* on September 4, 1901. Then adding, in the unselfconsciously racist parlance of the time, "The nigger in the fence should be smoked out." McInness had only to look at the board of the Fuller Company, where one of the directors was former New York Mayor and Tammany man Hugh J. Grant.

Likely the Fuller Company had convinced somebody down at Buildings to change their mind about the fire escapes. And, then they must have gone one further, even trying to get the fire code amended.

In any event, the amendment to the building code was now stalled, and not likely to go anywhere. So the Fuller Company must have gone back to their contact at the Buildings Department, because the next thing we know is that in October 1901, Fuller received a variance allowing them to use ordinary wood in their window frames for the Flatiron, and another skyscraper the company was now erecting, the new Jewelers' Building, on Maiden Lane in the Financial District.

The newspapers immediately picked up the story. The other, smaller construction companies—Thompson-Starrett, Fuller's main rival, most prominently among them—naturally cried foul. They accused politicians of giving special treatment to Black's skyscraper trust. And the story was getting bigger. Some fifty builders and architects banded together and hired a lawyer, who sued the Buildings Commissioner James G. Wallace, also a Tammany man, over the variance. In the city-wide elections one month later, a reformist coalition led by mayoral candidate Seth Low knocked out the Tammany machine. Commissioner Wallace, and all the Tammany men in city government, were fired from their jobs.

On December 17, a judge ruled that Wallace had failed to enforce the building laws, in effect voiding the variance that had been granted to the Fuller Company. The builders and architects also signed a petition opposing the amendment, which they presented at a hearing on December 20. There, Theodore Starrett, president of Thompson-Starrett, and brother of Paul, who worked for Harry Black, testified.

"There is no reason under the present law why any one firm of contractors should be granted special privileges. Our firm has complied with the law, and until the law is changed every other firm should be compelled to do the same," Starrett said. When asked if abolishing Section 105 would endanger the public, he answered, "Yes, in a great measure." Starrett also said that "a representative of the George A. Fuller Construction Company" approached Thompson-Starrett and asked them to sign a petition in favor of abolishing Section 105. But Thompson-Starrett, he said, refused.

Numerous fireproofing and insurance companies also showed up at the hearing to testify. A lawyer for the insurers specifically named the Fuller Company, criticizing it for its "selfish motives."

"The question of public life and safety," said the lawyer, "should be above the question of increasing the dividends of this company."

The Fuller Company, which always took pains to advertise the fireproof qualities of its skyscrapers, now had a serious public relations problem, and all of its own making. And it could only get worse, as the new Fusion Party administration would take office in January. Perez Stewart, appointed the new Buildings Commissioner, was vowing to go after every building violation in the city.

Paul Starrett reacted to Stewart's announcement by immediately ordering the Flatiron's window frames to be made of fireproof wood, and coated with copper.

On September 6, 1901, as Purdy was haggling with the Buildings Department over the revised Flatiron application, an anarchist shot President William McKinley in Buffalo at the Pan-American Exhibition. The news, sent by telegraph from Buffalo to newspapers around the country, was posted on all New York's Newspaper Row bulletin boards within minutes after being received, at a few minutes past four in the afternoon. Within the hour, as thousands of people were leaving their places of work for the day, the news began to spread quickly. Crowds stood in front of the newspaper offices, pushing and straining to read the boards. Newsboys clutching the evening papers rushed around the streets, shouting, "Extra, Extra!" The city felt tense.

Doctors removed one bullet from the president's breast without difficulty, but were unable to get at another, which had penetrated his abdomen. After the surgery, McKinley rallied. Doctors said that they expected him to recover. They assured the public that the inoperable bullet would present no problem. "If the slightest inflammation appears in the region of the lead, it will be immediately extracted. No difficulty is anticipated. One of Edison's best X-ray machines and his most skillful and trusted operator, Dr. H. A. Knolls, arrived today. The batteries were charged, and the machine is ready for instant use. With it the physicians say there is not the slightest doubt that the ball can be located perfectly for an operation," the *Times* reported. People expressed relief, and went on with their lives.

On September 11, 1901, the Buildings Department approved the Flatiron permit. In the meantime the president, according to his doctors, was continuing to improve. They issued regular reports to the reporters hanging about, describing his progress in minute detail. The possibility of blood poisoning, they said, was lessening. Why, he was even beginning to take solid food. And he had moved his bowels. After his breakfast on the morning of the twelfth, he even asked for a cigar. But on the thirteenth, he began to fail. Sepsis had set in. On September 14, President McKinley died. Vice President Theodore Roosevelt arrived in Buffalo from his Adirondack retreat, and was sworn in as President of the United States. He pledged to continue McKinley's policies.

McKinley's funeral took place on Wednesday, September 18. On Thursday, which was declared a national day of mourning, all business was suspended and schools were closed in New York City. People hung black buntings from tenement windows. Curiously, such displays were absent in the fashionable districts uptown. The reason was that most of the houses were still empty of their inhabitants, who did not as a rule return to the city for the season until October 1. Among those absent was Harry Black, who was now en route to Europe along with Allon.

People attended special memorial services in churches about the city. Afterward they wandered about the streets, or to the parks, where children played, enjoying their unexpected vacation from school. All of which made people feel as if they were celebrating a holiday. But then they remembered that their president had just been assassinated, and quickly substituted feelings of grief for happiness. Many people were wearing dark clothes or at least a mourning badge, and the men wore black ties. The most popular badge was a little American flag made out of silk, turned upside down to indicate distress.

At exactly three-thirty, the moment McKinley's coffin was being lowered into the ground in his birthplace, Canton, Ohio, all traffic—streetcars, elevated railways, cabs, even tugboats—came to a halt. People stood up, the men removing their hats. Military bands played solemn music in city parks. In Madison Square Park, the Seventy-first Regiment Band played "Nearer, My God, to Thee," which had been the late president's favorite hymn.

By the end of the day, people were feeling restless. Without work, they had nothing to do. All places of amusement—Coney Island, the penny arcades, the theaters—were also closed. The only places open were saloons, which by late afternoon became packed. There was, the *Times* reported, far more drinking than usual. The next day—Friday, September 20—New York returned to business as usual, and the wrecking company returned to the Flatiron, to finally complete the job it had begun four months earlier. As horses hauled away the remaining debris, workers moved in with pickaxes and shovels to begin excavation. First they dug up the layer of sand that lay over Manhattan's tough bedrock, which lies close to or at the surface until just south of Twenty-third Street. Then the bedrock starts to dip, finally to a depth of 155 feet below the surface at Manhattan's extreme tip, where most of the city's skyscrapers stood. There, *caissons*—huge, hollow piers made of steel or wood, pumped full of compressed air—had to be sunk through the sand, mud, clay, and gravel that lay on top of the schist. At the top of the caisson was a work chamber, which men entered and exited from through a vertical steel shaft. Once inside, they excavated the soil within the caisson, therefore causing it to sink, until it hit the bedrock.

Then each caisson was filled with concrete, forming piers that would support a foundation.

But at the Flatiron, you didn't need caissons, because you hit the bedrock at only thirty-five feet down. On top of the rock would rest a concrete-and-granite foundation. It in turn would support the Flatiron Building's steel skeleton, which would then easily carry thousands of pounds of beautiful terra-cotta bricks and tiles, as if they weighed nothing at all.

CHAPTER FIVE

BIGGER AND BIGGER

*H*ARRY BLACK SPENT A month in Europe, where he passed most of his time looking for opportunities to expand his company's operations. He met with potential investors in London, among them one Lord Revelstock, of the venerable banking house Baring Brothers, to whom Black proposed that the Fuller Company build several skyscrapers in various locations throughout London. "As an experiment," he told them. Black's idea was radical. To be sure, the British were fascinated with American know-how and ambition. Their newspaper correspondents sent frequent dispatches to London describing New York's frantic, constant movement in every direction, including upward, into the sky. But that didn't mean the British were ready for skyscrapers in their venerable city. Moreover there were practical considerations. For example, London's building law forbade any building to obstruct the neighboring building's light.

Black did not consider the law to be a serious hindrance to skyscraper construction in London. He was certain that once the British realized how much they stood to gain from building high, they would simply amend their laws. Just like people did in America. He told an

American reporter: "The owners of adjoining properties, however, whose light might be obstructed, fail to perceive that the value of their own property would be greatly enhanced by local improvement, and also by the practical illustration of their opportunity to build in a similar manner and thus obtain enormously increased rentals."

We have no record of Black's visit to Paris during that same trip abroad. But no doubt his attempts to extend the Fuller Company's operations there made no headway, either. Beautiful Paris, with its carefully maintained public spaces that were the envy of America's cities, and strict building codes—in 1898, when Cesar Ritz planned to start a hotel in an eighteenth-century *palais* on Place Vendôme, authorities told him he could do as he liked to the inside, but must not touch the outside, except to clean it—could not possibly accommodate skyscrapers. Indeed, New Yorkers visiting Paris immediately noticed the paucity of any private construction projects, especially in comparison to New York. But for all their insistence on uniformity, the French much admired American design. Indeed, at the Paris Exposition in 1900, the Fuller Company had won first prize for a model of Cass Gilbert's just-completed Broadway-Chambers Building. The new building was a particularly striking example of Beaux-Arts-inspired skyscraper design in New York. It had been one of Harry Black's first projects after he opened the company's office in New York. The prize-winning submission had been executed by Corydon Purdy, and it was actually two models. The first was a twelve-foot high skeleton frame, its beams made not of steel but brass. The second was a plaster replica, also twelve feet high.

What we do know for certain about Black's Parisian sojourn is that he met up there with his friend, the steel and wire magnate John W. "Bet-a-Million" Gates, so-nicknamed because of his gambling habits. There Gates and Allon, without Harry, shopped, perhaps together, since each purchased a pearl necklace. Gates's cost him $30,000, with Allon's topping Gates's, at $35,000. Gates returned to New York on September 17, where he paid the requisite 60 percent duty to U.S. Customs—$18,000—on the necklace.

The Blacks returned together to New York on October 19, aboard the White Star steamer *Teutonic*. But Allon, unlike Gates, failed to declare her new necklace to customs officials. Ten days later, a customs agent named Bidwell received a wire from Special U.S. Treasury Agent Theobauld in Paris. Theobauld had been looking for the necklace for three weeks, after being tipped off about its purchase by agents in Paris. Now, finally, the connection had been made to Allon Fuller.

New York's newspapers, now engaged in vicious circulation wars, jumped on the story of Allon Fuller's pearls, and how Black rushed to the Customs House at Bowling Green on October 29, with his wife's pearls in hand. Handing them over to Bidwell, he offered to write a check on the spot for $24,000 to the U.S. government, representing the amount of duty owed. What happened next is not clear. By some accounts Bidwell refused the money, saying that the pearls might be subject to confiscation, or, even if not, would first have to be appraised by the Treasury Department before any required duty was paid. So Black had to leave Allon's pearls behind in the Customs House. But this was not Black's version of events. When cornered by a reporter from the *World* later that day in the lobby of the Holland House, the luxurious apartment house at Thirtieth Street and Fifth Avenue where he and Allon maintained a suite, Black claimed that he had paid the duty, and "everything had been straightened out."

Headlines for the story had used the words "smuggle" and "seizure," words to which Black objected.

"It is all wrong to call this a seizure and to say that the necklace was smuggled," he said. "Yes, my wife bought the necklace in Paris. But she went abroad several months before I did, and of course a man doesn't know everything his wife buys." ("Mrs. Black is wealthy in her own right, and often purchases jewelry without consulting her husband about it, and he doesn't mind," wrote *The Sun*.) Black said the pearls were now in his possession. But he refused to show them to the reporter.

When asked to explain why he had brought the pearls back to the Customs House, Black said that his wife, "conscience-stricken" by her actions, had confessed to him that she had smuggled in the necklace. So naturally, he had rushed down to customs, in order to right her wrong. And that was, Harry said, the end of it.

The reporter persisted. Hadn't Black's friend Mr. Gates paid duty on the pearl necklace that he, coincidentally, had also purchased in Paris?

"Yes, Mr. Gates and I are good friends. If I didn't know him, Gates, perhaps I wouldn't have this bother," Black said.

"Do you mean Mr. Gates may have told the customs people about your necklace?" the reporter asked.

Harry Black laughed. "Mr. Gates and I," he said, "are good friends. And we were together in Paris."

Such, apparently, was Gates's and Black's idea of a practical joke.

By the time Harry and Allon returned from Paris, a huge, triangle-shaped hole, thirty-five feet deep, had been excavated on the former site of Eno's Cumberland Hotel. Eight-foot-high wooden boards surrounded the site. Traffic—electric streetcars, hansom cabs, horses pulling carts, pedestrians—streamed in all directions along each of the four broad thoroughfares that, by intersecting at three points, formed each of the triangle's sides. Here and there the fence had an opening, allowing workmen and machinery access to the site, and, to the curious passersby, a peek in. They saw, amidst a mass of mud, rocks, and piles of timber, the architect's shanty sitting atop a portion of the building's first floor, all wedged into the skinny angle formed by the intersection of Twenty-third, Fifth, and Broadway. Below would be the basement, and below that, the cellar, all enclosed with a six-foot-thick concrete retaining wall, which supported the bottom sec-

Erecting the steel columns, February 1902.

tions of the thirty-six rolled steel-support columns. Each column rested on two separate granite courses, the lower larger than the upper, and then a concrete pier, which varied in height because it in turn sat right on the bedrock, which was uneven. Each column, if you looked from above, was shaped like an "H," and measured no more than fourteen inches wide and long, and *a mere one inch thick*. This was then the standard size for structural steel columns in highrise structures, and still is.

The foundation excavation extended beyond each of the Broadway and Fifth Avenue lot lines by twenty and twenty-two feet, respectively, thereby creating vaults beneath the sidewalks, a common practice at the time that was later discontinued. (Corydon Purdy's rationale for enlarging the base was to strengthen the building's footing.) Timber struts temporarily braced the inner walls of the vaults, to "resist the heavy thrust of the outside earth," which was now being equally assaulted from the other direction, as men dug and blasted out the subway tunnel a mere one block to the east, on Fourth Avenue.

The Fuller Company, now erecting fifteen buildings around the city, and digging foundations for several more, was New York's, and therefore the world's, biggest construction firm, and winning more new contracts than any other builder, as New York's building boom continued. Erecting a skyscraper took on the average one year, if your crews worked both day and night, the latter now possible using electric lights. Harry Black insisted that his company could deliver a building faster than any other. Although so far, Thompson-Starrett, still Fuller's main rival and a nagging thorn in Harry Black's side, held the record for speed: Theodore Starrett's company had just finished erecting a fifteen-story office building at 68 William Street that, from start to finish, took a mere six months.

And, besides skyscrapers, contractors were now putting up public buildings: a new Hall of Records at Chambers and Center Streets, and, nearby, on Broad Street, a new Stock Exchange, on the site of the now-demolished old one, and a Customs House designed by Cass Gilbert, at Bowling Green, and Carrère and Hasting's New York Public Library at Fifth Avenue and Forty-second Street, where the old reservoir once stood. All the new structures were Beaux-Arts and Classical, and on the grandest scale, as befitted New York, the world's current commercial hub. But work on these structures was progressing slowly, in contrast to skyscrapers. ("Contractors Rush Skyscrapers While Public Buildings Creep," wrote the *Times* on November 30, 1902. "While the skyscraper grows before the eye, one has to live here for two or three years before he is conscious of any growth whatever, say, in the new Hall of Records, or the new Public Library.")

New York's building frenzy resulted in so much demand for structural steel that the factories in Pennsylvania could not keep up with orders. And once the steel was finally delivered, there was a shortage of men, who, positioned at terrifying heights above the streets, could then assemble the steel pieces into skyscrapers. The men, along with their brothers-in-labor who were building a second bridge over the churning East River, next to the Brooklyn Bridge, all belonged to Local 2 of the International Association of Bridge and Ironworkers, whether they wanted to or not. The boss of Local 2, a tall, skinny, broad-shouldered Irishman named Sam Parks, who was well known for his filthy mouth, tolerated no independents. Parks had started out as a construction worker during the 1880s in Chicago, where the battles over unionization were fought bitterly, and with violence, by both sides, as exemplified by the 1886 Haymarket riots, when seven policemen died from a bomb explosion at an anarchist rally organized to protest the killing of two striking workers by police.

In Chicago, George Fuller, then building his first skyscrapers, and some '93 Exposition buildings, had learned the hard way that he had better find a way to deal with unions. Otherwise strike after strike could put you out of business. Fuller found a solution: bribing a union boss. Whether the boss was duly elected by the rank-and-file, or ruled with his fists, was immaterial. All that mattered was that workers obeyed him when he ordered them not to strike at your construction site.

In Chicago, Fuller found Sam Parks, a willing recipient of kickback. People said Fuller and Harry Black had deliberately brought Parks to New York, along with the Fuller Company, in the late 1890s. This is likely true. Until then New York builders had managed to fight off labor leaders' attempts to organize workers, but it was clear that at some point, anybody building in New York was going to have to reckon with unions. Only a fool believed otherwise, and Fuller, no fool, doubtless decided that he needed a union leader who looked kindly upon him. In exchange, Fuller would give Parks free rein. He could go ahead and unionize if he wanted, as long as he left the Fuller Company alone. Parks was fine with this arrangement, because for this favor, Fuller would pay handsomely. It would be, simply, just another business expense, one that would cost far less than contending with constant strikes and the then-obligatory lockouts.

As soon as Parks arrived in New York, Fuller made him a foreman on a construction job. Parks now began to organize Local 2. He went from site to site, with a forbidding-looking friend or two, and his pet bulldog named Arbitrator on a leash, "inviting" unaffiliated workers to join up. "I like to fight," Parks once told a reporter. "It is nothing after you've risked your life bridge-riveting at $3 a day. In organizing men in New York I talked with them nice and pleasant, explaining how they could be better off in a union. Some did not believe unions would be good for them; and I gave them a belt on the jaw. That changed their minds. Lots of men can't be moved by any other argument." Within three months, all of New York's 4,500 ironworkers had joined up.

Parks did right by his rank-and-file by forcing up their wages. In 1901, they were making $3.76 for an eight-hour day, twice as much as the previous year's rate. For overtime, you made double, which meant that a rush job could net you $50 in a week. So you could forgive Parks if he sometimes smacked people around. The bigger story was that he looked out for his men. He made them, and their union, proud. "Fighting Sam Parks," they called him.

"Samuel Parks, of New York, was much in evidence at the Boston gathering and his vigorous outpouring of trenchant talk made the rafters ring like the rock-ribbed recesses of a Colorado canyon after a discharge of heavy artillery," gushed the union's *Bridgemen's Magazine* in 1901. *Bridgemen's* ranted frequently against trusts, in particular U.S. Steel. Yet for the George A. Fuller Company, tied inextricably to the steel trust, the union had only affection. "To an uninitiated outsider it would seem that the Fuller Company and the Roebling Company are like two gigantic pythons making goo-goo eyes at each other, and likely we will get up some morning and find they have formed one of Pierpont Morgan's community of interests or one has swallowed the other, and it can't come too soon," wrote *Bridgemen's* in July 1902. "It would be an ideal company in spite of the hue and cry to the contrary; we find that organized labor has little to fear from amalgamated millions. The larger the capital the greater the harmony."

Local 2 elected Sam Parks a "walking delegate" in 1901, which was a big deal for a union man. Each of New York's thirty-nine building industry–related unions had a walking delegate, who sat on a board together, and whose job was literally to walk around from site to site, to make sure that their union's rules were enforced, and then report back regularly to their union. In effect, the delegate acted as a liaison between workers and employer, a splendid idea as long as people on both sides behaved with decency, and an invitation for abuse if they didn't. In his role as walking delegate, Parks demanded graft, not just from his largest "employer," the Fuller Company, but now from many of the smaller construction operations, who were already struggling to survive as Fuller was controlling ever more of New York's construction business. If you refused to pay off Parks, he'd tell his men to strike, often without giving them a reason, and they obediently did his bidding. So small businesses were getting battered from two fronts. According to the journalist Ray Stannard Baker, a colleague of Lincoln Steffens and Ida Tarbell at the left-leaning *McClure's* magazine, Parks spent his union's money as he wished, and without giving any accounting. Local 2, Baker wrote, received $60,000 in dues in 1901, of which over $40,000 simply disappeared. When a member asked during an open meeting what had become of a certain sum of money, Parks threw a table at him. He was said to live uptown, in a luxurious apartment, walls adorned with paintings, and his wife bedecked in pearls. But these were just rumors. The truth, according to the *Times,* on September 9, 1903, was that Parks rented a six-room flat for $48 a month at Lexington and Eighty-third Street, a working-class neighborhood of grocery stores and saloons. His building neighbors consisted of mechanics and factory foremen. To him, power meant recognition, not expensive digs.

Thanks to Parks, there were no labor problems on any Fuller

construction projects. Although in November, two men had died on two separate Fuller jobs. At the Maritime Building at Pearl and Bridge, a derrick crushed William Ryan. And the breaking of a boom—one of the pieces that comprises a derrick—killed William Walters on a building going up at Wall and Water. Workers' fatalities were a fact of life in construction. That these were the days before the now-obligatory safety gear—goggles and hard hats—increased the dangers that went with the job. The average life span of an ironworker after he started working in the profession was ten years. Their motto was: "We do not die; we are killed."

Steel destined for the Flatiron Building was now rolling off the American Bridge Company mills in Pennsylvania, then cut and shaped into columns, girders, joists, plates, struts, knee-braces, and rivets. Each piece had holes drilled into it, to receive the rivets that would connect it with another piece as the building was being assembled. Some sections were assembled right in the shop, such as the bracing that Corydon Purdy had devised to protect the Flatiron from wind shear. One wall girder was laid across another, forming a cross, and the two pieces were then riveted together. Then diagonally across each of the four resulting corners was riveted another piece of steel, called a knee-brace.

Before shipment, a red number was painted upon each piece of steel. Then the pieces were assembled in bundles—all the beams for one floor together, all the rivets for one angle together, and so forth. So when a steel delivery arrived at the site, you knew exactly where the pieces fit. Therefore the skeleton would be assembled easily and quickly, which was how it had to be, as you couldn't have piles of steel lying in the street and blocking traffic. So the steel was being produced, then shipped, according to a careful schedule that Starrett and Purdy had earlier worked out, then piled onto freight cars that, pulled by giant steam locomotives, were now arriving every day, or every other day, at one of New Jersey's rail yards or ports. The steel was then loaded directly onto barges that crossed the Hudson, docking on Manhattan's West side rail yards, then trucked by teams of horses up Broadway to Twenty-third Street, and unloaded at the building site.

There the two foremen, Dan Dunn and Billy Dell, were waiting with blueprints supplied by Purdy, illustrating exactly where each numbered piece of steel would fit. Down in the cellar, work crews had installed heavy construction machinery, all powered by steam. Two gigantic, double-drummed engines operated the derricks, which were hoisting the steel beams from the street. An air compressor—a system of pipes, cylinders, and valves that sucked in air, and then held it in until it reached the desired pressure—would power the hammers driving in the rivets used to fasten beams and girders together, as well as other tools, for drilling through, reaming, cutting off, and chipping the steel. The pressurized air was delivered through a vertical pipe rising up from the cellar, like a tall tree rooted in the ground, with manifolds, attached to outlets, at every floor, like branches, from which short branches of screwed steel pipe and flexible hose extended, and attached to the various pneumatic tools.

It was now January, and the weather frigid, as the first tier of the Flatiron skeleton began to rise. By mid-month the temperatures rose to unseasonably mild levels, averaging around forty, and the days were sunny, ideal weather for construction. But now all work had stopped on the Flatiron, its skeleton as yet reaching only one story high. Workers could build no higher yet, because the first-floor girders had been missing from the last steel delivery. So there was nothing to do but wait for the next shipment from the American Bridge Company.

Several weeks went by before the missing girders finally arrived in New York, and work resumed, only to be again interrupted by a sudden nor'easter that blew into the city on the night of February 17. It would turn out to be the worst blizzard since 1888.

Heavy snow fell for twenty-four hours, which fierce winds shaped into drifts reaching five feet in height. As street sweepers continuously cleared paths through the snow, teams of horses pulling the trolleys through the narrow paths kept floundering in the drifts. Electric sweepers kept the tracks of the electric streetcars clear, but drifts blocked the intersections. Traffic at times backed up, before resuming again, very slowly. Still, in the midst of the storm, the city kept moving. People struggled to get to work. Attendance on the Stock Exchange floor—temporarily located at the produce exchange on Bowling Green, where it would remain until the new structure was completed—was way down, due to the train delays suffered by members who commuted daily from the suburbs. Brokers from Lakewood, New Jersey, arrived only minutes before the closing bell. Still, business on Wall Street continued as usual, because wire services and telephone lines for the most part functioned.

Construction on the new Stock Exchange had been going on day and night. But the blizzard had forced a halt to it and all other construction projects around New York as well. At the Flatiron, we can picture the beginnings of the steel skeleton—consisting, so far, of two rows of steel columns riveted to the first level of girders, with an elliptical steel panel rounding the corner at Fifth and Twenty-third—sticking up out of the drifts. All around and straight through the building site, the wind howled, whipping the snow into blinding sheets.

Five more days of storms followed the nor'easter. Sleet, alternating with more snow, rain, or sometimes a mixture of the two, lashed the entire Eastern seaboard. In New York, the snow-piled streets melted into seas of dirty, ankle-deep slush. By now it was the end of February. Then, during the first week of March, another messy winter storm blew into New York. And again, people managed to get to work and then back home again through the sleet and snow, thanks in part to the advance warning that the weather bureau had sent out, which gave the sanitation department sufficient time to ready thousands of street cleaners and carts for trucking away the snow. So the trolleys and streetcars ran, and so did the railroads, although as much as five hours behind schedule. Freight continued to arrive, even fruit from Florida, although prices were high—$4.50 for a dozen peaches, and thirty-five cents for a quart of strawberries, which one grocer down on Fulton Street advertised with a placard balanced on a snowdrift, less than a foot away from where the fruit was displayed, reminding winter-weary passersby that spring was coming.

Steel for the Flatiron job was arriving regularly in New York, and the skeleton was quickly taking shape. The architect Charles McKim, now working on the plans for the new Pennsylvania Railroad Station together with his partners Stanford White and William Mead in his office at 160 Fifth Avenue, just across the street from the Flatiron site, every day observed the ongoing construction from his window. "The only other building higher than your Fifth Avenue and 23rd Street building that I have ever heard of is the Tower of Babel," he wrote to Burnham on April 30, 1902. (McKim was misinformed. The twin-towered Park Row building on City Hall Park, completed in 1899, at 391 feet, measured one-third higher than would the new Fuller skyscraper.) "They are adding at the rate of about a story a day, and there are four more stories, they say, to go." All over the city, buildings were going up just as quickly as the new Fuller skycraper. But this oddly shaped work-in-progress was capturing the public's attention as none other.

Crowds watched as a derrick lifted a steel column that swung from a chain grasped a little above its middle "like a pencil between the fingers." Meanwhile, in the cellar, an engineer was working the hoisting machine, which powers the derrick. He could not see what was going on high above him, but "bellmen" pulled on cables attached to bells to indicate to the engineer where exactly the steel was, so that, with his controls, he could hoist, or lower, or move the load left or right, in order that men waiting high above the city on wooden platforms—the iron men call these temporary supports *false work*—could catch the column with hooks, or in their hands. Then they carefully guided the column to its corresponding girder.

Then the riveting gang took over. It used to be that men drove in rivets by hand, but now they were using pneumatic hammers. People walking about New York wherever construction was going on had grown used to the sharp *rat-a-tat-tat* sounds coming from above, as if giant woodpeckers were hitting their beaks against steel branches. George Fuller began experimenting with compressed air for construction in Chicago during the 1880s. The results were astounding: one pneumatic hammer, operated by two men, could drive in almost twice as many rivets in a day than an entire gang of men using the old manual method. Now, at the Flatiron, the riveters were standing by, ready, like dancers in the wings, watching for the cue to begin their carefully choreographed movements. The so-called *heater* was now stoking the fire of a little coal forge by cranking in air, cooking the rivets to temperatures up to 2,000 degrees Fahrenheit. When a rivet glowed white-hot, the heater grasped it with a pair of tongs, whirled it around his head, and tossed it into a metal bucket—*pling!*—held by the *catcher*. The latter then grabbed the rivet with his tongs, tapped it against the steel beam—to get rid of cinders—and stuffed it into one of the beam's prefabricated holes—all done quickly, before the rivet began to cool down, and harden. Ernest Poole, in a 1908 article in *Everyman's Magazine,* described what happened next:

> A third man lifts a tool called a "gun," a ponderous pneumatic hammer, the compressed air that drives it coming through a five-hundred-foot hose from the world below. He holds the tube firmly against his stomach, while with a deafening *rat-a-tat-tat* the hammer began its fierce pounding, welding the red-hot end of the rivet flat against the steel. Meanwhile, a man stood (on the opposite side of the beam) with a "Dolly bar," one end pressed on the rivet head, the other end tight against his waist. So he holds the rivet in place, taking the rapid succession of shocks from the stroke of the "gun" inside, his feet braced firmly on the planks, his body bent forward to meet the blows that are bucking him off into space.

Every movement of each *rivet rapper,* as the ironworkers union affectionately called its members, had to follow precisely on the previous one's. So you'd better pay close attention, and move with the rhythm. Otherwise, the burning rivet might whizz past you, or strike and injure you or another worker, or cause you to lose your balance, and fall to your death. "Once, just as the man with the tongs had started to whirl them to toss off his missile, the man with the keg threw up his hand as a signal that he was not ready," wrote Ernest Poole in *Everyman's Magazine,* November 1908.

Poole, a brave soul, had followed a riveting crew working hundreds of feet above the sidewalk, to observe them first-hand. "And then, as though doing just what he had intended, the man with the tongs let the rivet fly straight up into the air with a throw so precise that a moment later it dropped down toward his upturned face. Like a ball player catching a 'fly,' he watched it come, made a quick step aside, caught it adroitly in the jaws of his tongs, and plunged it back into the forge, just as a bit of byplay." And, most of all, a rivet rapper had better stand steady on his feet, way up in the sky, as the traffic hummed more than a hundred feet below, and all around him the winds blew, especially hard now in the springtime.

The Flatiron's steel frame was rising higher and higher. The Pennsylvania plant had manufactured the steel so exactly to specifications that the thousands of pieces were fitted together "without so much as the alteration of a bored hole, or the exchange of a tiny rivet," wrote the *Times.* The Flatiron's sides were now temporarily braced by ten-inch-thick wooden struts, placed diagonally in alternate directions in every transverse bend of every story in the outside column panels. It was as if the skeleton were wearing a herringbone tweed coat, to keep it warm, which was being removed, section by section, as masonry workers began to clad the Flatiron with the thousands of yellowish-gray, glazed terra-cotta tiles, even as the steel frame was still being assembled on the topmost floors. At the top of the third floor the workers now started installing a frieze, studded with *dentils,* so-called because they resemble teeth. It was carved out of Indiana limestone, which would also clad the base. But the remainder of the Flatiron's skin would consist only of terra-cotta.

The workers were now standing on wooden platforms attached to ropes hanging along the length of the shaft, waiting to receive the terra-cotta tiles arriving in gigantic wooden crates from Staten Island. Another team of workers have carefully unpacked a batch of tiles, each one numbered for assemblage, brushing off the straw that protected the pieces from breakage during their journey from Tottenville to Manhattan. The pieces now stood on the ground, lined up. Workmen, under the supervision of their foreman, loaded them onto platforms and hauled them up, into the hands of their brothers-in-labor. They, in turn, working downward, first covered the sixth, and then the fifth story with rectangular tiles, one at a time. They surrounded each window space with terra-cotta jambs, sills, lintels, and spandrels. When finished, the Flatiron would have more than 700 windows, which would cover the entire building, like the holes of a honeycomb, and even curve around each of the three angles. Light would stream into the Flatiron all day, and never be obstructed by other buildings, because it stands in the middle of an intersection.

When the workmen were finished encircling the fourth floor with tiles, they began to install another frieze around the building, this one far more complex than and at least twice as wide as the one just below, on top of the third floor. The second frieze had small dentils outlining the top side, and a wide *guilloche* border—that is, circular interlaced bands—and it hugged the building like an elaborate pearl necklace around a woman's neck. In between the two friezes, separated by pairs of windows, workers were attaching tiles with fantastic designs: medallions, buttons, sheaves of wheat, rosettes, sunbursts, and, most striking, a woman's face—her expression serious, her hair coiled into serpent-like ringlets. There were four of these tiles, each affixed to the building just where its corners begin to gently curve, at Twenty-second and Twenty-third Streets. These Medusa-like creatures stare straight out, two facing east and two west, oblivious to the pe-

Workmen covering the Flatiron skeleton
with terra-cotta tiles, spring 1902.

destrians and vehicles that were rushing along and across the streets
that form the triangle.

That the architect Frederick Dinkelberg had designed the Flatiron's
three angles to curve gently around the periphery of each curb, Chicago-
style, had left just ninety-three square feet empty at the intersection
of Twenty-third, Broadway, and Fifth. And ever since Harry Black
had first seen Dinkelberg's design back in March 1901, the financier
had been after Daniel Burnham to alter the plan in some way, in order to squeeze some financial return from this awkward little sliver
of unused real estate. Black's idea was for Dinkelberg to construct
some kind of extension at the northern tip, thereby utilizing every bit
of the lot.

That Black, who knew nothing about architecture, should make such a suggestion infuriated Burnham. In the hopes that Black, with all the ongoing Fuller projects and deals on his plate, would forget about his ninety-three square feet of unused space, Burnham had, over the last year, kept putting off responding to Black's request.

But Black didn't forget. Finally, in April 1902, he grew tired of waiting. He had somebody at the Fuller offices do a rough sketch showing the Flatiron's first floor retail space extending all the way to the lot's northernmost point, by means of a tacked-on one-story glass and cast-iron-framed storefront extension, twenty-five feet long and thirteen feet high, with a metal roof. Its windows would project nine inches beyond the lot line. Black then ordered the sketch and an accompanying letter sent to Burnham, instructing him to make architectural drawings of the amended Flatiron design, which the Fuller Company would then submit to the Buildings Department for approval.

Burnham, upon receiving this correspondence, must have seethed. As pragmatic a businessman as the architect was, Black, who knew nothing about architecture, had crossed the line. Not only was the proposed extension wildly out of scale with the building, it would have to be attached right at the middle of the pair of two-story-high Classical columns that had already been installed. They stood at street level, right at the curve of the Twenty-third Street intersection. The motif would be repeated at the top, where two more columns would support the cornice. This was a typically Burnham design flourish that he had used in Chicago, on the First National Chicago Bank and the Commercial National Bank Building, and on the Frick Building in Pittsburgh. Cutting off the bottom half of the sidewalk-level columns by extending the storefront would, naturally, destroy the symmetry of the Flatiron design.

"We have very carefully considered the projection of the shop windows around the first story of the Flatiron Building," Burnham wrote on May 2, after receiving the sketch and accompanying letter. He continued, tersely: "There is no way to project these without very seriously injuring the artistic effect of the building. It can be done, of course, but it will be at considerable loss of appearance."

But Black refused to back down. Burnham, inasmuch as he worked for Black, had to do what Black wanted. Within a week or two, the altered plan had been filed with the New York City Buildings Department, which promptly rejected it, on the grounds that the extension's walls were not thick enough. The Fuller Company appealed the department's decision, which was based on the fact that the code did not address the kind of structure that was now being proposed. "We would respectfully ask your consideration of the fact that this extension is nothing more than a show case and is the only means we can see to utilize our property at the extreme point," somebody at Fuller wrote, adding that all materials to be used—iron, plaster, tile, and metal roof— were fireproof. Finally, at the end of June, the Buildings Department would give the go-ahead to construct the extension. By then, Black's and Burnham's relationship, never good, had become very tense, indeed.

Just at the time that Black was forcing the issue of the Flatiron extension, he applied to have the Fuller Company listed on the Stock Exchange. Wall Street had been expecting this ever since Black had turned what started out as a Chicago construction company into a skyscraper trust, back in March 1901. Now, one year–plus later, the stock market was still active, but jittery, one reason being the recent suit filed by the Roosevelt administration against Northern Securities, J. P. Morgan's new railroad trust. Ever since the new President's first address to Congress the previous December, in which he had alluded to enforcing antitrust regulations that up to now the government had ignored, industrialists had been sitting on their hands. Everyone was waiting to see what trust the President would go after next, and conservative voices, among them *The Wall Street Journal,* were cautioning investors about overvalued stocks. The *Journal* now specifically advised its readers to avoid Fuller stock, even though the company's earnings during the past year had been substantial. "It is a matter of common knowledge that few businesses are more subject to extreme fluctuations of profits than building," the paper wrote. "We have to consider the stock as essentially very speculative in character . . . We think a company of this sort is not altogether suitable as an investment for the public, and much more suitable for private ownership by its own managers."

The *Journal* could say whatever it liked, but in the meantime, the Fuller Company was buying up properties all over town, knocking down whatever existing structures stood on them, and erecting new ones, as high as possible, because only in that way would investors get maximum return on their dollars. Most recently, Black, along with "Bet-a-Million" Gates, and a third investor, the German-born Bernhard Beinecke, who had made his fortune in the meat business, had put together a deal resulting in the acquisition of McKim, Mead, and White's deluxe 400-room hotel at the Grand Army Plaza, at Fifty-ninth and Fifth. They had paid $3 million for the Plaza, which *King's Handbook of New York City* declared one of the grandest hotels in the world. "Mahogany appears extensively in the finishing and in the furniture, and there is much carved wood, with brass trimmings in the old Colonial style. The dining room is in gold and white, with stained glass windows and an arched ceiling, thirty feet in height, fretted in gold." But the gorgeous hotel, completed in 1890, was technologically antiquated, because it was constructed with no steel frame, and therefore had only eight stories. In its place, the Fuller Company would erect a modern twenty-story hotel, which would give them a much greater return on the land.

Black was saying that the new Plaza, just like any Fuller Company project, would be built fast, faster than anyone could imagine possible, because speed counted as everything in the struggle among construction firms to outdo each other. That Theodore Starrett's company for now held the speed construction record rankled Black. He would show Starrett, and Wall Street, that the Fuller Company was not only the biggest, but the fastest contractor in town.

And if adhering to a completion date that Black had promised a client—for example, the Straus family, owners of the new Macy's store

McKim, Meade, and White's beautiful Plaza Hotel, at Fifty-ninth Street and Fifth Avenue, which would be demolished in 1905. On the site, Harry Black would build a new, grander structure.

that the Fuller Company was constructing—meant that your workers would have to work overtime, and cost you way more than you'd budgeted at the onset, the men who worked for him would just have to, so to speak, sharpen their pencils. Black believed that profit was inevitable, as long as you wanted it badly enough. But the Macy's project, now half-finished, was already deep in the red, and driving Theodore Starrett's brother Paul, who was overseeing it, and the Flatiron Building, and everything else that Fuller was working on above Fourteenth Street, completely mad. Without consulting Starrett, Black had earlier negotiated a contract with the Strauses, guaranteeing that the building would not cost them more than twenty cents a cubic foot. For whatever reason, Black believed that this figure would result in a profit for the Fuller Company. "But this was a dangerous assumption," Starrett wrote later in his autobiography, where he described the Macy's project's endless complications. "As I juggled steel, cement, and argument in putting up the Macy store, I began to realize that, no matter what I did, no matter how much I fought to keep down the costs, we would lose heavily."

But Black reasoned that despite the huge cost overruns, the Macy's job would profit the Fuller Company, just by virtue of association with what was going to be the biggest, most elegant, most famous store in the world. Its ongoing construction at Herald Square, one of New York's busiest hubs, which thousands of pedestrians and vehicles—trucks, vans, pushcarts, automobiles, auto cars, trams, trolley cars, bicycles, and express wagons—crossed every day, was eliciting intense interest among New Yorkers. Newspapers, closely following Macy's progress, often mentioned the name of the company building it, to Harry Black's delight. And in business, visibility means everything. When people see, and like, the concrete results of a corporation's labors, they have confidence in that corporation. And so it will grow. And in fact, on Wall Street the talk was that Black was currently negotiating with some of America's biggest corporations—among them U.S. Steel and J. P. Morgan's bank— to invest in his skyscraper trust, which, very soon, was going to be housed in its own headquarters, which could actually be seen from the Broadway side of the new Macy's site if you looked toward downtown.

In the meantime, nobody was buying Fuller Company stock.

By mid-May, the new Fuller Company headquarters' narrow, V-shaped steel skeleton was surrounded with scaffolding, and half-covered with thousands of terra-cotta tiles. And even with construction going on all over Manhattan, no project was attracting people's attention like the "Flatiron," which is how people persisted in calling it, refusing to give in to its new, official name, "the Fuller Building." When a streetcar ran down Broadway and passed the Flatiron, every passenger rubbernecked, craning their necks to catch a glimpse. Nine blocks north, guests entering or exiting the Waldorf-Astoria Hotel marveled at the Flatiron's original design. And in Madison Square or in front of the Fifth Avenue Hotel, hundreds of people could be seen milling about for five and ten minutes at a time, day or night, pointing and staring up at the building.

Among them were always a few of those types New Yorkers called "sidewalk superintendents," "gentlemen of leisure," as *The Brooklyn Eagle* described them, "superintending its construction and explaining things to one another or to any passersby who would listen." The site also attracted "more intelligent visitors: architects and engineers from all over the country, armed with permits and usually officially escorted by some one competent to give official explanation of the theories involved," the *Eagle* wrote, adding that people often shivered at the Flat-iron's "apparent instability: as often as any comment on the gigantic enterprise, or the splendid engineering feat accomplished, one has heard from passersby: 'I'd hate to be in the top of that in a high wind.'" But the structure, the *Eagle* emphasized, was perfectly safe. "A triangle is the safest possible form of building, as the triangle is the strongest of the geometric forms. An engineer will tell you that a triangle supports it-self, and braces itself against any possible pressure . . . He will try to explain that from its very shape, the greater the pressure on a triangle at any point, the greater its resistance at all points." The *Eagle* reporter had it right.

Such reportage doubtless pleased Harry Black greatly. Already his skyscraper had turned into a splendid advertisement for the Fuller Company. It would be even better if people would only start calling the building by its proper name. The moniker "Flatiron" also dis-pleased the men actually building it, but for a reason different from Black's. "To call the magnificent structure now being erected at 23rd Street by the Fuller Company the Flat Iron building is decidedly a mis-nomer," a member of the practically all-Irish Local 2 proudly wrote in *Bridgemen's* that month. "It looks a great deal more like a 20-deck Irish man-of-war sailing up Broadway, the iron being painted an emerald hue as a compliment to Michael Patrick O'Briody and Walter A. Smith, the gang of Feniems [sic] erecting it."

Two months earlier, in March 1902, Sam Parks had sat down in a Brooklyn saloon with Nels Poulson, the Norwegian-born president of the huge Hecla Iron Works in Williamsburg—major supplier of stairs, railings, gates, canopies, elevator cars and enclosures, and all kinds of grilles to the buildings trade. Hecla had won the bids for the Flatiron's elevators and stair railings.

"You've never done anything for the walking delegates," Parks told Poulson. "Ain't it about time?" Hecla, Parks claimed, was violating union rules, by allowing its bronze workers, who belonged to a different union, to install the work that they had made, rather than defer it to the members of Parks's union. Still, Parks would look the other way for $1,000.

Poulson gave Parks two minutes to get out of the saloon. He then wrote a letter to his trade organization, stating that Parks had tried to extort $1,000 from Hecla. Parks in retaliation now ordered the iron workers at Hecla to strike, which forced the shutdown of the entire operation, and idled some 1,200 men. Parks also filed a $10,000 suit against Hecla for slander, on account of Poulson's letter.

Poulson held out for several weeks. By now it was late April, and the strike had cost his company some $25,000. The president of Parks's union now called Poulson and apologized to him for the strike. Parks's grievance, he told Poulson, was a sham. But what could the union do? The men had to obey Parks.

Parks now was demanding $2,000 as the price for ending the strike. That amount, he said, would cover every day that the workmen went out on strike. Poulson was desperate. If the strike lasted much longer, he'd be out of business. Somebody at Fuller—probably Ex-Judge Mc-Connell, who was serving as president of the company, and rumored to be Parks's contact—asked him to see Parks one more time, to try to end the strike. Poulson met with Parks in an unfinished room at the Flatiron Building. Parks greeted the contractor cordially, addressing him as "Mr. Poulson."

"Why did you order a strike on our works when the president of your union himself admitted that there was no ground for a strike and apologized for the one you ordered?" Poulson asked Parks, who suddenly changed his form of address.

"You fucking son of a bitch," he said. "I do not give a damn for the president of the union and I don't give a damn for the laws of the country. I'm Sam Parks, I am. You go to work when you pay me and not before."

What happened next is that Poulson met with a Mr. William Mc-Cord, who worked for the American Bridge Company, a subsidiary of United States Steel. Poulson paid McCord $2,000, drawn from the Hecla Iron Works funds. McCord then wrote a company check, payable to his son, Robert McCord, who then endorsed it over to Parks. Robert and Parks then met at the Fuller Company offices, where at first Parks refused the check. He wanted, he told Robert McCord, cash. But in the end he accepted it. In exchange, Parks agreed to call off the Hecla strike. The Fuller Company then cashed the check for Parks, on May 1, 1902.

When Poulson received back the cashed check, he had it framed, with glass on both sides, so as to have both endorsements visible. He knew that some day that check would prove valuable.

In the meantime, Hecla Iron Works was back in business, supplying the Flatiron, the Stock Exchange Building, the Chamber of Commerce, and all the other construction projects with which it had contracts. By some accounts, the rank-and-file really did get some of the Hecla money. They also sent Parks a diamond ring, on which was engraved: "Victory, Strike Hecla Iron Works."

At the Flatiron, laborers were attaching the thousands of remaining terra-cotta tiles to the building's upper half. The late spring weather was cool and clear, perfect for the task, but marred by an excessive amount of soot in the air, due to a coal strike in the Pennsylvania mines that, causing shortages everywhere, was forcing people to burn the cheap stuff—soft bituminous coal—from emergency stockpiles, instead of the usual anthracite, which, being hard, burned clean. The Sixth Avenue El, which ran one block west of the Flatiron, was emitting nasty clouds of black dust as it rattled by, which stung the eyes of the men perched on platforms hanging flush along the building's elevations, and made them cough, as they worked higher and higher up, as fast as they could, affixing each tile to its proper place.

By June the men had reached the uppermost section, which corresponds to the capital of a classical column. They were tiling terra-cotta shields, fleurs-de-lis, medallions, lion's heads, and glowering masks around the tall, arched spaces where windows would soon be installed. Frederick Dinkelberg had varied the design at the two next-to-last floors of the Twenty-third Street point, by setting back the three oblong windows in the front. He turned the space thereby created into two small porticoes, one atop the other, so that you would be able to step out, and see the views all around, from the Hudson to the East Rivers.

Workers were now fitting terra-cotta columns with ornate, Corinthian-style capitals onto the porticoes. Then, on the roof, they attached a multilayered cornice that protruded by four feet. If you looked up from below, the soffit—underside—revealed a rich pattern of dentils alternating with rosettes.

During the third week of June, workers took down the scaffolding that, up to then, had prevented an unbroken view of the building's vertical lines. Now passersby could for the first time see the Flatiron in its entirety, rising straight up from the sidewalk, and into the sky, like a classical column that had been pounded down, reshaped into a skinny triangle, and plunked down in America.

CHAPTER SIX

THE SKYSCRAPER TRUST

At the end of July, Harry Black, accompanied by Allon, spent a few days at the fashionable Fort William Henry Hotel in Lake George, New York. The hotel was drawing more visitors than ever this year. The *Times* wrote, "Every week day evening the parlors are devoted to dancing, and each Sunday evening sacred concerts of a high order are given." From these genteel surroundings Black hoped to proceed directly to nearby Saratoga for the start of the "season," where a man spent his Sundays at the races and the casinos, rather than listening to church music.

Black loved to gamble, and he loved Saratoga. He always spent as much of August there as possible, along with scores of other rich and powerful men who gathered there from all over the country. People said that more money changed hands at Canfield's Saratoga Club, America's most luxurious and expensive gambling establishment, than at Monte Carlo. And if you needed a break from gambling, the Town Hall Theatre featured a minstrel or vaudeville show almost every night. During the day, you could take the waters at the spa. Or you could drive your automobile—Saratoga was filled with them, "at least half a hundred," according to the *Daily Saratogan*—up and down Broadway, a pastime that especially delighted Black. By now he owned five, of which his favorite was a French Panhard.

Saratoga was just what Harry Black needed after his grueling year in the real estate business. But, as it turned out, he did not go directly there from Lake George. First he would have to return to New York City for a few sultry late-July days, to attend to some important business.

For months, a rumor had been circulating on the Street that another huge real estate consolidation involving Harry Black was in the works.

Ever since Black had merged Fuller with Henry Morgenthau's Central Realty back in March 1901—thereby increasing his company's capital to $20 million, and making it the largest realty operation in the world—Black had been busy, very busy, always looking for ever more sources of capital. Now, just fifteen months later—July 29, 1902, to be precise—he held a meeting in New York City, the culmination of all his recent hard work. Present was the Fuller board—which, besides Morgenthau, included the banker James Stillman, former Tammany mayor Hugh J. Grant, and Black's friend Ex-Judge McConnell, from Chicago—and some other exceedingly wealthy men as well, who represented some of America's largest corporations.

If all went well, Black's company was about to get a lot bigger, and a lot richer.

It was deep summer, and an inconvenient time to be conducting major business in New York. The wealthy had long departed for their various vacation destinations. Since the end of June, throughout Manhattan, all but a few theaters and restaurants had closed down, not to reopen until September. Except for the roof gardens, there was no place for a respectable person to go for a little amusement. Newspapers were so starved for entertaining news that when a young woman walked down Fifth Avenue wearing nothing but a bathing suit and sandals, they turned it into a story.

Black, perhaps, could have postponed the meeting he was now chairing until September. But he didn't want to wait. His new Fuller Building would be ready for occupancy in the fall, and he had a million other projects on his plate besides, all of which required huge infusions of capital. His company would have that capital, as long as everybody now came on board with him. The deal involved two additional real estate companies—Alliance and New York Realty—which had agreed to merge with the Fuller Company. Harry Black's newly enlarged skyscraper trust would be worth $66 million.

According to the newspapers, this latest consolidation involving the Fuller Company went through that day, July 29, without a hitch. Black and company named the new, huge entity the United States Realty and Construction Company. Thompson-Starrett, the Fuller Company's main competitor, was conspicuously not among the companies that U.S. Realty had just absorbed. Whether Black had tried to lure in Thompson-Starrett is not known.

The men who would make up the new U.S. Realty's board represented an astonishingly wide cross-section of American money, old and new. In addition to all the members of the Fuller board, U.S. Realty's included Charles M. Schwab, president of U.S. Steel; Charles Steele of J. P. Morgan's bank; the banker James Speyer, like Morgenthau a member of New York's exclusive circle of German Jewish financiers, whose family had been bankers in Frankfurt-am-Main for centuries; and Augustus D. Juilliard of the Mutual Life Insurance Company, who would later endow the world-famous music school. Albert Flake and Robert Dowling, principals of New York Realty, also joined the board of U.S. Realty, which also absorbed their company. Cornelius Vanderbilt, as well as Charles Tweed, chairman of Southern Pacific, would represent railroads. And the aristocratic Charles Francis Adams, great-grandson of John, and grandson of John Quincy Adams—he had fought as a

Union general in the Civil War, and was former president of Union Pacific—would represent, as the *Times* said, "Boston interests."

Black gave a statement to the newspapers late in the afternoon of July 30, one day after forming his new company. "U.S. Realty's operations will be confined very largely to New York, with the exception of the construction business of the Fuller Company, which will be carried on as usual throughout the important cities of the country," Black announced. He emphasized that the Fuller Company would function as an independent entity within its new parent corporation.

He then added: "The new company will undoubtedly enter foreign fields, with the view of introducing steel construction in cities like London, Paris and Berlin. Its relations will be very close to the United States Steel Corporation, and naturally, as we will be the largest consumers of structural steel in the world, our terms as to price and delivery will be most favorable."

By bringing so many powerful financial interests together, U.S. Realty would, Paul Starrett later wrote in his autobiography, "cultivate neglected opportunities" in the real estate business. "If a man owned a piece of metropolitan real estate and had no money with which to put a modern building on it, the corporation would finance a building for him and take a mortgage on it. If a man had no money and no land, the U.S. Realty would show him how he might acquire a valuable corner and erect a profitable skyscraper. If a bank or an industrial company had outgrown its quarters and required a larger space, the U.S. Realty would show the directors how they might trade their present property in on a more desirable plot and finance a new and larger building with rentable space that would carry the investment." U.S. Realty, said Black, would even manage its own properties, and improve their physical plants.

But Starrett's view of U.S. Realty as potentially benefitting anybody in the real estate business didn't necessarily apply to those with just a few modest properties. There were hundreds of such owners, even in New York's heated-up real estate market. They no doubt worried that the skyscraper trust would, just like any trust, stifle competition, corner the real estate market, and drive them out of business.

Black and the U.S. Realty board were preparing to have the company stock listed on the exchange. Even though the public had given the Fuller Company stock the cold shoulder, Black was certain that this time it would be different. Now that his skyscraper trust was truly gigantic, with ties to the likes of U.S. Steel, people would rush to buy shares.

There was another reason for Black's optimism: everybody wanted to buy New York real estate. It was sexy and exciting, owning a piece of the city that the whole world looked to. And some wanted land simply to improve, and use, for a business or residence. But most of all, investors wanted land for speculation. The *Real Estate Record and Builders' Guide* reported that people were holding on to lots, even vacant lots in shabby neighborhoods, for only a few weeks, before flipping them at a profit. The constant buying and selling of property contributed to New York's fluidity, a place where everything was changing, and for sale. All these processes were being further encouraged by the interborough rapid subway line now being constructed, which was causing the expansion of residential neighborhoods into what was still farmland all the way uptown. In anticipation of the new underground train, retail establishments from Union Square to Broadway and Twenty-third, since the Civil War New York's center of retail trade, were moving up to Fifth Avenue, from the Twenties to the Forties. There, the brownstones in this formerly residential neighborhood were now, one by one, being demolished, and replaced with commercial buildings. On the Lower East Side, immigrants were buying and selling tenement houses. Speculation was now the main force driving the New York real estate market, pushing the value of New York property higher and higher.

Speculation was the raison d'être for Harry Black's skyscraper trust. All the big real estate investors, Black reasoned, could not fail to see equally promising opportunities in real estate stocks, especially in a continuing bull market that showed no signs of cooling down. Black had been especially heartened by what the *Real Estate Record and Builders' Guide*, a must-read for anybody in the industry, had said after the Fuller Company went public back in April: "Whatever the fortunes of this particular venture, it shows whither the business of buying and selling the securities of construction and realty corporations on commission is drifting, unless realty interests do something to intercept it. So far they have given no sign of sincere intention to keep this business to themselves, which is not in accord with their ordinary energy and enterprise."

The *Real Estate Record and Builders' Guide*'s implication was that all the money to be made building, buying, and selling New York real estate had to end up somewhere. And what more logical destination than Wall Street?

Before wrapping up business in New York, U.S. Realty's board had to name a president. Black had naturally assumed that the job would be his, but the board passed him over for Bradish Johnson, president of New York Realty, who had inherited a family fortune in the sugar business. Their choice came as a great and unpleasant surprise to Black. He would, however, remain president of the Fuller Company.

"His new associates, while granting his ability, feared he had too much the reputation of a speculator," Paul Starrett would later write in his autobiography, *Changing the Skyline*. "Though, no doubt, they were quite willing to reap the profits of speculation, they wanted somebody as a 'front' who would, so they said, inspire public confidence."

On August 1, Black caught a Friday night train to Saratoga from New York's Grand Central Station. Allon was already in Saratoga, awaiting him. We don't know what Black's mood was when he left New York. Probably he felt a mixture of elation for pulling off the U.S. Realty consolidation, and hurt caused by his new board's show of ingratitude toward him. It was as if they were refusing to crown him king of the kingdom he had won for himself, and them as well, through his hard work and gift for dealmaking.

The racing season in Saratoga would begin the following Monday, August 4, and Black's train was filled to capacity with people with names such as Belmont, Gould, and Wanamaker, "rich people, fashionable folk, gay coteries . . . who would ignite the banknotes and set-a-spinning the wheel of gaiety and splendor," gleefully wrote Julian Ralph, the young *Times* reporter assigned to Saratoga. Up to now, the resort had been, in Ralph's words, "deadly dull and stagnant," not only due to a stretch of unusually rainy and miserable weather, but, as a newsboy on Main Street told him, "de real high muckers ain't come yet." But now, on the eve of the opening races, Saratoga was, in Ralph's words, "gay at last," as trains kept arriving from New York—one carrying only race horses—and Boston, Montreal, Philadelphia, Buffalo, Chicago, Albany, and Cleveland, continuously depositing at the station "more of the same sort of people, bent on being royally and rapidly entertained." Decked out in their evening clothes, the visitors filled the dining rooms of Saratoga's grand hotels. At the New Yorker hotel, "negroes, always the favorite servants here, file up and down the middle of the room beneath a brilliant line of electrollers like the dead planets of the Milky Way," wrote Ralph. "They are the best colored waiters I have ever seen. They grin whenever they move, go about as softly as so many kittens, and speak even more softly than they move."

As soon as he arrived in Saratoga, Harry Black ran into his good friend John W. "Bet-a-Million" Gates, who had apparently squealed on Black to U.S. Customs the previous summer regarding the sneaking in of Allon's pearl necklace. Black had laughed off Gates's calumny as if his friend had simply pulled off a harmless practical joke.

Gates, one of Wall Street's most flamboyant players, had just settled in for the summer at the United States Hotel, where Harris Gates & Company, a firm that set up telegraph systems, had installed private wires in his rooms, so that he could continue his habitual manipulation of the stock market. Born a farmer's son in Illinois, Gates had arrived in Texas at age twenty-one, selling a new product called "barbed wire" to cattle ranchers. *Cosmopolitan* magazine described how Gates started his business: "He put a spool of the wire in his trunk and carried it as baggage to Texas. He arrived at San Antonio, obtained a permit from the Mayor to erect a corral in the plaza—the first barbed-wired fence put up in Texas—hired twenty-five steers and was ready for business. People came from miles around to see the show. They were to be convinced against their wills that the slight barbed-wire barriers could avail against Texas steers. Cowboys drove the cattle in every direction except through the prickly wire. They had come to jeer and remained to buy."

By the time Gates was thirty-one, he had founded the American Steel and Wire Company, and was worth millions. J. P. Morgan bought out his company, American Steel and Wire, in 1901, but Gates, angling for more money, held up its consolidation into U.S. Steel. Finally, Judge Gary, a U.S. Steel board member, called Gates's bluff. Gates relented. In retaliation, Morgan refused to allow Gates on U.S. Steel's board. "You have made your own reputation, we are not responsible for it. Good day, sir," Morgan reputedly told Gates when the latter complained about his exclusion. Gates, furious at the snub, vowed to get back at Morgan.

Newspapers friendly to J. P. Morgan—and most were, because they were afraid of him—caricatured Gates as a vulgar Westerner, who belched, spit, and ate his peas from a knife. Gates didn't care, in fact, he relished his image as a crude and self-made millionaire. The waiters and bellhops and cigar clerks who served him adored him, because he always left them big tips. Gates was a big, fat man who loved cigars—he had them specially made in Cuba—and women. He wore three diamond buttons in his shirtfront, and three more diamonds in each suspender buckle. He lived at the Waldorf-Astoria, where he paid $20,000 a year for his apartment. When the stock market was slow, he and his cronies played bridge at the Waldorf every afternoon. Sometimes Harry Black joined him.

Gates's gambling habits were legendary. "Life is a gamble," Gates

John W. Gates, cigar in mouth, with an unidentified companion, undated.

once said. "Everything is a gamble. When the farmer plants his corn he is gambling. He bets that the weather conditions will enable him to raise a good crop. Sometimes he loses. Sometimes he wins. Every man who goes into business gambles. Whenever a man starts out on a railway journey it's a gamble whether he ever reaches his destination." In the city elections the previous November, Gates had bet $75,000 on Mayor Seth Low, the Fusion Party candidate. Anecdotes about how Gates had earned his moniker "Bet-a-Million" abounded. Some said he had bet a million dollars on an English racehorse; others, on which of two drops of rain would first reach the bottom of a window in a train that he was riding. What was uncontestable was that he only bet for huge stakes. "There's no fun in it unless I risk getting hurt, or can hurt the other fellow," he supposedly said.

In July, Gates had tried, but failed, to drive up the price of corn to $1 a bushel. With August always a quiet month in the markets, Gates wasn't counting on spending much time inside his Saratoga hotel suite, waiting for wire messages from his brokers. Instead he planned to pursue his usual routine at Saratoga: daily trips to the race track, followed by evenings at Canfield's, the glittering casino.

Some time during that first week in August, Black offered Gates a piece of U.S. Realty, no doubt as a way to stick it to the board for not making him president. Gates accepted. "The era of combination will prove the golden era for the United States, not only for capital, but for labor," the wire magnate two weeks later told a reporter for *The Philadelphia Inquirer*, who was querying him about America's industrial situation. Gates was waiting in the Saratoga station for a train that would take him to Colorado, where he would attend the annual meeting of Colorado Fuel and Iron, one of the various conglomerates in which he had a stake. He was, he told the reporter, sorry to cut his vacation short. "For labor, industrial combination is its savior," Gates said. "It includes reasonable wages, reasonable hours, and steady employment."

After meeting Gates in Saratoga, Black again interrupted his vacation, returning briefly to New York, where he announced two additional appointments to U.S. Realty's board: John W. Gates and P. A. Valentine, vice president of Armour and Company, the meat company, who would, the newspapers reported, represent the Chicago interests.

Black remained in New York for a few more days, to meet separately with the Fuller Company directors. The men voted to formally name the Flatiron Building "the Fuller Building." Black had press releases sent to all the newspapers, noting specifically that the building's new name was in honor of George A. Fuller, the founder of the company. Most of the papers, with no other real estate news to report in the dead of the summer, obediently ran the story, if you could call it that. "Now the Fuller Building," read *The Sun*'s headline, under which was written: "The directors of the Fuller Company have decided to name the famous Flatiron Building the 'Fuller Building.'"

But New Yorkers paid no attention, which was hardly surprising, and continued to call it the Flatiron Building.

During the last two days of August, Grand Duke Boris, cousin of the Tsar, arrived in New York for a visit. Nattily dressed in a blue serge suit and a straw hat, and carrying a cane, the duke was escorted about town by detectives and Secret Service, to shop and sightsee. He bought two Tiffany vases and lunched at the University Club. Afterward, stepping out onto the sidewalk, he smiled at the pedestrians who had stopped, briefly, at the sight of a visiting royal, surrounded by his bodyguards, and saluted them with his cane. Then, to the surprise of his security entourage, he shunned the carriage that had been provided for him and stepped into a hansom cab, just like a New Yorker. It took him to the Russian church, to attend a service in honor of his sister's wedding to Prince Nicholas of Greece, which had taken place the previous day in Russia. The priest kissed the duke's right hand.

Later the duke was taken to the glamorous Casino Theatre, a massive terra-cotta mixture of Moorish and Romanesque at Thirty-ninth and Broadway, for a performance of the musical comedy *A Chinese Honeymoon*. Two chorus girls in the show had telephoned him the previous day at his hotel, the Waldorf-Astoria, to issue him a special invitation. The duke particularly enjoyed the song "Mr. Dooley," performed by the popular actor Tom Seabrook. Afterward, he asked for, and received, a copy of the sheet music, autographed by the singer. During an intermission, he went out to the sidewalk, and bought five boxes of matches from "Matches Mary," a New York institution who went from theater to theater selling her wares. Clearly, the duke was having a grand time.

"The portion of the metropolis which came into contact with His Highness was charmed by his gentility and good humor," the *Tribune* wrote the following day. The duke especially loved the city's tall buildings. "The American architects' ambition," he remarked, "is to penetrate the sky." During an after-dinner speech at the Union Club, he made special mention of New York's newest skyscraper—he called it "the Flatiron building"—and marveled at its strange shape.

While the Grand Duke was running around New York, wealthy summer vacationers were busy settling up their hotel bills in Saratoga, or closing up their "cottages" in Newport or their Adirondack great camps. It was time to return to New York for the start of the autumn season. Fifth and Madison Avenues, deserted during the summer months, would soon come alive again as people moved back into their mansions and apartments. The theaters that had been shuttered during the hot weather were now reopening. Sherry's and Delmonico's would again be filled with diners. John Gates would return to the Waldorf and play his endless card games.

Train after train was now arriving in Grand Central Station from various vacation spots. Passengers debarked into the crowds milling about among piles of huge trunks and endless pieces of luggage. Among those returning was Harry Black.

At this moment he was feeling particularly exhilarated. U.S. Realty's initial public offer was about to be posted on the stock exchange. And the Fuller Building's first tenants were scheduled to move in shortly. The building was not yet fully leased, but it didn't look like all the floors were going to be ready for occupancy on that date in any case.

Black was pushing Paul Starrett to get after the subcontractors to quickly finish up, so that the building could begin paying out income as quickly as possible. In the meantime, the Fuller Company was going to begin distributing a glossy six-page pamphlet to brokers and prospective tenants. It would also run frequent and very large ads in all the big daily newspapers. The ads announced that on October 1, the Fuller Building, a "Modern Building unequaled in Location Comfort Appointments and Convenience," would be ready for occupancy, and were ac-

An advertisement for the "Fuller Building."

companied with a sketch of the new skyscraper (newspapers were not yet using photographs). Some days the ad filled up an entire page of a paper's real estate section.

The Fuller Building, the ads said, was the strongest building ever erected. It would have its own steam and electric plants, which would furnish free heat and light to tenants. It would have six hydraulic elevators, manufactured by the world-famous Otis Company. Otis had invented hydraulic systems, which had superseded their original steam-operated elevators. Hydraulic elevators were fast and efficient for the time, and needed no electricity, instead running on water pressure that moved pistons up and down within a vertical pipe, thereby activating a system of ropes and pulleys. As for the woodwork, "It is of mahogany and quartered oak, and has all undergone a process of fireproofing, in order to eliminate the possibility of fire," the ads assured its readers.

As the ads began making the rounds, somebody—we don't know who—made Harry Black an offer to buy the Flatiron that would have netted him a profit of $1 million. Black turned it down. The reason, according to Paul Starrett in his memoir, was that Black was absolutely sure that the Flatiron neighborhood would remain New York's commercial heart. Perhaps this is what Black told Starrett, but surely it was not the financier's real motive for refusing to sell. Anybody could see that the city's center of gravity was continuing to shift uptown, and would, inevitably, continue to do so, as work progressed on the new subway, which would whisk New Yorkers up Broadway in a fraction of the time it took them now on a streetcar. The subway would deposit them right at the theater district at Longacre Square, or at the new Macy's department store at Thirty-fourth Street, now almost finished. And more department stores would surely follow Macy's, deserting Ladies' Mile for New York's new shopping district.

But for whatever reason, even for a million dollars profit, Black, so notorious for his gambling ways that his own board refused to make him president of his own company, could not let go of the Flatiron. Perhaps he, like everybody else, was taken by it. And he must have been elated that with all the new, grand buildings going up all over Manhattan, it was the Flatiron that everybody was talking about. So assiduously had everybody followed its progress during construction that the *Real Estate Record and Builders' Guide* on September 6, 1902, reported a surprisingly detailed technical knowledge of the Flatiron by the man in the street. People were talking about engineers' calculations and wind stress.

Yes, New Yorkers loved the Flatiron. That is, all the ordinary folks did. But those formally entrusted to make judgments on what constituted good art felt otherwise. Forget about popular opinion, they said. What did the average person know about the aesthetics of architecture? Suddenly, everybody who looked at the Flatiron Building considered himself an expert.

The critics believed that the Flatiron's sole merit was how ingeniously its builders had managed to exploit such an odd site as a business investment. But as a work of art, they dismissed the Flatiron as a failure. The well-known sculptor William Ordway Partridge, who had executed the statue of Admiral Farragut that stood in Madison Square, called the Flatiron "a disgrace to our city, an outrage to our sense of the artistic, and a menace to life." (What exactly could Partridge have meant by "a menace to life"? Was he one of those who persisted in believing that the building would tip over in the wind?)

Montgomery Schuyler, the tall, handsome, mutton-chopped and very patrician editor of *Architectural Record,* devoted an entire article to a scathing assessment of the building as soon as it was finished, even before any tenants moved in. The scion of an old upstate New York Dutch family, Schuyler first came to New York City during the Civil War, where he worked as a newspaper reporter and editor, first at the *World* and then the *Times,* and also contributed to highbrow magazines such as *Harper's.* Observing New York's drastic physical changes as he covered the city, he developed an interest in architecture. Along with several others, he had launched *Architectural Record* in 1891.

In his critique of the Flatiron, Schuyler acknowledged that the site had presented an enormous challenge, but the Flatiron's architect, Schuyler wrote indignantly in the magazine's October 1902 issue, without ever mentioning Dinkelberg or Burnham by name, had left the building's "awkwardnesses entirely undisguised, and without even an attempt to disguise them, if they have not even been aggravated by the treatment. That is, in fact, the peculiarity and the misfortune of the present erection, the fact that the problem does not seem to have presented itself to the architect as a problem." Schuyler hated the building's curved edges—"the wedge is blunted, by being rounded. But it might as well have been produced to the actual point. The treatment of the tip is an additional and seems a wanton aggravation of the inherent awkwardness of the situation." Schuyler did however admire the "rusticated" masonry, that is, its rough, irregular surfaces, and terra-cotta detail. But, he continues, "this praise is all limited to the assumption, which the architect inscrutably chose to make, that he was designing elevations and not a building. Either of the principal elevations, taken in conjunction with the edge upon which they converge, has not the aspect of an enclosing wall, so much as of a huge screen, a vast theatrical 'wing,' which conceivably rests upon Titanic castors and is meant to be pushed about, instead of being rooted to the spot."

What a clever simile, of a Flatiron Building rolling along the sidewalk! How apt, and how ironic! It was precisely the Flatiron's fluid nature—from every angle, it looked different—that made people love it so. The building embodied New York, where every day people arrived from across the sea, or from the farms of rural America, swelling the city's population, and continuously remaking the city into something else, that kept evolving with each successive wave of new immi-

The just-completed Flatiron Building, 1903.

grants. New York, the *Evening Post* had recently declared, was a "fluid city." It had not yet been able to settle down, either industrially or socially. New York did not have clearly defined neighborhoods, like Paris, where "people of common tastes and similar resources find near at hand their natural associates. . . . You will find an Italian, a Chinese, a Hungarian quarter, but where will you find an aristocratic, an artistic, or a university quarter?" New York as yet had no zoning laws—the first would be enacted in 1916—which meant that any quarter could change suddenly into something else entirely. Retail businesses, now on the move uptown, were replacing block after block of brownstone residences between Fifth and Madison Avenues. The new subway and bridges to Brooklyn meant that people could live further away from their places of work. And any quarter in New York had the potential to become aristocratic, as long as people were making real money.

Change was the essence of New York, and the Flatiron was part of that change. It looked different from any other skyscraper. If you were walking toward it on Twenty-third Street, going west, it seemed like Schuyler's huge theatrical screen, rising straight up in front of you. If you were north of the building, on Fifth Avenue or Broadway, the Flatiron appeared to be moving toward you, like a huge ship. Perhaps you would imagine that it had just arrived from Europe, filled with immigrants, plowed right through the harbor and was now continuing its journey, on land, uptown. "It's just like a great wedge of strawberry shortcake, with windows for berries," one young girl was overhead saying. "A tall thin wedge of a building, for all the world like a slice of a gigantic layer cake, a boarding house slice, very thin and tapering," wrote *The Brooklyn Eagle*. A *Times* reporter, watching a man walking down Fifth Avenue with his girl, heard him trying to persuade her that the Flatiron Building was architecturally superior to l'Arc de Triomphe on the Champs-Élysées, and just as beautiful as the Washington Monument on the Potomac. Nonsense, she replied; to her, it resembled a clothespin that fastened Fifth Avenue and Broadway jointly onto the clothesline of Twenty-third Street. Her boyfriend replied: "Granted its scale, it is architecturally well designed. It will be to the travelers on the two great highways of our metropolis a column of smoke by day, and by night, when the interior is lighted, a constellation of fires." She said, "The Flatiron will probably be used to advertise electrically a patent for weak backs and sore feet." "But there is something spirited and commanding in it," persisted the young fellow. "It gives an accent to the vista of two great thoroughfares."

"But the accent," his girlfriend said, "is so very American."

That remark, the reporter later commented in his article, "was taken as a complete justification of the Flatiron Building, for what greater virtue can native architecture have than to be conceived and executed in the native vernacular?"

Real Estate Record and Builders' Guide, applauding the current and unprecedented popular interest in architecture caused by the Flatiron Building, wrote: "No amount of approval or disapproval on the part of a few interested and competent people can compensate for the (up-to-now) widespread lack of interest in architecture. An architect's design must appeal to a lot of people, not just the elite. And this can only have a good effect on popular taste. No art can be thoroughly wholesome in a democracy that has not a good basis in popular taste."

CHAPTER SEVEN

—————

THE FLATIRON OPENS
FOR BUSINESS

O<small>N OCTOBER</small> 8, 1902, a photographer named Robert Bonine halted his horse-drawn wagon on the west side of Madison Square Park. There he took in the gorgeous view of the Flatiron's eastern flank, which rose straight up in front of him. After unloading a tripod and a camera—a "kinetograph"—from the wagon, he set up the equipment on the pavement, in preparation to do a shoot of the building. Not still photos, but a moving picture.

They were the latest craze, movies, as people were beginning to call them. Photographers, among them Bonine, were now traveling the country and world to create this latest form of entertainment. The catalogue of films shot—their length varied from one to three minutes— now numbered in the thousands. You could watch films of flamenco dancers performing at the 1901 Buffalo Exposition, young boys diving off cliffs in Hawaii, and dog sleds speeding over the snow in the Klondike. Moving pictures were being shown everywhere, from music halls, in between the live acts, to so-called "theaters" charging a nickel admission that entrepreneurial types were now setting up in vacant stores and abandoned shooting galleries. It was easy: all you needed was a canvas sheet, chairs, and the machine that projected the film, and you were in business. Along Coney Island's main drag, showmen stood on the sidewalk, shouting: "Ladies and gents, step this way, and I'll explain to you the wonderful moving pictures. The photos is first took by instainious [sic] process. Then they is transferred to a film and the result is most realistic."

The technology for movies was invented during the last two decades of the 1890s, in part by Thomas Edison, but others played a major part, too, and it is impossible to ascertain precisely who contributed what. The pictures were taken with a kinetograph camera, which, in its earliest form, was operated with a hand crank, but was soon improved upon by the addition of a motor. The motor continuously advanced a three-inch-wide strip of celluloid film by two inches, which took only one-hundredth of a second, then stopped it for one-sixteenth of a second, during which time the shutter opened and closed, thereby capturing the image before the lens on the film, and then again advanced the film by two inches, and on and on, until you had a strip of image after image, which, when viewed in sequence, would produce the illusion of motion. A one-minute moving picture consisted of 1,800 separate images of the subject, and filled up 320 feet of film.

At first, moving pictures were viewed through peepholes in free-standing machines called kinetoscopes, invented by Edison's employee D. K. Dickson. Dickson filed a patent for the machine under his name in 1891, but on behalf of Edison's company, which then began to manufacture the machines. Investors, smelling money, pounced, placing their orders. Their venture proved an instant success. On the first day, August 14, 1894, at the first-ever kinetoscope parlor—ten machines set up in a former shoe store at 1155 Broadway in New York, at the corner of Twenty-seventh Street—proceeds totaled some $120, with each ticket costing twenty-five cents. Each machine had cost $250.

More parlors soon opened in New York, then a few in Chicago, then another in San Francisco. Soon you could view so-called "peepshows" all

over the United States. Before long, the term took on its present con-
notation, because the kinetoscope turned out to be the perfect device
for viewing dirty pictures. The machine acquired a tawdry association,
which caused the kinetoscope craze to quickly ebb. And there was
another reason: its success had proven the enormous money-making
potential of the moving picture business, thereby encouraging imitation. People were rushing in to try and reap their own profits from the
invention. They made changes in the design, to avoid a patent infringement lawsuit from Edison. Dickson, for example, who by then had left
Edison along with a handful of other defectors, invented the "Mutoscope," also a viewing machine, but, unlike the kinetoscope, which ran
on an electric motor, had a hand crank. They received a patent for it in
1895. In the meantime, they had been working on a machine that
would project moving images onto a screen, much as an old-fashioned
magic lantern did for slides. In 1896, they came out with such a machine:
the "Biograph." The young men opened a new company—the American
Biograph and Mutoscope Company—on Broadway and Thirteenth Street,
and began producing motion pictures.

In the meantime, a student in Washington, D.C., named Thomas
Armat was working on his own version of a projection camera. The
investors backing him persuaded him to bring on board Thomas Edison, who up until meeting him had resisted the idea of a projection
machine. Armat's camera was given a name, not just "Vitascope," but,
"Edison's Vitascope." Affixing the famous inventor's name to Armat's
invention, his backers insisted, would assure its success.

Edison's Vitascope had its debut on the night of April 27, 1896, at
Koster and Bial's Music Hall on Thirty-fourth Street and Broadway.
(Koster and Bial's, incidentally, was later demolished to make room for
Macy's department store.) *The New York Times* described the scene:

> An amazed assemblage of New Yorkers burst into applause and
> loud cheers as a shaft of light pierced the darkened theatre, struck
> the scene, and there was revealed the familiar and popular figure

of Annabelle Moore, a serpentine dancer who pirouetted about, waving endless yards of silk in a distinctly proper manner. "Why, it's Annabelle herself," several persons in the audience exclaimed . . . (then followed) a flash of Charley Hoyt's popular Broadway farce "A Milk White Flag," another dance by Mae Lucas from the "Gaiety Girls," and some bits of scenery. The best picture shown was the hit of the evening. It depicted waves rolling on the rocks of Manhattan Beach. The seat holders in the first two rows actually ducked their heads and prepared to get wet.

Edison quickly registered "his" Vitascope with the U.S. patent office. After he received the patent in 1897, he instituted a suit against the American Biograph and Mutoscope Company, claiming copyright infringement. He would win his case on the first round, but in 1902 lost on appeal.

Bonine, also an Edison defector, was working with American Mutoscope in 1902. He, and other photographers like him, were roaming around New York, making films of whatever they saw that grabbed their interest. *Actualities,* they accordingly called their unstaged, plotless films, some lasting only twenty-five seconds, and at most one minute or so. They captured for the ages startlingly vivid images of life in New York, as it was happening on the streets: a busy fish market on the Lower East Side; a boatload of European immigrants filing off the gangplank at Ellis Island, carrying babies and leading children by the hand, loaded down with bundles, and looking right into the camera lens recording their first steps on the soil of the New World; a police parade passing by Union Square; grime-covered workmen digging out a foundation for a skyscraper, the air around them thick with steam from a crane hoisting up a cart filled with construction material that a gang of men, awaiting it on a plank, ease down from a giant hook. It was Bonine who had made the latter actuality, of the skyscraper excavation, in the spring of 1902. He had also shot a panorama of skyscrapers on lower Broadway. And now, in October, here he was, standing in front of the Flatiron Building—New York's latest skyscraper, just now completed, the one that people couldn't stop talking about, and surely would keep talking about for a long time to come. Thanks to him, they would be able to see what it looked like, in October 1902, just as it was opening for business.

Bonine started his shoot by pointing the lens right where the building's northern point met the sidewalk. The glass-and-cast-iron extension that Burnham had tried in vain to prevent was now in mid-construction. Because this was the middle of a workday, Bonine's film captured the images of all manner of traffic that was passing by, diagonally up and down Broadway, and across Twenty-third Street—streetcars, horse-drawn carts, an occasional automobile—as well as clusters of pedestrians, some looking directly into the camera as they crossed Broadway. Then Bonine, leaving behind the chaos on the sidewalk, shifted the camera's gaze. He was panning his camera upward, craning his neck, up along the building's eastern elevation, pausing first at its midsection, and, then, finally, moving all the way up, where the camera's gaze lingered for a few seconds, shooting frame after frame of the top of the Flatiron Building.

As Bonine was shooting his Flatiron movie, the first tenants were moving into the building. Among them was the publisher Frank Munsey, who had leased the entire eighteenth floor. Munsey, a six-foot-tall, skinny, impeccably dressed man in his late forties, with a long face, large mustache, and an intense expression in his gray eyes, had been raised poor on a farm in Maine. As a young man he had gone to work as a clerk for the Western Union Company in Augusta, then the publishing capital of trashy fiction magazines printed on pulp paper, "serving principally as advertising catalogues for gold-filled watches, bosom pins, rings, music boxes, card tricks and books on beauty and pugilism, all of which were to be ordered by mail from the publishers themselves."

Some people had gotten rich off these ventures, a lesson not lost on Munsey. He arrived in New York in 1882, with, as he would later love to brag, only $40 in his pocket, and the grand idea of publishing a juvenile fiction magazine. Although he was not bookish by nature—in fact, he hardly ever read for pleasure—he had, in his words, "the publishing germ." He was convinced that publishing could make him rich. After convincing people with money to back him, he launched his new magazine, *Argosy*. Among the manuscripts that he purchased for it was a serial, "Do and Dare, or a Brave Boy's Fight for Fortune," by Horatio Alger Jr. In 1884, Munsey launched a second magazine, *Munsey's Illustrated Weekly*.

Munsey managed to keep both of his publications going for a few years, all the while constantly tweaking their respective formats. "With me there has never been anything very terrible about changing a publication as often as conditions warranted, and in making the change as radical as possible," he later wrote in a short and cloyingly laudatory history of his publishing empire. Sometimes he turned a profit. But he had had to borrow heavily to pay for all the start-up expenses—paper, shipping, printing, binding, paying writers, rent, a stenographer—and the debt was crushing him. Still, he hung on, even upping the ante in 1887, borrowing yet more money to send men across the country to go from town to town, then door to door, selling copies of *Argosy*. His instincts were good. After his homespun sales campaign, *Argosy's* circulation rose, resulting in net profits of $100 a week, good for the time, but still not enough to even begin paying off his debts.

When creditors hounded him, he got them off his back by bouncing around his loans from one bank to another. He fired his stenographer. Except for one editor, Malcolm Douglas, to whom Munsey paid $10 a week, he literally put out both magazines himself, spending eighteen hours a day in his office; his lanky frame bent over a beat-up wooden desk that he'd bought for $8. He even began writing the *Argosy* stories himself, at night in his rented room, under his own name, so that he wouldn't have to pay writers. Munsey's prose had a breathless, earnest quality. To save money, he moved the *Argosy's* offices to cheaper quarters—"the second floor at 81 Warren Street, sandwiched between a cheese store and a maker of dessicated cocoanut"—and his digs across the Hudson River to Jersey City, where rents were cheaper.

In 1893, after ten years of struggling to make it, now thirty-nine and more than $100,000 in debt, Munsey decided to relaunch *Munsey's* as a monthly, just like the stately *Harper's* and *Century* and *Scribner's*, except that he would undercut his competition by pricing his publication at ten cents, whereas the going rate was twenty-five. He was taking a huge risk. The country was in the midst of a depression. Yet this was also the time to do it. His retooled magazine would use wood pulp paper, the cheapest kind, and half-tone engraving. The audience was there: the working classes, a large, untapped market, hungry to read stories. Munsey placed a huge ad in *The Sun*, announcing the magazine's drop in price. "Why we can do it," blared the ad, in boldface. "Because we deal direct with news dealers and save two profits you pay on other magazines. *No middlemen; no monopoly.* On all news stands." The monopoly that Munsey was referring to was the American News Company (ANC), which controlled all magazine distribution, and thereby had set the going newsstand price for monthlies at twenty-five cents, which guaranteed it a healthy profit. The ANC was now refusing to distribute *Munsey's* at its new low price. Munsey responded by bypassing the ANC, handling the circulation himself.

His experiment worked. Circulation numbers soared. There was only one problem: at ten cents a copy, *Munsey's* was losing money. To make up for the difference, Munsey came up with a brilliant and revolutionary idea: he would sell advertising space in his publication, not just a few discreet ads in the back, like the highbrow magazines, but throughout the pages.

And so was born the ten-cent "pulp" magazine, an idea that Munsey based on what he had learned in Augusta, and then vastly improved upon. The fiction in his "pulps"—mostly fast-moving action stories—was far superior to the junk in the "dreadfuls." He also used lots of illustrations. And, like the "dreadfuls," Munsey's publications depended not so much on circulation to turn a profit, but advertising. Of each issue's 160 pages, 80 to 100 consisted of ads. Munsey had changed the rules of magazine publishing forever. Soon other magazines—*McClure's* and *Cosmopolitan,* to name two—were forced to also drop their prices to ten cents. He also remade *Argosy* into a magazine for adults, offering "good red-blooded fiction for the millions." A regular contributor was Edgar Rice Burroughs, with his series about two characters who lived a carefree life in the jungle, far from the ills of civilization. Their names were Tarzan and Jane.

Munsey became immensely rich. He began to buy newspapers. Some he merged with others, and others he killed, if they didn't prove profitable. Sometimes he fired entire staffs of the newspapers he acquired. He also invested in a chain of grocery stores, and U.S. Steel stock. He soon had the distinction of being one of the most hated men in publishing, both for his lowbrow taste and complete command of the business aspect, for which he was envied.

Munsey was a bachelor. He had no known relationships with women, or men. He lived to work. He loved talking about how much money his publications made, but cared nothing for the writing that filled them. In fact, those who worked for him said that he didn't even read his own publications. One of his editors told of Munsey firing one of his best writers, on the grounds that he was too fat. Munsey, skinny as Abe Lincoln, hated fat men.

He had an apartment at the Sherry-Netherland, "furnished in tasteful elegance. Books, rugs, statuary—all indicate a mind in touch with the real thing in its respective realm of human endeavor," wrote *Town and Country* of his living quarters, on September 8, 1906, also duly noting that he had "reached the half-century mark unmarried, yet he takes keen pleasure in society." Since 1895 Munsey, having ascended to the top of New York's social ladder solely by virtue of his fabulous and entirely self-made wealth, had been listed on the Social Register. He remained on it for the rest of his life. The grandes dames of New York society kept introducing him to available women without success. He liked Paris, where he visited for the first time in 1895, after his daring business move had paid off. From then on he went back, year after year. Paris had a booming industry in naughty postcards, and no doubt

Frank Munsey, 1887.

it was there that the enigmatic bachelor discovered that he liked looking at pictures of naked women. During *Munsey's* first several years, he
regularly placed images of nude or semi-dressed women into his otherwise banal magazine, a daring move in those Puritanical times. Circulation soared, and finger-waggers criticized *Munsey's* for its immodesty.
Some libraries cancelled their subscriptions. In response, Munsey
toned down his magazine's depiction of the female form, now shown
never completely nude, but with parts discreetly covered.

Prior to 1902, Munsey's headquarters were located at 111 Fifth Avenue. No doubt the brouhaha over the Flatiron as it was being constructed a few blocks north was a factor in his relocating there. That
the acknowledged czar of the publishing world was one of the Flatiron's first tenants was a real gift to the building. Munsey's presence
would surely attract more tenants.

Munsey had a platform built at the point of the Flatiron, on which
his desk was placed, so that he could see easily out the windows, and
take in the view, which fanned out in three directions, clear to the East

and Hudson Rivers, and beyond. Below, the leaves on the trees in
Madison Park had turned red and gold in the autumn air, a refreshing
contrast to the grimy chaos of the surrounding streets, filled with hur-
rying people, and the buzz of traffic, and the earsplitting sounds of
steam drills as more skyscrapers were being built and the tunnels for
the new subway were being dug out, all mixed in with the *slam-bang*
noise of the Sixth Avenue El.

Each of the Flatiron's twenty floors was divided into small offices, all
entered from a center corridor. And each office, no matter how small,
received light, thanks to the building's design. So there was nothing to
obstruct the light from entering any of the building's more than 700
windows, which were all arranged in closely spaced pairs, yet one
more feature of the Flatiron that displeased the critic Montgomery
Schuyler. The poor tenant, Schuyler wrote, "can, perhaps, find wall
space within for one roll top desk without overlapping the windows,
with light close in front of him and close behind him and close on one
side of him. But suppose he needed a bookcase? Undoubtedly he has a
highly eligible place from which to view processions. But for the trans-
action of business?"

One by one, people were leasing offices. A tenant named Sercombe
operated a vanity press in Room 1005 ("I will pay the highest cash
price for all AI freak books published at author's expense, and written by
bookey stiffs, literary bums, and self-appointed dealers in Sweet Singers
of Michigan, or elsewhere."). Books and other publications—including
ten-cent magazines, the *American Architect and Building News*—poured
from the Flatiron. And the thriving popular music industry, now expanding beyond the block of Twenty-eighth Street between Broadway and
Sixth known as Tin Pan Alley, was also finding a home in the Flatiron.
Hallways were filled with the *clinkity-clink* of piano keys accompanied by
singing, as songwriters plied their compositions to music publishers, who
might, "please God," say "yes," and turn your tune into a piece of sheet

music. Then people would buy it for ten cents, take it home, and play it on their pianos. Soon thousands of pieces of sheet music were being turned out at the Flatiron, and some even used the instantly recognized image of the building, whether in the tune's title—the "Flatiron March and Two-Step," by J. W. Lerman, a church organist and composer of Sunday school hymns, who dedicated his song to the George A. Fuller Company—or simply picturing it on the cover of "Father Knickerbocker: A New York Rag," which depicted the character in the tricorne and knickers* who personified New York cavorting in front of the Flatiron.

The other Flatiron tenants represented a hodge-podge of New York businesses. There were ticket agents for railroads and steam ship companies. Most of the third floor was leased to the Equitable Life Assurance Society, except for one office, which housed the Imperial Russian Consulate. Mrs. G. M. Dana had an office on the fourteenth floor for her Bohemian Guides Society, which, in her words, "supplied timid men in New York on business or pleasure with female escorts familiar with highways and byways." She described the girls as good-looking, well-dressed, and intelligent, and, above all, respectable. "They will not tolerate any funny business." On the tenth floor was Daniel Langton, a landscape architect. The Bromonio Company, a patent medicine concern, leased an office. On the fifteenth floor, the J. E. Gardiner Company offered shares in racehorses, at an unbeatable 260 percent interest (the following year, Gardiner would skip town). The Western Specialty Manufacturing Company, another tenant, made all kinds of small and clever devices; in 1908 the company would come out with the "Little Wonder," a hot water bottle made of rubber-lined silk that folded up into the size of an envelope, but, when filled, held a full quart of hot water. The United Cigar Store had signed a lease for the retail space, which included the still-under-construction north point extension. The

---

* Knickerbocker was the invention of Washington Irving, who used the character as a narrator for his 1809 satire *A History of New York*.

newspapers reported that United was paying a huge amount of rent, but did not specify the number. United was following the lead of other tobacco companies renting retail space in equally sexy and expensive locations: the northwest corner of Thirty-second Street and Broadway, two blocks from the construction site of the new Macy's department store, and in the St. James Building, also on Broadway, three blocks north of the Flatiron, and on the same side of the street. The tobacco companies realized that the expenditure paid off, since these stores functioned as advertising to the thousands of daily passersby.

A luxury restaurant leased the cellar, a huge space that extended into vaults beneath the surrounding sidewalks. The Flatiron Restaurant was a vast operation, open for breakfast on through after-theater suppers. Patrons entered it via the building lobby, down a grand stairway, and through a vestibule finished in marble, cut glass, and solid brass, with potted plants placed to the sides. An orchestra played from lunchtime until the last guests departed. The restaurant seated 1,500 people, who ate off specially made china decorated with Flatiron logos. Its ventilating system was a marvel. In the summer, the entire space was cooled by electric fans that drove the air over refrigerating pipes. In the winter, the moving air was first heated by coils. "So perfect is the ventilation that smoking is permitted at all times, there being no discomfort to the ladies or other guests," wrote *The Sun* on August 2, 1908. In fact waiters distributed complimentary cigarettes, imprinted with the words "Flatiron Restaurant," to patrons after meals. The huge menu boasted a "cosmopolitan kitchen," which in 1902 New York meant mostly German, and heavy on the meat. There was all manner of game, caviar—"our own importation"—and a dozen kinds of oysters. Beverages included over thirty kinds of Moselle and Rhine wines, fifteen different German beers (served in specially made souvenir steins embossed with an image of the building) and thirty-five brands of whiskey. For dessert, the *pièce de résistance* was the "Flat Iron Souvenir Ice Cream," a seventy-five cent extravaganza molded in the shape of you-know-what.

Harry Black took the entire nineteenth floor for the new Fuller

The Flatiron Restaurant, 1905.

Company headquarters. Above Fuller, the top floor housed an office of
the Whitehead & Hoag Company, which had a large factory in Newark
that produced celluloid souvenirs. The company specialized in buttons
and badges for all kinds of organizations—among their clients, it so
happened, were the iron workers—and gorgeous bookmarks decorated
with images of flowers. All were made of celluloid, a highly flammable
material. Also in the Flatiron was the main office of the Roebling Construction Company, which manufactured fireproof building materials—
floors, roofs, and partitions made of concrete. Roebling was owned by
the sons of Richard "Boss" Croker, the Tammany leader who had ruled
New York for sixteen years, until Seth Low's Fusion Party finally threw
Tammany out in 1901.

As the first tenants were settling into the Flatiron Building in October,
Macy's was moving from its old Fourteenth Street location uptown, to
its new colossal store at Thirty-fourth and Broadway.

For four days, the Straus firm's 200 delivery wagons, each loaded up
with merchandise, made trip after trip up and down Sixth Avenue,

transporting the entire contents of the department store. (Huge automobiles were also used in the move, traveling up Seventh Avenue instead of Sixth, because the former had "asphalt and a less obstructed thoroughfare.") During the nights, mountains of packing debris— wooden boxes, straw, and paper—were piled up on Thirty-fifth Street, between Broadway and Seventh. There, women and boys were standing on line, waiting for the sky to become light, when the foreman would permit them to gather as much of the rubbish as they could carry in their arms. They piled their takings into empty baby carriages and wagons, to cart it home, and use as kindling. Some then returned for more, until, by ten in the morning, the pile was gone.

It had taken the Fuller Company just one year to build Macy's, the largest store in the world. It employed 4,000 people. The building weighed two million pounds. If all its floor planks were placed end to end, they would stretch from New York to seventy-five miles beyond Detroit. It had thirty-three elevators and four escalators, which all together could move 40,000 people in one hour. The Fuller Company was especially proud of the store's ultra-modern fire safety system. All in all, the new Macy's represented a great engineering feat. But it resulted in a heavy financial loss to the Fuller Company, because of Black's insistence on winning the bid for the job at any price. The contract Black signed with the Straus family to build Macy's guaranteed that it would cost them no more than twenty cents a square foot. That translated into $3,000,600, quite a reasonable sum, even in 1902, to build the biggest store in the world. The real cost of construction, Paul Starrett wrote in his autobiography, was far greater, and the Fuller Company had to eat the difference. (What it added up to Starrett didn't specify. He wrote only: "All I knew was, we would lose heavily.")

Macy's opened its doors on the morning of November 8. The next day, the *Times* described the scene: "The thousands that had hurried in and out of the doors of the old store at Sixth Avenue and Fourteenth Street went early to the new place, eager for an inspection. But they did not overcrowd the store, as it has a floor space of twenty-four acres."

Macy's, the world's largest department store. To the right is the
New York Herald Building, 1905.

A few weeks later, Harry Black's new company, United States Realty
and Construction, embarked on its first project: the purchase and immediate demolition of the fifty-year-old five-story brick Trinity Building,
which stood on an oddly shaped, narrow lot at 111 Broadway, abutting
Trinity Church. Both structures had been designed by the architect Richard Upjohn in the 1840s.

The Trinity Building's dingy basement had long been where the
city held its real estate auctions. Buyers purchased everything from
tenement houses to, say, Eno's flatiron, which the Newhouses bought
from Eno's heirs when they were liquidating his estate in 1898. In place
of the Trinity Building, U.S. Realty would soon build a double-towered
twenty-story office building, designed by the architect Francis Kimball,
yet one more in New York's rapidly increasing roster of skyscrapers.

Early one Sunday morning in November 1902, a team of fire trucks
pulled by giant work horses arrived at the Flatiron to conduct a test of
the standpipe, a six-inch-wide wrought-iron pipe that ran from the

cellar to the roof. It had connectors at each floor for attaching fire hoses, and another one, a "Siamese," outside, at the sidewalk level. Among the crew was the fire chief, Edward Croker, nephew of Richard, the former Tammany boss. Edward Croker himself would oversee the test of the device.

Standpipes had been mandatory in all new buildings over one hundred feet tall since 1899, after a series of skyscraper fires had proven the old equipment woefully obsolete. Fire hoses could not lift water beyond the seventh or eighth story. This was most spectacularly proven during a conflagration at the Home Life Building on lower Broadway in 1898. When firemen dragged the hoses up to the higher levels of a neighboring building to douse the fire, gravity forced the water back down the hoses, which then met the upward pressure from the pumping engines. One after another, the hoses had burst.

But metal standpipes, if functioning properly, could withstand a thousand pounds of pressure to the square inch, twenty times what a twenty-story skyscraper such as the Flatiron required. Skyscraper owners were asking the fire department to test their standpipe systems, and pronounce their buildings safe. The public, always nervous about fires, was particularly jittery now, after a recent disastrous fire in February 1902. Seventeen people had died, all guests at the Park Avenue Hotel, which burst into flames that had migrated from another fire already raging at the Seventy-first Regiment Armory, across the street. The hotel's owner, the department store magnate A. T. Stewart, had touted the eight-story structure to be one of the city's safest. ("A substantial and absolutely fire-proof hotel" is how King's Handbook of New York described it in 1893.) Stewart had built it originally as a hotel for single working girls, and he had made sure to use only fireproof materials. In the rear of the building was a large iron stairway, for egress. But it had no external fire escapes, which were technically not required because of the building's "fireproof" classification. The hotel had no fire hoses, an indication that it had no recent safety inspections.

Chief Croker was now busy going around the city, present at each test of every system. Even the most staunch anti-Tammanyite declared that nobody was better qualified for the fire chief's job than Boss Croker's nephew. It was Edward Croker who had successfully fought to get the standpipe requirement written into the city building code in 1899. Fire safety was his mission, and passion. He drove around the city in his little trademark red automobile at a time when fire trucks were still horse drawn. It was a justified rarity, as it enabled him to arrive quickly at the scene of a fire. He was known for his tactlessness. Once, a newspaperman accompanied Croker to a burning building. When Croker arrived, he saw that the blaze was getting away from the men already there. The fire chief sprang from his auto and raced up to the top floor of the burning building. A reporter described the scene: "Two sets of men were playing two lines of hose on the flames from the hall before the elevator shaft. With a bellow of rage Croker sprang upon the rear man at the nozzle of one hose, pulled him back a little by the slack of his coat, and then, using him as a battering ram, hurled the whole crowd into the flat and close up to the flames. 'That's the place to fight a fire from,' he yelled. 'Get close up to that blaze and eat it up!' He said more than that, but that's the printable part." In 1911, Croker would testify after the Triangle Shirt Company fire.

On that Sunday in November, Croker's firemen began unwinding foot after foot of canvas-covered hose from two engines, Numbers 1 and 14, the department's most powerful. After hooking up one to hydrants on the Twenty-third Street and Broadway sides, and another to the standpipe's Siamese connection at the sidewalk level, the men opened up the hydrant valves. As water began gushing from the mains and through the hoses, another crew started up the steam pumps. *Puff-puff-puffing* away, the machines pumped thousands of gallons of water straight up the Flatiron's 300-foot standpipe, to the top of the building. All the while the pumpers on the trucks were violently rocking to and fro, seeming at times to nearly jump off their bearings. Number 1, the largest fire engine in the country, attained a pressure reading of 295 pounds, the highest ever recorded in New York. (Later, firemen found a two-inch live crayfish in the pump, that had been sucked out of the water main.)

Next, firemen attached hoses to the standpipe, beginning at the thirteenth, and at each floor up to the top. They sent out a stream of water from each, simultaneously. Thousands of gallons of water were now spurting out of the inch-and-a-half hose nozzles, out the Flatiron windows and cascading off the roof, "sending up mist and foam with a roar like a high waterfall." Broadway was a gushing river. The standpipe and pumps were working so effectively that a gauge that Croker had attached to the hose registered the water pressure on the roof at forty-seven pounds, more than four times the pressure of a sidewalk hydrant, and four times greater than had been predicted possible.

Guests at the Fifth Avenue and Bartholdi Hotels, across Fifth Avenue, upon hearing the sputter of the pumping machines, had rushed to their windows. Passersby stopped and gaped at the sight. Many fire insurance men, and hundreds of fire fighters, both active and retired, had come especially to observe the test. The spectacle lasted two hours. By the time it was finished, thousands of people were standing around, watching. Some had rushed home and returned with hand cameras, to take photos.

There had been no official ribbon-cutting ceremony to mark the Flatiron's opening. But, with all the grandeur of the fire safety test, nothing more was needed. Croker was jubilant. The Flatiron test, he said, was one of the most successful that he had conducted to date, adding that its standpipe functioned so well that it could help fight fires in the surrounding neighborhood as well as in the building itself. The efficacy of the Flatiron's standpipe was proven in April 1904—by then, the building was fully rented—when a fire broke out on the twentieth floor, in the offices of the Whitehead & Hoag celluloid novelties company. The fire department, arriving on the scene, immediately attached their hoses to the Siamese on the sidewalk. Firemen then rode the elevators to the twentieth floor, where they attached more hoses to the standpipe couplings. Water immediately began spouting from the hoses, with such high pressure that the fire was extinguished in only fifteen minutes.

The Flatiron's tenants did not have to worry about fire. But the wind that whipped around the building was another matter.

CHAPTER EIGHT

23 SKIDDOO

*T*HE PUBLIC COULD NOT let go of the fear that the Flatiron might topple over in the wind. It looked so vulnerable—a towering, skinny wafer of a building, standing all by itself, with no neighboring structures to buffer it. And its location, at Twenty-third Street, was famously windy to boot. But there was nothing to fear. The Flatiron was probably the most overbuilt building in the world, capable of withstanding four times the maximum wind force than it would ever actually come up against. During a sixty-mile-an-hour windstorm that battered the city one morning soon after the first tenants moved in, you couldn't feel the slightest vibration in the building. One tenant claimed that not even the filament in the light bulb above his desk quivered.

So the Flatiron stood like a mountain, impervious to even the strongest winds. In fact, the building's presence strengthened the gales. Everybody was now talking about how treacherous Twenty-third Street had become because now, from whichever direction winds were blowing, they converged at the Flatiron. If the winds came from the north, upon reaching Twenty-third Street, they rammed right into the Flatiron's skinny northern angle, which then, like a knife, sliced each blast in two. Both currents then continued rushing southward, which, reaching the back of the building, ran smack up against columns of hot air rising up from the Flatiron's vaults through sidewalk grilles, which caused them to gain strength, and then join back together again into one blast, which then got sucked into the short stretch of Twenty-second Street behind the building, turning it into a wind tunnel.

The winds sometimes would then shoot down and across Fifth Avenue and Broadway with such force that they blew open shop doors and smashed plateglass windows. Some merchants resorted to dividing their windows with wooden planks, as bracing against the wind. One, a Mr. Gibson N. Vincent, sued the Flatiron owners for $5,000 in damages, after the windows on his clothing store were shattered in the wind for the second time. The rain then poured through, he claimed, ruining his inventory. In his complaint he wrote: "The said 'Flatiron' building, by reason of its extremely peculiar and unusual shape and form of construction, is a public and private nuisance." Such litigation was unprecedented. Lawyers, intrigued, watched closely. "Personally we have grave doubts as to whether the foregoing facts constitute a cause of action," the *American Lawyer* wrote. "To hold otherwise would be to determine that the owner of the particular lot could not utilize his ground to put up the structure that the shape warrants."*

At the base of the Flatiron, the wind blew total strangers into each other's arms, causing much embarrassment. Hats sailed off heads, and umbrellas turned inside out and blew away. A cameraman even shot a one-minute actuality entitled *At the Foot of the Flatiron,* which showed pedestrians walking by the glass-paned cowcatcher, being buffeted by the

---

* *Life* magazine wrote in February 1903: "What the Flatiron and the other cloud-capped edifices need is a wind-storage apparatus, which, instead of turning aside brisk breezes to the detriment of the neighbors, will gather their vagrant energy and turn it to account in running elevators and making electric light." Talk about prescience.

wind. The tip of the building—the "prow," people called it, acknowledging the building's resemblance to an ocean liner—proved the most vulnerable place to be on a windy day. One stormy February afternoon a fourteen-year-old messenger boy named John McTaggert made three attempts before finally rounding the prow, toward Broadway. But then another wind blast came up that blew John back around the prow, and then, back first, right into the middle of Fifth Avenue, where he was run over by an automobile that belonged to the New York Electric Transportation Company. An ambulance rushed him to New York Hospital, where the poor child died.

Then there was the unfortunate Mrs. Nellie Grant Sartoris, daughter of Ulysses S. Grant, who was in New York on a visit one April day in 1904. She had tucked under her skirts a bag containing brooches, earrings, a pearl necklace, and a diamond ring, all gifts of her father. While she was crossing Fifth Avenue, at Twenty-third Street, a wind came up, nearly knocking her off her feet, and lifting her skirts over her head. Later, she realized that her bag of jewels was gone, apparently blown away by the wind, and doubtless retrieved by some lucky passerby.

She ought to have been more careful. By then it was long common knowledge that if you walked by the Flatiron on a windy day, at the very least your skirts were going to end up over your head, and your legs exposed. It was now all the rage for groups of men of a certain character to loiter at the foot of the Flatiron, expressly to catch a glimpse of feminine flesh. A story persists that this is the origin of 23 skiddoo, slang for "beat it!," which policemen supposedly yelled out at these no-goodniks as they shooed them away. But that explanation for this expression cannot be true. In 1899, the humorist George Ade, writing in The Washington Post, mentioned a new slang expression that meant "GO AWAY!" that he had just heard, used by a newsboy. "A small boy with several papers under his arm had edged up until he was trespassing on the territory of the other," wrote Ade. "When the big boy saw the small one he went at him in a threatening manner and said: 'Here! Here!

Twenty-three! Twenty-three!' The small boy scowled and talked under his breath, but he moved away."

If the men hanging around the Flatiron waiting for the wind to kick up didn't move on when they heard "23 skiddoo," the police arrested them. "If you ask me," a cop stationed next to the Flatiron told a reporter, "these young women are asking for it. They come down here in patent-leather slippers, opera silk stockings and lots of fluffy white stuff over that. Then they march around the block looking for the wind. Sometimes it does not come and they're a disappointed looking lot. When it does blow hard enough to gather a crowd of rubber necks they seems to be having the time of their lives." For the more modest damsel, Miss Elizabeth White, president of the Dressmakers' Protective Association of America, located at Fifth Avenue right across the street from the Flatiron, devised a "wind-defying" skirt. It resembled a lily, with a wide flounce around the bottom, which was lined with a band of haircloth about seven inches wide. "This does the trick. It does not add perceptibly to the weight of the skirt, but it holds the pesky thing down," wrote the *Chicago Daily News*.

The image of the wind-whipped Flatiron was now being incorporated into New York's popular psyche, and turning up everywhere: in newspaper comic strips, on some of the thousands of Flatiron-themed postcards that people were now sending back home as proof that yes, they had seen that marvelous building that people all over were talking about, in the souvenir beer steins for sale at the Flatiron Restaurant, embossed on one side with the prow of the building, and the other with a girl, her skirts whirling above her head. And shops around the city were now stocking a pair of two eight-inch delicately tinted plaster figures, meant to be sold together: the Flatiron Girl, in sepia and green, and the blue-toned Flatiron Cop, "a delightful representation of one of the 'Finest' " wrote the *Times* on May 18, 1904.

A Tin Pan Alley composer named Herbert Walter wrote "A Breezy Corner," a two-step dedicated to "the corner of 23rd Street, Broadway,

A Flatiron-themed postcard, 1905.

and 5th Avenue." *The New York Times,* with a nod to Shakespeare, immortalized the winds with "A Flatiron Soliloquy," which appeared in April 1903 ("To stand or tumble down? That is the question.").

With the image of the Flatiron Building popping up everywhere, visual artists were beginning to incorporate it into their various media, too.

One snowy day in 1902, Alfred Stieglitz stood in Madison Square Park, gazing up at the Flatiron Building.

The thirty-nine-year-old photographer was famous. He had exhibited his works all over Europe and the United States, winning over 150 medals. And the inaugural issue of the magazine *Camera Work,* his creation, had just been published, to much acclaim. He had decided to devote the beautifully designed magazine not just to photography, but other fine arts as well. Because for him, photography *was* art, at his time a cutting-edge idea.

Stieglitz was an iconoclast. The son of progressive-minded German-born Jews whose Hoboken home functioned as a makeshift salon for artists and writers, Stieglitz had learned to use a camera while studying mechanical engineering in Berlin as a young man. He remained in Europe for nine years, traveling about and taking hundreds of photos. Returning to New York in 1890, he realized, to his dismay, that cameras in the United States were considered mere machines, good only for pragmatic uses. Whereas in Europe, these machines were used to create art.

Stieglitz went about New York, taking photos of icy sidewalks and misty streetscapes, and turning photography in America into a new artistic medium. Photographs, he argued, constituted art, and therefore could be called "pictures," to be hung in galleries alongside paintings. A 1902 show of his work at New York's National Arts Club—he spontaneously gave the exhibition the title "Photo-Secession," that is, "secession from the accepted idea of what constitutes a photograph"—was a knockout success, spawning an entire "Photo-Secessionist" movement.

While the Flatiron was being built, Stieglitz had felt no desire to photograph it, despite all the fuss people were making over it. But now, seeing the building in the middle of a snowstorm, he was suddenly transfixed. For some time now he had been experimenting with taking photos, often of moving figures, in gloomy, wintry weather: snow, fog, mist, rain, and sometimes even at night. And the Flatiron now seemed to be *moving*, toward him, in the snow, "like the bow of a monster ocean steamer, a picture of the new America, which was in the making," he would later say. With his camera, he caught the image that was captivating him: the tall, straight Flatiron, its soft-gray façade perforated with black windows, against a wintry-white sky, its top frieze clearly delineating the shaft from the capital, and the prow pointing toward Fifth Avenue. But all the angles are softened by the whirling snow-

Alfred Stieglitz's famous photo of the Flatiron.

flakes, and circles of park benches and naked, snow-topped trees at the building's base. And then the Flatiron's sharp edges leap out at you, again, in the form of a tree in the foreground, very close to the lens— its trunk branches creating also a V-shape, repeating the triangle motif.

He ran the photogravure in *Camera Work* on October 1903, along with an essay and poem—"To the 'Flat-Iron' "—by his friend, the pro- lific art critic Sadakichi Hartmann. The son of a German father and a Japanese mother who had died giving birth to him, Hartmann grew up in Germany and came to America as a teenager, where he became a jour- nalist, author, playwright, painter, and photographer, all the way ask- ing questions about beauty, identity, and America.

" 'Estheticism and the 'Flat-Iron.' Isn't that a paradox at the start?" Hartmann wrote. "Surely you do not mean to tell us that the eyesore at Twenty-third Street and Broadway has anything to do with art? some of my readers will incredulously ask . . . Never in the history of mankind has a little triangular piece of real estate been utilized in such a *raffiné* manner. It is typically American in conception as well as execution. It is a curiosity of modern architecture, solely built for utilitarian purposes, and at the same time a masterpiece of iron construction. . . . A curious creation, no doubt, but can it be called beautiful? That depends largely on what is understood by beautiful. Beauty is a very abstract idea. . . . Why should not the time arrive when the majority without hesitation will pronounce the 'Flat-iron' a thing of beauty? I know I will not make many friends with these lines today. It is only a small circle which will acknowledge that my claims are justified."

Hartmann explored the still-evolving idea of beauty in America, specifically in New York, exemplified by the city's bridges and skyscrapers. "The huge office-buildings of lower New York make one think of the vision of some modern Cathay"—Hartmann was alluding to China's crowded cities—"caught up in the air . . . And as the night descends, catching a last glimpse of the bridge glinting like a fairy tiara above the waters of the East River, you feel that the City of the Sea has put on her diamonds—and then you notice the words 'Uneeda Cracker.'

"As yet everything is saturated with the pernicious habit of industry, yelling and writing before the juggernaut of commerce. In France things are shod with velvet, but on Broadway they are not . . . (instead there are) towering office-buildings with narrow frontage, and certain business structures made largely of glass and iron. And amidst all these peculiarities of form a new style is quietly but persistently developing. Thousands work unconsciously towards its perfection, and some day when it has freed itself from a certain heaviness and evolved into a splendid grace it will give as true an expression of our modern civilization as do the temples and statuary of Greece."

Over the next few years, Stieglitz would take additional photos of the Flatiron. In 1904, Edward Steichen, another member of Stieglitz's "Photo-Secession" movement, took his own photo of the building, which Steiglitz ran in *Camera Work* in 1906. The two photos are similar—Steichen was certainly paying homage to Stieglitz, whom he much admired—but Steichen took his on a rainy evening, and then tinted it with gum-bicarbonate. The result was a strange, very dark composition, contrasted here and there with a pinpoint of light from street lamps or automobiles, that cast reflections on the pitch-black, wet street.

Once, Stieglitz's father, Edward, walking down Fifth Avenue, bumped into his son, who was standing in front of the Flatiron. "How can you be interested in that hideous building?" demanded Edward.

"Why, Pa," Alfred replied, "it is not hideous, but the new America. The Flatiron is to the United States what the Parthenon was to Greece."

Yet the art establishment continued to deride the Flatiron—"a disgraceful blot upon our civilization," the sculptor William Ordway Partridge called it, speaking one evening at the Municipal Club. But nobody was listening, except for other high-brow critics. The public in the meanwhile only embraced their adored Flatiron Building all the more. In March 1904, five months after Stieglitz's photo appeared in *Camera Work,* women were rushing to millinery stores to buy that year's most coveted Easter hat, modeled after the Flatiron Building. "It tapers over the forehead to a knife blade, tall and sharp, cutting the wind. Its likeness to the building is unmistakable. It is tri-cornered, with a wide back, the sides steep and high, the jutting point more audacious than dignified. Every woman will wear it, but it should belong with the short skirt of the girl with the tip-tilted nose, say the critics. Except when it succeeds in being piquant, the flatiron hat runs the risk of being rude." The hat was made of rough straw, trimmed with velvet ribbon loops and rosettes, paint brush quills and fancy feathers. Some models sported gold cord and tassels, reported *The Kansas City Star* on March 19, 1904.

Stieglitz wasn't the first to idealize the Flatiron in a photograph. That same winter, in 1902, Arthur Hewitt, a member of Stieglitz's Photo-Secessionist circle, took his own photo of the Flatiron, which was published seven months before Stieglitz's, in a March 1903 issue of *Outlook,* a classy weekly newsmagazine geared toward the *Scribner's* crowd. Nighttime, when New York was all lit up, fascinated Hewitt. His

Flatiron was shot in the dark, its outline barely visible, and delineated by rows of lit windows. His description of the actual process is worth quoting:

> I had previously arranged the night for the photograph with the owners of the building, as they had kindly consented to light up the entire structure. A strong and bitter wind was blowing when I set up my camera on the roof of a neighboring building. It required a stout heart and strong determination to go ahead with my work; for after a few moments (one cannot well work the mechanism of a camera with gloves) my hands were numb with cold. I recollect that the wind was so strong that it obliged me to hold my camera, to steady it, during the entire six minutes of the exposure. . . . I cannot remember a longer six minutes in my life.

And now, in the wake of Stieglitz's and Hewitt's published photographs, something was changing. Artists of all kinds were now drawn to the Flatiron Building. They were using it in all kinds of ways, from idealized subject to backdrop. Edward Steichen and Alvin Langdon Coburn, both member of Stieglitz's circle, and Jessie Tarbox Beals, the first female photojournalist to be hired by a newspaper, photographed it. The etcher and lithographer Joseph Pennell, who during World War I produced a series of Liberty Loan posters, sketched it. A newspaper illustrator named John Edward Jackson used watercolors, reproducing the image over and over again, in various weathers, including one of pedestrians struggling against the wind at the building's prow. Jackson was one of a wave of young artists that included a Philadelphian named John Sloan, who were now landing in New York, and turning the images of everyday life that they were observing on the streets into gritty, thrilling urban art. Sloan painted the Flatiron at least four times. Everett Shinn and Ernest Lawson also painted it, both members of Sloan's renegade artists' group "The Eight"—so-named after they and five other artists mounted their own wildly successful exhibit in 1908 after their paintings had been rejected by the Academy of Design. (Later, Sloan and company would be called, derisively, the "Ashcan" artists.) So did the Tonalist Paul Conoyer, and American Impressionist Childe Hassam. The Flatiron was painted, and, most of all, photographed, far more than any of New York's buildings, of which some were, to be sure, quite wonderful.

And why is this? Is it because the Flatiron was free-standing, therefore fully accessible to the eye on all its sides? And if you walked far enough back and aimed your camera, you could catch all twenty of its stories in the frame? And depending on where you were viewing it, say, from the window of a nearby building, or a rooftop, or from any number of angles at street level, the building's shape appeared completely different, as if its shape were constantly changing, like Proteus, the monster in Greek mythology?

Yes, all these reasons ring true. And the architectural critics could not see this. To them, the Flatiron was, simply, an artistic failure. But the public recognized, and loved, that the building was different from all the others. And their verdict had prevailed. The Flatiron Building was now considered worthy of imitation by artists of all kinds. It could be rightfully called a work of art.

CHAPTER NINE

WATER AND WIND

$\mathcal{A}$T THE END OF October 1902, three months after the creation of U.S. Realty, active trading in its common stock had begun on Wall Street, at $32 a share. Before the day was over, the price had fallen to thirty. Six months later, it was at $22. The public had no confidence in Harry Black's new company. And who can say why? The company was backed by some of America's biggest capitalists, and constructing buildings everywhere.

Black, seemingly oblivious to his company's declining stock, was distributing dividends to its shareholders, most of whom were also board members. They in turn accepted the dividends, even though logic dictated that what with the falling price of U.S. Realty shares, they hadn't been earned. At the same time Black was trying to make U.S. Realty even bigger, and therefore, worth even more. He was now trying to acquire Thompson-Starrett, the conservative little construction company headed up by Theodore Starrett, whose brother still worked for Black. Thompson-Starrett was valued at $1 million, literally one-sixty-sixth of Black's giant corporation. Yet it was U.S. Realty's main rival in New York. Among the buildings Theodore Starrett's company had erected during the last few years was the Atlantic Building, a skyscraper on William Street, and the Aeolian Building on Fifth and Thirty-fourth. It was now building the Algonquin and St. Regis Hotels.

It galled Black that Thompson-Starrett, with such modest capital, could beat out Fuller on such conspicuous contracts. And there was also the added insult that Theodore Starrett was trying to lure his brother Paul away from the Fuller Company, to join him, and the three other Starrett brothers, at their family company.

So Thompson-Starrett was naturally a thorn in Black's side, and he just had to have it. In the meantime, he had a big problem: Sam Parks, the boss of the ironworkers who should have been in the Fuller Company's pocket, was raising hell in New York.

In the spring of 1903, labor unrest was rocking the building industry all over the country. Power struggles between management and workers had led to the rise of trade unions, which set the stage for another layer of conflicts, but between unions. In the midst of this chaos, Sam Parks controlled all sides, through a combination of fear, blackmail, and reward.

Parks by then was president of the Board of Building Trades, the trade union that controlled thirty-nine member unions, including the ironworkers. Totaling 60,000 men, it was the most powerful trade union in the country. He was suffering from tuberculosis now, but his illness seemed to only drive him harder. During the last four years, Parks had called over 1,000 strikes. Now they were growing more frequent, and he kept upping the ante, like a compulsive gambler unable to walk away from the game. If you didn't pay him his graft, he would go right to the building in question, accompanied by his bull dog and his thugs—*rumdums*—and pull the men right off the job. If the men balked, Parks's rumdums would break their ribs. Once they grabbed a worker who was ignoring Parks's strike order. The thugs pushed him into a dark alley, where they tore the skin off his face. He was scarred for life. But it wasn't only fear that made the rank-and-file obey Parks. They had also done well by him. By now, in 1903, ironworkers were making $4.50 a day. Two years earlier it had been $3.76.

And now, Parks, after calling one strike after another during the spring of 1903, was threatening another one. This one would be the biggest ever. He would, he said, call out all 60,000 men of the Board of Building Trades, unless employers agreed to wage increases for all member unions, ranging from 10 to 20 percent.

Parks had finally crossed the line. The builders estimated that every day a construction project stood idle because he had called a strike, an owner bled an average of 30,000 wasted dollars. If they gave in to the increase that Parks was now demanding for the unions, many would be forced out of business altogether.

The owners knew that they had to act together to smash the Sam Parks machine. This was difficult, because their interests often collided, and they fought among themselves. But now, they set aside their differences. Nearly 800 owners, representing every major builder in the city, including the Fuller Company, their combined net worth totaling more than half a billion dollars, met one evening in mid-May They voted to form a new organization that would represent all of them: the Building Trades Employers Association. Every builder in New York joined, with one exception: the Fuller Company.

Thanks to its special relationship with Parks, Fuller had been immune from the strikes that Parks had been calling since April. One word from Parks was enough to shut down construction projects all over the city. But at Fuller sites—among them was the new Times building going up at Longacre Square—everything was moving forward, without a hitch. And Harry Black had no intention of jeopardizing this arrangement. He would not be pressured by the employers to join their new organization.

Soon after the owners' meeting, they met again, at the Building

Trades Club, at Broadway and Twenty-sixth. The Fuller Company did not attend. They invited the newspapers to attend, an unusual gesture for management. Their perception up to now had been that no good could possibly come of talking to those bums called reporters, and so employers routinely refused. So newspaper stories about labor disputes were based only on the unions' version of events. And the unions had plenty to say. What is more, they loved saying it.

The president-elect of the new organization, a man named Charles Eidlitz, realized that the employers' reticence was putting them at a huge disadvantage in the court of public opinion. He told his colleagues that they had better start talking to the press. The more conservative ones balked. But Eidlitz prevailed. At the meeting, the employers issued a public statement, declaring the walking delegate "a parasite on the body public to be exterminated." They vowed to force the striking unions into accepting arbitration. They called on the district attorney, William Travers Jerome, to prosecute Sam Parks for the crimes that he had committed.

Jerome, a member of a patrician clan—his aunt was Jennie Jerome Churchill, and his first cousin her son, Winston Churchill—received them happily. He had political ambitions, and was now working hard to make a name for himself as a crusader against corruption.

One month after the employers' association meeting, Neils Poulson, president of Hecla Iron Works, who the previous year had paid Parks $2,000 to call off a strike, was sitting in his office early one morning, when his friend Robert McCord, who had acted as his go-between with Parks, dropped by.

"Mr. Jerome," McCord told Poulson, "is now close on the trail of your friend Parks."

Poulson accompanied McCord to the D.A.'s office. Poulson carried with him the framed $2,000 check that, courtesy of McCord, had been signed over to Parks, and cashed by the Fuller Company. Poulson was hoping that the check would give Jerome all the evidence of bribery that the ambitious D.A. needed for an indictment.

Jerome, ecstatic over Poulson's check, pounced. At three that same afternoon, police entered a saloon at Fifty-fourth and Third, where Sam Parks was sitting with a group of labor men. He was arrested, and arraigned a few hours later downtown at the criminal courthouse. From there police escorted him over the Bridge of Sighs and into the Tombs. The next day, the story ran in all the newspapers, complete with the texts of affidavits that the D.A. had taken the previous day from McCord and Poulson. What happens next to Mr. Parks, Poulson told the *Tribune,* was up to Mr. Jerome, adding: "But I think that check is in just the right place."

The following day, Parks's friend, the cigar-chomping, corpulent, walrus-mustachioed former police chief William "Big Bill" Devery, bailed him out. It cost Devery $5,000, which he paid in cash, right at the Tombs. Flashing his bankroll before a crowd of reporters, he pronounced Sam Parks the best friend the workingman ever had. Devery, like many a corrupt New York politician, had come up through the Tammany machine, which now, after being trounced by the Fusion ticket in 1902, was already regrouping, under the rule of boss "Silent Charlie" Murphy. Devery was now challenging Murphy's position, and also had his eye on the mayoralty. In return for Devery's favors, Parks would deliver union votes.

The next day Jerome handed down another indictment, for extorting $500 from the Louis Comfort Tiffany Glass and Decorating Company at 333 Fourth Avenue in exchange for settling a strike. Four days later, two others followed, and then a fourth. The last one was brought by a skylight manufacturer named Josephus Plenty of Hudson City, New Jersey, who testified that he had paid Parks $200 to get the union back to work in his factory.

For each indictment, Devery posted bond. In between, Poulson testified at a hearing at the Court of Special Sessions, where he supplied more detailed evidence about Parks. Poulson said that he'd met with Parks at the Fuller Company offices in the Flatiron Building. The Fuller Company, Poulson told, had specifically requested that he meet Parks, because the company wanted the strike at Hecla, which was supplying ornamental iron for all the Fuller projects, settled.

The Sam Parks drama was providing great copy for New York's newspapers, and serious problems for the Fuller Company. With U.S. Realty stock's already steadily sinking, the revelation that its subsidiary was doing business with a corrupt labor leader was hardly going to convince people to buy. Feeling the pressure, on June 17 Fuller announced that it would halt all work on its construction projects, to show its solidarity with the other employers. It locked out 10,000 union men off Fuller jobs. But the company had yet to join the employers' association.

The ironworkers refused to turn against the leader they called "fighting Sam Parks." They re-elected him walking delegate of Local 2 on June 22—he had held the post since 1896—even though by then he had been indicted four times. "The fact of the matter is that Mr. Parks is one of the ablest and most aggressive of our great labor leaders," wrote the union publication *Bridgemen's Magazine*. It dismissed the charges of extortion brought against him by Jerome as sensational, adding: "Parks' vindication is certain to be speedy and complete."

Three days after his re-election, Parks, in a truly spectacular show of belligerence, led forty walking delegates on a parade around the city, pulling men off whatever construction jobs he had forgotten to include among his latest strike orders. The spectacle was not lost on the Fuller Company. A few days later, it signed a separate agreement with the unions that left the power of the walking delegates intact. Workers now returned to all the Fuller jobs. Jerome publicly censored the company. "The Fuller Company has done many peculiar things which may be explainable. If they have not committed any crime they are morally guilty of acts not right," Jerome told the *Tribune* on July 3. The D.A., relentless, continued handing down indictments on Parks for extortion and assault. Each time, Devery bailed out Parks.

Finally, in August, Parks went on trial for extortion. Ex-Judge McConnell, the Fuller Company president, a small, wiry man, modestly dressed, with close-cropped gray hair and gray eyes, sat among the crowd that packed the courtroom. One of the witnesses, Louis Schmidt, superintendent of the Tiffany studio, testified that Parks, demanding $500 from him, had told him: "I have kept the men in the Hecla iron works on strike for a year and a half, and I will ruin that concern yet before I am through. I can do the same with you and if you prefer to take your medicine you're welcome to it."

The trial lasted seven days. The jury, after deliberating for fifteen minutes, convicted Parks. The judge sentenced him to two and a half years in Sing Sing. But his lawyer went back to court, and obtained a certificate of reasonable doubt based on a technicality. Parks was released from Sing Sing, after Devery, once again, posted his bail. Jerome set to work on getting new indictments to retry Parks, who, for now, was a free man.

Labor Day came around, and this year, Sam Parks would serve as grand marshal for the annual parade. Dressed in the Bridgemen's uniform, a red silk shirt and white hat, Parks, sitting on a white horse, looking sallow and shrunken from his advancing tuberculosis, led the parade down Fifth Avenue, past the Flatiron Building, and under the Washington Square arch. Across his chest he wore a wide white-and-gold silk sash, on which his initials were embroidered in huge gold letters. Behind him, 3,000 members of his own union marched, also decked out in red and white. Coming up the rear were thousands of other men representing other unions. Spectators lined the sidewalks, asking "Which is Parks?" "Is Parks there?" Everybody wanted to see the man who had the power to stop all building in New York. Whenever somebody in the crowd shouted "There he is!" people cheered, and Parks turned, smiled, waved his riding whip, and bowed. And always, at the same time, others jeered or hissed. Once, when the parade halted, an onlooker, noticing the letters "SP" on Parks's sash, yelled: "Does that stand for 'Sing Sing prison'?"

Sam Parks, grand marshal of the 1903 Labor Day parade.

Thirty unions had marched in the previous year's Labor Day parade. But this year's had only fifteen, and people were saying that it was all because of Sam Parks. The president of Local 2 was among those who had refused to march. Parks's power was eroding, his union now split into factions. His once-loyal men had been worn down by the constant strikes. They wanted to sign the arbitration agreements that the employers were now offering them, get back to work, and feed their families, now hungry on account of all the lost wages. But Parks refused. He continued to call out strikes. In September, he pulled his men from a Fuller job at the sixteen-story Butterick Building, at 161 Sixth Avenue, at the corner of Spring and MacDougal Streets. The building's interiors were designed by Louis Tiffany. But the strike was short-lived. A few days later, he called another strike, on the Metropolitan Life Annex, just east of the Flatiron Building. This time, the workers ignored him.

In November, Parks was convicted. When he was once again sent to the Tombs to await sentencing, he got in touch with Devery, expecting that his old friend would bail him out. But this time Devery refused. Parks had been avoiding "Big Bill" ever since the latter had failed to wrest control of Tammany from Murphy. Devery told the papers: "Parks has acted the part of an ingrate to me. He has never done anything for me, but has been in constant receipt of my favors. He done me dirt and threw me down."

Parks was sentenced to two years and three months at Sing Sing. He would die there in May 1904 of tuberculosis.

During Parks's trial throughout the summer of 1903, U.S. Realty's stock, already falling, had dropped lower. By July, less than one year after its initial public offering at $32, it was selling at only $9 a share. Board members feared investors would panic and dump the stock. Nor was it only U.S. Realty that was in trouble now. All stocks, even the most blue-chip, had been falling since the spring.

In August, the company issued its first annual report. It revealed what a Harvard economist later called "vicious accounting practices." The directors had paid themselves generous salaries and unearned dividends, based largely on projected profits from buildings still in progress. Wall Street quickly reacted. "U.S. Realty has been conspicuously in the public eye in the last few months, chiefly as the place at which Samuel Parks' checks were cashed," wrote the *Evening Post* on August 5, 1903, then adding: "Over half its capitalization of sixty-six million dollars is pure water and wind." And the company was no longer paying dividends on its preferred stocks.

No question about it, Harry Black's skyscraper trust was in big trouble, and everybody was reading about it in the newspapers and magazines from all sides of the political spectrum. Ray Stannard Baker, who was exposing the dark side of American capitalism in a new form of journalism that would soon be called "muckraking," along with his colleagues Ida Tarbell and Lincoln Steffens at *McClure's,* called Parks a "tool of the trusts." For U.S. Realty, Baker railed, "corruption is a good investment." *The Wall Street Journal* praised Thompson-Starrett, the company that Harry Black had tried, but failed, to acquire. Thompson-Starrett, the *Journal* wrote in a headline, "Illustrates the Wisdom of Conservative Capitalism." The article then pointedly contrasted its success with the "disappointing financial results" of U.S. Realty.

By November, shares of U.S. Realty common stock had dropped to $5.50 a share. Board members became alarmed. They had entered into this deal with Harry Black because he had assured them that they were making a rock-solid investment. New York real estate, he had insisted, could only increase in value, and so would the money they were investing into the skyscraper trust. But now they were wondering if they had been had. A lot of people said that Harry Black was nothing but a gambler.

The inescapable fact was that the public didn't have confidence in U.S. Realty, especially now that its subsidiary, the Fuller Company, was associated with Sam Parks, the convicted felon. And confidence is everything. No amount of capital can make up for the lack of it. Without the public's confidence, no business, no matter how large, can survive.

Some board members, among them the blue bloods—Hyde, Juilliard, James Speyer, and James Stillman—now broke away and formed their own committee. On November 19, 1903, they sent around a circular to all stockholders, asking them to "confer upon us powers which will enable us to secure some radical changes in the administration, especially in the construction department, in order to secure the confidence of the communities in which its business is to be transacted."

"Especially in the construction department," meant the Fuller Company, and everybody knew it. During the next month and a half, infighting among the directors grew increasingly bitter. Black, who up until now had insisted that everybody should just hang on, because he predicted nothing but the rosiest future for the company, was changing his tune. He was saying that things looked so grim that people

Paul Starrett, 1904.

should cut their losses. He even urged Paul Starrett to resign. He was telling him this as a friend, Black said.

Starrett refused. He pointed out that the Fuller Company was still going strong. Several projects, he told Black, were going to make them a lot of money. Starrett did, however, follow Black's advice on the financial side. Starrett sold the 1,000 shares of common stock that Black had given him when he made him vice-president of the Fuller Company. Members of the board also dumped their stock at Black's urging. Among them was Ex-Judge McConnell. Prices, accordingly, kept dropping.

While Black was urging everybody to sell, he was secretly buying. By the beginning of 1904, he held a controlling interest in U.S. Realty. In mid-January, during a raucous board meeting, ten members, who together represented most of the banking interests backing U.S. Realty, all of whom had sold their shares in the company at a great loss, stood up, presented their resignations, and together walked out the door.

They felt fury at what they considered Harry Black's duplicitous business practices, mixed in with shame at having now lost their substantial investments in his real estate trust. The truth was, they had been seduced by Harry Black. Seduced, and dumped. "Bet-a-Million" Gates remained, as did James Stillman, who only recently had aligned himself with the anti-Black faction, but now, apparently, was having a change of heart—and Ex-Judge McConnell. But McConnell had, under pressure, resigned as president of Fuller. He, along with the other board members who had sold their stocks for next to nothing, had taken a beating. Black found it hilarious that his old friend McConnell had fallen for his tricks. It was as if McConnell had lost at poker, among friends. It was all a game, and all in good fun.

Just as "Bet-a-Million" Gates had played a trick on Black back in September 1902, when he had ratted on him to the customs agent over Allon's pearls.

Of the thirteen members out of the original twenty-three who did not resign were the well-respected real estate tycoons Albert Flake and Robert Dowling, who in 1902 had merged their company, New York Realty, into U.S. Realty, and were now sorely regretting it. Dowling told reporters: "We must protect our own interests and the interests of those persons who became identified with the company through our influence." Two days later he added: "We are going to stand by the company with more fervor than ever. Harmony now prevails, and under such conditions our work should be marked with great success."

The next thing Black did—of the thirteen board members who had not resigned, he had the backing of all but Flake and Dowling—was to call a meeting. He named a new board of directors, filling the vacancies created by the defections with men he knew would support him, along with a new set of executives. The new board elected him president, and restored Flake and Dowling to their previous positions as vice-presidents, doubtless to keep them from leaving along with the other defectors. U.S.

Realty was now worth only $16 million, compared to its $66 million assessment of the previous year.

"The water has been squeezed out of U.S. Realty," the *Evening Post*
wrote. But Black didn't care. The company still existed, its main subsidiary, the Fuller Company, was still the biggest building firm in New
York, and Black now controlled all of it. Moreover, the retention of
Flake and Dowling had reassured the stock market. By the end of January, the stock of the drastically downsized U.S. Realty was beginning
to rise, amidst rumors that the company, now trimmed of its fat, was
about to be reorganized, and its shares repackaged into bonds. There
were even rumors that Black was looking for a buyer for the Fuller
Company. Black ended up holding on, but made drastic cuts. Most of
the clerical staff was fired, and, for the time being, Fuller took on no
new jobs. The company was now admitted into the Building Trades
Employers Association. "The welcome accorded the big construction
company was scarcely with open arms. It sounded more like a box on
the ear," wrote the *Real Estate Record and Builders' Guide* on January 23,
1904. The association fined the company for past infractions, and, in a
show of how little it trusted Harry Black, the Fuller Company had to
pay an amount ten times greater than the usual join-up fee required of
all members.

In October, during the second trial of Sam Parks, a vicious nor'easter
had slammed into New York. At Twenty-third Street, the wind rushed
headlong into the Flatiron Building, turning the area around the triangular structure into the storm's center. And then, the *Times* wrote: "the
wind came piping through Twenty-second Street, turned the rear corner of the structure in Fifth Avenue, following the western side of the
triangle until it reached the apex at Madison Square, shot out in the
square about 200 yards, and then bounded back, striking the apex,
which cut it in two. One half was shunted into Fifth Avenue, the other

into Broadway, and anything that came near enough was picked up by either of these currents and hustled down town."

Harry Black was up in the Fuller Company offices during the worst of the storm. Afterward he told *The Sun* how pleased he was with the Flatiron's resilience. Even with gale force winds, he said, he felt no vibration in the building, and therefore no anxiety. He had, after all, endured far worse.

CHAPTER TEN

ALLON

$\mathcal{I}$T WAS NOVEMBER 23, 1903, opening night at the Metropolitan Opera. For the last hour, the three-block stretch of Broadway near the opera house—the building occupied the entire block bounded by Broadway and Seventh Avenue, from Thirty-ninth to Fortieth Streets—had been choked with all manner of vehicles, horse-drawn and horseless, moving back and forth from one position to another. "Cursing cabmen yelled invectives at belated teamsters, motormen stood at their posts in surly silence waiting for the mass to open and let their cars through, flunkeys scurried to and from the doors of the Opera House, and blue coats twisted in and out of the shapeless, intricate tangle of vehicles, and gave directions in commanding tones," the *Times* wrote. On the sidewalk, people were pushing eagerly through the crowds, then through the entrance to the huge opera house, which quickly filled to capacity. Hundreds of disappointed people were turned away.

The orchestra, where the "merely ordinarily rich" sat, resembled "a garden of fair women," wrote the *Herald*. The *World* described the standing room, located in the uppermost galleries, where "tenor worshippers—sons of France and sunny Italy—stood like packed sardines in Cranks' Alley." Meanwhile, New York's high society filed leisurely into their boxes: August Belmont and his children (the newspapers the next day describing in luscious detail everybody's finery, said that his daughter-in-law wore "the famous Belmont pearl necklace and pendants"), Alice Roosevelt, various Goelets, Juilliards, and Vanderbilts, and J. P. Morgan and his daughters. One of the last to arrive was Mrs. William Astor, whose habit it was to arrive late on opening night. Resplendent in black-and-white velvet brocade and diamonds, and carrying a large white ostrich fan in one hand, the acknowledged arbiter of New York society, now seventy-three years old, took her seat in her box, number seven. Everybody had been waiting for her. Only when she appeared could the performance start.

Seated nearby Mrs. Astor was "Mrs. Harry S. Black," as the society pages politely called Allon. Harry, however, was not there. Perhaps, being now in the thick of the problems plaguing U.S. Realty and the Fuller Company, he was tied up on the evening of the twenty-third, and had told Allon to go to the opera alone. Whatever the reason for his absence, it was doubtless noted, and remarked upon, by many present this evening, especially those women of a certain type that we all know and recognize, who were now peering through their lorgnettes to see who was sitting in whose box, and wearing what. Surely they paused when they glimpsed Allon, sitting alone. New York society had long gossiped about her marriage. She was said to be unhappy.

Opera patrons were also "oohing-and-aahing" over the elegant interior. It was new, installed just this past summer, designed by Carrère and Hastings, one of the city's most celebrated architecture firms. "The new decorations make it a place of festal and dignified appearance," the next day's *Times* wrote approvingly. "The dull gold and its touches of deep red and the red of the boxes make a glowing setting for the audience, and the proscenium arch, with a design that shows the brain and skill of an artist, instead of the fretted and meaningless filigree that has adorned it in recent years." A new dome chandelier, festooned with over 900 lights, hung from the ceiling.

The audience sat, restless, waiting for the opera to begin. The performance was *Rigoletto,* and the part of Rodolfo would be sung by a Neapolitan tenor who was making his American debut here tonight. His name was Enrico Caruso. He had sung all over the Continent during the last three years, and the Europeans were mad for him. Heinrich Conreid, the Metropolitan Opera's new manager, had hired Caruso away from Covent Garden the previous year. The terms of the tenor's contract with the Met were not made public, but it was common knowledge that they were far less generous than Covent Garden's, which had paid him the incredible sum of $1,000 for each of forty performances. Yet Caruso had agreed to defect, because he wanted to come to America.

Enrico Caruso, circa 1908.

And now, the new red-velvet curtain finally opened, revealing a ballroom scene. The faces of the audience, who were seeing Caruso for the first time, clearly revealed disappointment at his physical appearance. The Italian was short, round, and, frankly, homely. But when he sang the aria "Questa o quella" in the first act, people warmed. His intonation was perfect, his voice filled with warmth. And in the last act, he completely seduced the house with his rendition of "La donna è mobile." "He sang it as it should be sung, in devil-may-care fashion, sipping his wine, tossing his cards and with striking changes of tempo," wrote the *World* the following day. The audience went wild, standing up, clapping, and shouting, among them his countrymen, who were yelling "Bravo! Bravo!"

Afterward, when asked by a reporter to describe his feelings about his New York audience, Caruso was ebullient. "Splendid! Magnificent! Such a gracious reception! Nothing could be kinder than New York has been to me! I have heard much about the city, but this night goes far beyond anything that I have pictured."

Allon would always remember this extraordinary night, but not because she witnessed the American debut of the great Caruso. Rather, for her, it marked the beginning of yet one more sorrowful chapter in her life.

Ellen Fuller died of pneumonia on January 22, 1904, in her suite at the Waldorf-Astoria. During her illness, which had lasted a little over a year, a twenty-nine-year-old nurse named Lucy Kennard cared for her. Allon, now twenty-seven, and Harry often visited her ailing mother. Lucy caught Harry's eye. Physically, she was the same type as Allon: slim, tall with black hair, and dark eyes.

Ellen Fuller's body was sent back to Chicago by train, where she was buried next to her husband, George Fuller. Then Allon departed immediately for Palm Beach, where she could recover, and grieve. Allon liked the Florida resort, where she and Harry always spent part of each winter. But Harry went back to New York. He told Allon that he would join her at the end of February. First, he had some business to attend to.

Two weeks after Ellen Fuller's death, Lucy Kennard received a call from Harry Black. He told the young woman that he was sick, confined to his Madison Avenue apartment (building number 667, at the corner of Sixty-first Street), and he wanted to hire her to nurse him. She obliged, remaining with him for six days. Lucy slept in a separate room, opposite his. By the sixth day, Harry felt better. The two went out for a drive.

They returned home to his apartment, and had dinner. Harry retired to his bed. After a while, he got up. He told Lucy that he felt nervous. "I don't want to be left alone," he said. "Might you sleep in the room with me?" His bedroom had an extra bed. Lucy agreed. She entered the room, and lay down on the unoccupied bed. Within minutes, Harry was on top of her. Lucy left his apartment the next morning. That afternoon, Harry got on the train, and left for Palm Beach, where he joined Allon.

One month later, at the end of March, Harry returned from Florida. He immediately telephoned Lucy—she lived with a married sister on Columbus Avenue—and asked her to have dinner with him, in his apartment. She refused.

"I've already had dinner," she said.

Harry kept at it. "At the very least," he said, "let me come over and see you." Lucy agreed. By the time he arrived, she was no doubt second-guessing herself, because when he begged her to go out on the town with him, she refused. A few days later, he called her again, to ask her one more time for a date. Again, she refused.

Harry Black did not give up on Lucy. He kept calling her, first at her sister's home, and, then, one May day, at a hospital, where she was then working, taking care of a private patient. We don't know how Black came by this information. Perhaps Lucy herself had told him. In any event, when he got her on the telephone, he somehow convinced her to meet him when she got off from work, at three o'clock, at the "ladies' entrance" of the Vendome, an apartment hotel at Forty-first and Broadway. Because of the Vendome's convenient location—the center of the theater district—and comfortable accommodations, its clientele included out-of-town businessmen and people connected with the theater. In addition, the Vendome was known as a place where businessmen could carry out trysts.

At the Vendome, Harry showed Lucy into the ladies' reception room. "Wait here," he told her. After half an hour or so, he came back. He escorted the young woman up to a suite of rooms. They had a drink. Harry then briefly excused himself. He went into another room, where he made a telephone call. Then he returned to Lucy, and the two made love.

After they were finished, the phone rang in the other room. Harry got up to answer it. He returned to Lucy, who was still lying in bed.

"I have to go," he told Lucy. "I had a business appointment scheduled for four o'clock, and it's already ten past. I have to hurry."

Harry quickly dressed, and left the hotel, before Lucy. She went home by herself, in a cab.

Allon, in the meantime, had been growing suspicious. In April 1904, she had told Harry that she wanted to separate, and sailed, by herself, to Europe. We don't know where her nephew, now five, was during her travels. She likely left the child in New York with a governess.

Friends of Allon and Harry now interceded. They begged the couple to reconcile, so as to avoid the scandal of a divorce. Allon packed up and sailed back to New York, and to Harry. But things between them were not going well. At the beginning of the summer, Allon moved out of the Blacks' Madison Avenue apartment, into a suite of rooms at the Savoy Hotel. She and Harry now had contact only through their respective attorneys.

In the meantime, Lucy had not heard from Harry since their May tryst at the Vendome. Perhaps, with Allon having moved out, and by now probably threatening divorce, he was keeping his distance. In addition he had lately been preoccupied, yet again reorganizing U.S. Realty. It would be a new and smaller entity that he would rename U.S. Realty and Improvement Company. He had frequently gone head-to-head with Dowling and Flake, who had finally quit the board and would organize their own partnership in early 1905.* And while all this was happening, Paul Starrett, overseer of all Fuller Company projects, also decided that he, too, had had enough. Black's constant wheeling and dealing, Starrett later wrote in his memoirs, was affecting his work as a builder: "When I went out after building jobs, I was often turned down cold because of the impression that the Fuller Company was merely the subsidiary of a gambling outfit." Starrett decided to accept an offer to work with his brothers at Fuller's rival, Thompson-Starrett. He gave notice to Black, who told him that he was making a big mistake.

"You've got a big future here, Paul," Black told his employee, whom he had advised just several months earlier to resign, because U.S. Realty was never going to make it.

Starrett left to join his brothers at Thompson-Starrett. To his surprise, he discovered that his brother Theodore, the company president, had assumed that Paul would work under him, not with him. For Paul, such an arrangement was impossible. As soon as Black heard what had happened, he sent for his former employee. It was April 1904.

"Paul, I'm delighted!" Black said. "Will you come back with us? If you will, I'll make you president of the Fuller Company." Starrett accepted the offer. He would remain president of the Fuller Company for seventeen years.

"He probably had more influence on my life than any other man I have known," Starrett would write of Black years later in his memoir.

---

* In March 1905, Flake, age forty-four, died of pneumonia. Dowling went on to become a successful real estate man.

Starrett described Black as "having a smile that would charm the birds off the tree. He ignored anyone in whom he was not interested. He had a contagious sense of humor and told anecdotes illustrating his points effectively. He was bighearted and selfish and, according to my standards, rather unscrupulous. His contradictions had me baffled. Just when I thought I had him classified, he would astonish me with some unsuspected characteristic."

In mid-July, after Allon had moved out, Harry finally telephoned Lucy. He asked Lucy about her plans for the summer.

"I'm going to Europe in a few days," the young woman told him. She had tickets for the *Cedric,* a White Star ocean liner, a vacation way beyond the means of a working girl like herself, and no doubt courtesy of Harry Black.

"I'm awfully sorry," Harry answered. "I'd been planning that we would go on a trip together. But at least, I want to see you before you sail." He convinced her to meet him at seven-thirty that evening, in the ladies' reception room of the Plaza Hotel, which he and "Bet-a-Million" Gates had purchased two years earlier. Soon the Fuller Company was going to start demolishing the exquisite hotel. On the site, the company would erect a new, much larger Plaza, a French-chateau-like confection designed by Henry Hardenbergh.

From the Plaza, Harry and Lucy went out to dinner at Burns' Restaurant. Afterward, Harry hailed a hansom cab. Lucy asked where they were going.

"To a friend's place," Harry answered. "It's very quiet there, and we'll have a very pleasant evening." His friend was a Mrs. Nellie Ferguson, a thirty-eight-year-old woman who operated a boardinghouse in a handsome brownstone on West Fifty-fourth Street. Among her renters were men like Harry Black, who used her house for a place to conduct their love affairs.

Lucy sailed for Europe a few days later. Upon her return at the beginning of September—on the *Majestic,* no less, another luxury steamship— she and Harry resumed their affair. During September they had two more trysts at Mrs. Ferguson's. They didn't meet again until the end of November, when Harry called on Lucy on a Sunday evening at her sister's apartment.

Lucy asked Harry if he had seen the story in all the newspapers the previous month, that Mrs. Ferguson's house had burned down. The owner, Mrs. Ferguson, had died in the fire. "Yes," said Harry, adding that he felt sorry about Mrs. Ferguson's death. The newspaper accounts had included the fact that a man inside the house jumped from the top floor, breaking both legs. He was stark naked, and lay helpless in the backyard for almost an hour, until the firemen found him. He was taken to Roosevelt Hospital, wrapped in a red tablecloth. He gave his name as John Smith, living at 176 West 73 Street. But when a reporter checked out the address, he found it did not exist. The man was not "John Smith," but some wealthy and prominent New Yorker, caught, literally, *in flagrante delicto,* who managed to keep his identity a secret.

The following Sunday, Lucy left for Croton Falls, where she would care for a private patient. A few days after she arrived, a young man came to her employer's home. He introduced himself as Mr. Gates, and requested that Lucy accompany him to the Croton Falls Hotel. Somebody there, he told her, wants to talk to you. "It will only take a few minutes," he said.

Lucy obliged. (God only knows what she was thinking when she got into the motor car with Mr. Gates.)

When they arrived at the hotel, Gates accompanied Lucy to a room. There, Allon Black was waiting for her. He left the two women alone.

Allon looked straight at Lucy, and accused her of having an affair with her husband. Lucy denied it.

"Oh, but I can prove it," Allon said. "I've had Harry followed for months. Several witnesses saw you at the Fifty-fourth Street house with Harry. You know, the one that burned down. So it's better for you to just tell the truth." Suddenly, Mr. Gates entered the room. Allon, clearly on cue, presented Lucy with a summons and complaint that her attorneys had prepared.

Lucy, by now thoroughly agitated, looked through the legal document, which was addressed to Harry S. Black, defendant, and Lucy Kennard, co-defendant. It stated that Mrs. Harry Black, because she suspected that her husband was being unfaithful to her, had hired two private investigators in August 1904 to follow him. They had performed their job well: the complaint listed the exact date and time of each tryst that Harry had arranged with Lucy at Mrs. Ferguson's house.

Poor Lucy, now cornered, broke down. "It's true," she sobbed. "I've been intimate with your husband." She then signed her name to an affidavit that Allon presented to her, which attested to the facts in the complaint. During all this, Gates remained in the room, a witness to Lucy's oral and written confession. Clearly, everything had gone according to plan.

Allon went back to New York. Having no more need to shadow Harry, she dismissed the two private detectives. The next thing she did was to tell Harry that she had all the evidence she needed to divorce him.

The first thing Harry did after Allon confronted him was to hire James Daly, one of the detectives Allon had hired to follow him, to now shadow Allon. Whether he did this out of revenge, or because he was thinking that the detective might find something on her that might convince her not to proceed with her divorce suit, we don't know. But after following Allon for several weeks, Daly had nothing to tell Harry, except that once, he had seen Allon, a child, and another woman—surely these were Fuller Chenery, Allon's adopted nephew, now five, and his nursemaid—get into a hansom cab, drive up Fifth Avenue, and enter Central Park.

As for Lucy, she went back, shaken, to nursing her patient in Croton Falls. A month or so later, a man who said that he represented Harry Black came to see her. Black's man advised Lucy that she should get out of the state, so that Allon's lawyers could not subpoena her. Lucy refused.

Perhaps if Harry had not treated Lucy so crudely after their affair had been discovered, she would have helped him. But Harry Black was not a gentleman. Lucy never heard from him again.

For the second time, the couple's friends urged Allon to reconsider. They reminded her that as soon as she filed for divorce, the press would pounce on both of them. The Blacks were already regular fixtures in all the society pages. Their divorce would furnish tasty fodder indeed.

But Allon had made up her mind. "I shall not consider my friends in this matter," she told the *World*. "It is my own affair and the case will be prosecuted."

Harry sent his longtime counsel, the prominent trust attorney John R. Dos Passos,* to meet with Allon's side. All agreed that it was in both parties' interest to keep the proceedings as secretive as possible.

So when Allon filed for divorce, on March 24, her petition did not

Allon Fuller Black, 1905.

---

* Dos Passos, one of the attorneys behind the formation of the Havermeyer "Sugar Trust," had an eight-year-old illegitimate son, also named John, in Chicago, who would later become the famous novelist. But the elder Dos Passos would not acknowledge his son until just before the former died, in 1917.

state on what grounds. Rumor had it that Harry would not fight Allon in court. And that was all that the papers could get on the Black divorce. A photo portrait of a solemn-faced Allon, her dark hair topped with a large, soft-brimmed hat, with a single strand of large pearls—perhaps the now-famous ones that she had bought in Paris?—was now being splashed across front pages, along with headlines announcing the "mysterious" divorce case of Mrs. Harry Black, wife of the millionaire.

Waylaid at his Madison Avenue apartment by a reporter from the *Chicago Tribune*, Harry said: "I will not discuss my domestic affairs with anyone." Another reporter from the same paper went after Allon. When asked if a settlement had been made, Allon, the reporter wrote, "smiled and pulled a pearl colored rose to pieces. She was gowned completely in black, with a white rose in her hair and a great cluster beside her on the table. If she had been dressed in white she would have appeared a schoolgirl or a debutante at her first ball. With her head bowed slightly, now and then glancing up, Mrs. Black completed the destruction of the flower. 'Why, I don't know,' she said, holding the rose up to her lips. Another petal of the rose floated downward. Mrs. Black smiled and again glanced up. 'I never talk—for publication,' she went on. 'Didn't you know that? You'll have to pardon me for not discussing personal affairs.' And with that, the last rose petal fluttered to the floor."

In April, the Blacks reached a settlement that netted Allon $6 million. The lawyers based the figure on how much the $2.5 million that she had inherited from her father, George Fuller, back in 1900, was now worth, thanks to Harry Black's aggressive expansion of the Fuller Company.

One would like to know what Harry Black was feeling now, during the spring of 1905, as his impending divorce was making headlines. Even though the papers could not get the whole story, that Allon had caught him *in flagrante delicto* had surely knocked him off balance. He had in fact taken special precautions against just this sort of thing happening to him, paying off Colonel William d'Alton Mann, publisher of

Allon

the weekly gossip sheet *Town Topics*, which tracked the whereabouts of society figures all over New York. Mann cultivated sources close to rich people, in particular their maids and drivers, to keep in the know of who was being seen where, with whom. *Town Topics* was the *People* magazine of its day, eagerly read each week by all of New York society, and everybody else besides. But if you were a member of the crowd targeted for *Town Topics* and wanted your affairs kept private, you could arrange it so with Mann, for the right price. You could think of it as taking out an insurance policy against gossip. In fact, Mann in 1905 had published a companion volume to *Town Topics*, a gorgeous leather-bound tome called *Fads and Fancies* that chronicled the lives of various society figures, all of whom had paid a lot of money to be included. Among them was Harry Black, whose entry, detailing his married life with Allon, had been rendered obsolete by his pending divorce. It was all very embarrassing for him.

Unlike *People*, *Town Topics* and *Fads and Fancies* together formed a lucrative blackmailing scheme for its publisher. If you refused to

Colonel d'Alton Mann, undated.

subscribe to *Fads and Fancies* you were going to find the details of your life reported on in *Town Topics*. But Harry Black's current situation proved that Mann's "insurance policy" had not been foolproof.

Perhaps Black was genuinely feeling sorry for having wronged Allon. That he didn't fight her in court, and also worked out a fair settlement, showed that at the very least he felt indebted to her, at least to some extent, for his fabulous successes as a real estate mogul. After all it had been her father, George Allon Fuller, who had invited him in as his business partner. It seems that he wished to do right by Allon, at least by his own standards of what constituted right and wrong. And his shabby treatment of Lucy Kennard, the object of his fling, was equally revealing. Like many men who are hungry for, and then amass great wealth, he had grown used to grabbing and devouring whatever, really whomever, he wanted.

That Lucy had not followed the advice given her by Harry's agents to get out of New York, and therefore avoid being subpoenaed, had to have rankled him. In fact, when the time came for her to testify she was happy to oblige. She spelled out all the salacious details of her affair with Harry for Allon's lawyers. They used Lucy's testimony to obtain a favorable settlement for their client.

So along with his remorse for what he had done to Allon, he doubtless was feeling resentful that the price exacted for having sex with a beautiful young woman had proven far too high.

Above all, as his lawyers were finalizing the details ending his ten-year marriage to Allon, Harry must have been feeling exceedingly lonely. Looking for distractions from his divorce proceedings, he attended the opening of the Hippodrome, a huge pleasure palace that would make its predecessor, which had stood on the lot where Eno later built his Fifth Avenue Hotel, look like a one-ring traveling circus. The new Hippodrome was generating all kinds of buzz around New York. Black's friend "Bet-a-Million" Gates had been the primary mover behind this, another Fuller project. He had first conceived of the idea after meeting Fred Thompson and Elmer "Skip" Dundy. These two business partners, betting that real money was to be made by offering cheap entertainment for the masses, had built Luna Park on twenty-two acres in Coney Island in 1903. The *Times* called the new amusement park "a realm of fairy romance in colored light, so beautiful that the rest of Coney Island will have to clean up and dress up." Luna Park had a Venetian city, complete with canal and gondolas, Japanese gardens, a German village, a monkey theater, and three giant buildings housing shows such as "a trip to the moon," which the *Times* described as "an electro-scenic mechanical illusion." Amidst all was "a tower rising two hundred feet, and literally crusted with lights, making a shaft of brilliance that can be seen for many miles."

Thompson, who since childhood had tinkered with machines, had learned to build amusement structures at various World Fairs, starting with Chicago's Columbian Exhibition in 1893. He met and paired up with Dundy in 1901, at the Buffalo Exhibition. Thompson was known as the "boy wonder." Paul Starrett remembered Dundy as "something of a regular circus man, a slim, dried-up person—not unlike a frost-bitten persimmon—with a streak of vulgarity."

When Luna Park opened in 1903, it immediately began raking in money. Gates, always on the lookout for new ventures to bet on, decided that he wanted to build something comparable in Manhattan, under Thompson and Dundy's management. Gates convinced the now greatly decreased U.S. Realty board to back the venture. Thompson and Dundy were ecstatic at the opportunity Gates was handing them. To top it off, the board granted them complete artistic control over the new theater, along with unlimited financial resources. To Thompson and Dundy it all seemed too good to be true. And the timing was just right for another venture like Luna Park. Ever since arriving in New York in 1901, Thompson had wanted to build a hippodrome-type structure in Manhattan. He compared his mass-market entertainment vision to another capitalist idea now coming of age, the department store, which, with its wide variety of merchandise, pulled the entire spectrum of society through its doors. His hippodrome would likewise attract everybody, and most of all, the millions of New York's quickly expanding middle class—the clerks, office workers, garment workers, and all the others who performed the tasks that drove huge corporations—who could not afford to pay $2 to go to the theater, but wanted something classier than cheap vaudeville shows. "Nice, respectable, intelligent, people," Thompson called his prospective and up-to-now untapped audiences.

The Hippodrome would fill this huge marketing gap, presenting fabulous shows that freely mixed high-brow and low culture, everything on a huge scale, and all for only twenty-five cents. Thompson's "gigantic toy," as he put it, for the people of New York, was being equipped with all kinds of mechanical marvels: electric cranes for moving scenery around its 200-foot stage, and a 60-foot-diameter, 14-foot-high water tank cleverly hidden below the stage to be used for water shows. Also under the stage were built stalls housing horses and elephants that would appear in the Hippodrome shows.

Construction on the theater had begun in late June 1904. Now, only ten months later, in the spring of 1905, the Fuller Company was racing to finish up the huge project, literally painting the ceiling while the plaster was still wet, in time for the April 12 opening. The gargantuan red-brick-and-terra-cotta, vaguely Moorish pleasure palace, with its red, gold, and ivory interior, occupied an entire block along the east side of Sixth Avenue, between Forty-third and Forty-fourth Streets, and could seat 5,200 spectators (the Metropolitan Opera, by comparison, had a capacity of 3,000). The Hippodrome was being billed as the world's largest theater. To publicly claim something as the largest anything is always dicey, but perhaps in this case it was true. The scale was so huge that even the elephants, viewed from the far reaches of the audience, looked small.

On opening night, every seat in the Hippodrome was taken, from the 1,500 twenty-five-cent seats in the family circle, to the boxes holding some of New York's glitziest denizens. As part of a publicity blitz conducted during the previous weeks (the opening-night show, proclaimed an ad that appeared in the *World*, would reach "the limit and climax of theatre realism"), some of the boxes had been auctioned off the day before, fetching prices up to $575. Harry Black, doing his part to publicize his investment, had bought two, at $525 and $425. Black was now seated in one of his boxes—we don't know whom he invited to fill the other—in full view of the entire audience, of whom many doubtless recognized him, and pointed him out, wondering why his wife was divorcing him, and how come the newspapers couldn't get the story? Gates, naturally, was there, too. Also, in a right-hand box near the stage, sat a man, M. A. Marcel, and next to him, his charge, a baboon in a blue sailor suit and hat, named Coco. Both had just arrived from Europe, where for the last six months, the five-year-old baboon had been performing at the music halls of Berlin, Paris, and London. Coco, who dressed and acted just like a human being, had utterly charmed European audiences. Now he was scheduled to make his debut in America, here in the Hippodrome, the following week.

The four-hour opening-night extravaganza consisted of "A Yankee Circus on Mars," about a bankrupt New England circus rescued by five space ships that transport it to the planet, where the circus performs for the Martian King Borealis and his denizens, who spend their lives in perpetual play, in contrast to the earth, whose poor citizens only work. The spectacle featured the trademark Thompson and Dundy elephants, horses, the antics of the famous English clown Marcelline, a sixty-piece orchestra, a choir with hundreds of singers, and acrobats, all attired in gorgeous costumes. At the end, Thompson, in a nod to high culture, had thrown in Ponchielli's ballet *Dance of the Hours*, performed by 150 dancers. It all added up, the *Times* wrote, to a scene of "kaleidoscopic color."

After the gigantic curtain fell, an intermission followed, during which Coco and Mr. Marcel walked through the corridors. The trainer introduced the baboon to the crowds of people, who were staring and pointing. Among them, Coco showed an interest only in the little girls. He kept trying to kiss them, but Mr. Marcel held him back.

Then the bells rang for the second act, "Andersonville," a spectacle about the Yankee raid on the notorious Civil War prison camp, that featured a cast of 500, a bridge "dynamited into atoms," and, as the climax, hundreds of Yankee cavalry troops on horses plunging into a lake—the water tank—and swimming safely to the other side, all while under Rebel fire. The audience went wild with clapping. Coco, too, was seen clapping his gloved hands. What the ads had claimed—that the opening show would attain "the limit and climax of theatre realism"—had proven true.

A few days later, and the night before Coco was to make his debut at the Hippodrome, Thompson hosted a reception to introduce the baboon to New York society. Thompson invited all the newspapers to attend, too. The party was a great success. Everybody lined up to shake Coco's hand. Among the guests was Harry Black, who, after greeting

Coco the Baboon at the Hippodrome.

the animal, suddenly had the idea to host his own dinner party the following week in Coco's honor. He immediately announced his intentions, which reporters duly recorded in their notepads. The item would appear in the next day's newspapers. Black felt elated. A party was just what he needed. Ever since his separation from Allon, followed by the divorce, he had been suffering from bouts of melancholy.

Coco's party went off as planned, but it did not lift Black's spirits, as he had hoped.

———•❖•———

CHAPTER ELEVEN

UPTOWN

 IN THE SPRING OF 1905, an artist named Vernon Bailey, who made his living selling finely detailed pen-and-ink drawings of city views to newspapers and magazines, stood upon the Flatiron roof. From here, you had a panorama of the entire city, unobstructed. Bailey walked around the balustraded edges of the roof, looking out from each of the three sides of the triangle. From there, from each angle, he took in the different vistas, each one encompassing an astonishing mixture of perspectives, from the streets far down below, crawling with cars, streetcars, horse carts, and people, all tiny like ants, and the roofs of nearby buildings, on which stood wooden water towers, and all the way to the rivers surrounding Manhattan Island, and beyond. From the southern end, he could see across the East River to the slums of Williamsburg, in Brooklyn, and the skyscrapers that rose up at Manhattan's southern tip, and then, turning slightly west, the Statue of Liberty, and finally, the piers of New Jersey. Then he moved around to the point, facing north, where Fifth Avenue and Broadway crossed, and continued uptown, each thoroughfare veering, respectively, east and west. First his eye followed

Vernon Bailey's view from the Flatiron, looking north, 1905.

Fifth Avenue, "Millionaires' Row," up to where the green rectangle of Central Park began, at Fifty-ninth Street. Right there, where the old Plaza Hotel had stood, a huge hole had just been excavated. It was now filled with noisy machinery and crowds of laborers, as the Fuller Company embarked upon construction of the biggest, most luxurious hotel that the world would ever see.

Then Bailey shifted his gaze slightly west, to Broadway, where he could make out Macy's, and opposite it the Herald Building. And then, eight blocks farther north along "the Great White Way," as people now called Broadway, directly facing him was the just-completed New York Times Building, at 476 feet high the city's tallest structure, a distinction that never lasted for long in New York. People were calling the Times Building "the New Flatiron," or the "Andiron"; because, like the Flatiron Building, it stood at an intersection of three great thoroughfares—in this case, Broadway, Seventh Avenue, and Forty-second Street. That intersection was Longacre Square, which was renamed Times Square in 1904 when the new Times building was completed.

Times Square's theaters, luxury hotels, and lobster palaces, at night all ablaze with electric lights, had been made more accessible than ever via the city's new subway. A subway station had been built right in front of the Times Building, which had been excavated deep down, to a depth of fifty-seven feet below the curb. The subway tunnel ran directly through the basement. Underneath were two additional subbasements, and in the bottommost, the great presses rolled out the papers. People were now calling Times Square the center of New York, even the world.

Corydon Purdy, who had so aptly executed the Flatiron Building, was now, as a result, highly respected in his profession. He was often invited to deliver papers to engineering societies and universities on modern structural design. The Fuller Company had hired Purdy to do the Times skyscraper. Like the Flatiron, the Times Building was a marvel, designed to withstand all variety of stress that it endured. Steel girders braced it against the force of the wind on each of its three sides, the constant traffic that passed around it at street level, and the vibrations of the subway roaring through its basement. The steel frameworks for the building and the subway had been carefully constructed to be completely separate from each other. Sand cushioned the subway columns to absorb building vibrations.

From the Flatiron roof, Bailey made a series of eight sketches, each depicting a view from a different angle. His drawings had been commissioned by the publishing mogul Frank Munsey, whose offices were housed on the eighteenth floor, and would soon be featured in *Munsey's*, to accompany an article by the popular and prolific writer Edgar Saltus.

"The Flatiron's front is lifted to the future. On the past its back is turned. Of what has gone before it is American in its unconcern. Monstrous yet infantile, it is a recent issue of the gigantic upheaval that is transforming the whole city," wrote Saltus, who was famous for his flamboyant prose and the exotic and sometimes racy subject matter of his novels. It was as if the Flatiron, by the very fact of its pointing northward, was thereby acknowledging the continued movement of New York's glamorous commerce in that direction, even as the building sat just beyond the edge of Madison Square like some huge cast-iron paperweight, securing the constantly changing neighborhood. Amos Eno, by building his Fifth Avenue Hotel in the late 1850s, had made Madison Square into New York's most fashionable, vibrant public space, an honor it could claim no longer. It had lost its preeminence to Times Square. But the latter did not fulfill what had been Madison Square's most precious function, that is, as a beautiful and comfortable space, in the city's center, where people gathered and socialized, and showed off. Brightly lit, noisy, and traffic-choked Times Square offered no place to stroll, and sit, and talk. It was a place to get to, and then rush by.

"There is about Madison Square the charm and distinction of a glory that has indeed passed, but passed to no successor. It is a place of memories, but not of memories only. It still lives, and its current life is vigorous, and it has a future that promises to be in a different way as brilliant as its past," wrote a journalist named E. S. Martin in a pensive essay for *Harper's* in October 1907 entitled "Moods of a City Square."

But different how? New York was changing too quickly to predict the future of a city space now in flux. The theater district had moved north, leaving Madison Square's surrounding streets largely quiet at night. One by one, the restaurants were closing. The landmark O'Neil's, where all manner of businessmen went for the then-cheap and basic New York fare of lobster and roasted oysters, shut its doors in February 1906. A dry-goods store took its place. But during the day, the park was filled with people. And it was still lovely, a tree-filled oasis, surrounded on three sides by brownstones, and on the fourth, the east side, stood the Palladian-style Appellate Court Building, and the old brownstone Gothic-style Parkhurst Presbyterian church, with its needle-like spire,

Illustration by John Edwin Jackson for "Moods of a City Square."

where Theodore Roosevelt had been baptized. Across Twenty-fourth Street from the old church, stood another, a new one, also Presbyterian, but in a startlingly different style, with a multicolored terra-cotta façade and a green-tiled Byzantine dome. It had been designed by Stanford White in 1903, to replace the old, which was soon going to be torn down. On that lot the Metropolitan Life Company would erect its new tower, which, when completed, would stand nearly 700 feet tall, therefore much surpassing the Times building's height, snatching from it that ephemeral distinction: New York's tallest building. In fact, at that time the Met Life Tower would be the tallest office building in the world.

In the meantime, tourists were still flocking to the Flatiron Building, to see it, and to photograph it. They might also book one of the auto coach tours that left from the curb every hour, seven days a week. You purchased your ticket, which cost $1, in the Flatiron lobby. A brochure described several tours, each going a different direction. Downtown took you to "the odd sights of Chinatown and the Bowery—Oriental Restaurant, Chinese Opera House, The Tombs Prison, the Bridge of Sighs, Little Italy, the Ghetto, Five Points and the Mission." Uptown was "an exhilarating dash in and out, around and about Central Park, the grand boulevards, Fifth Avenue, Riverside Drive, Millionaires Row, Homes of Prominent Men of the past and present."

Everybody still loved the Flatiron, and Madison Square Park, too. On a beautiful day, it was filled with office workers sitting on benches as they ate their lunches, and lovers meeting and embracing, and moth-

A 1905 brochure advertising "Seeing New York" automobile tours,
which started at the Flatiron Building.

ers, with their babies and children in tow. There were always children playing there, in the summer until late in the evening, of all sorts: ragamuffins from the tenements beyond Third Avenue, and the cleaner, well-dressed variety, who were accompanied by nursemaids. Always, too, the same old men and women showed up every morning, stayed the day, and disappeared when it got dark. In the spring, thousands of tulips adorned the flower beds; on summer evenings, bands performed concerts. On the park's south end, a thirty-foot-diameter tiered fountain, surrounded with decorative iron railing and large stone planters holding flowers, spouted water. John Sloan, another artist who made his living as a freelance illustrator, originally for newspapers, and now for the magazines *Leslie's* and the *Century,* twice painted the "throbbing fountain," in 1907 and 1908. One depicted beautifully attired little girls admiring the splashing water as they lean on the rail, and the other, genteel New Yorkers enjoying the park on a warm summer night, the women in gauzy white dresses, and the men sporting straw boaters. In the background looms the Flatiron, partially obscured by a tree, from behind which shine, here and there, a row of lit windows.

Sloan often painted Madison Park and the Flatiron. Earlier, in 1905, he had done *The Coffee Line,* which depicted homeless men—of whom there were always some hanging around, staking their territory—on an inky black winter night, waiting on line for free coffee being doled out from the back of a cart. In the background, you can just barely make out the Flatiron, from the few feeble lights outlining the top floors of the eastern flank. Snow covers the ground. Looking at the painting, you feel the chill of that bleak night, just like the waiting men. It was just such unglamorous, everyday city scenes that most attracted Sloan, and he found them in abundance around the Flatiron, and a bit farther west, in Chelsea, where he lived, on Twenty-third Street between Sixth and Seventh Avenues. Chelsea was a mecca for writers and artists, with its cheap hotels and boardinghouses, its streets alive with dance halls, brothels, department stores, and sweatshops.

Soon after Vernon Bailey did his sketches for *Munsey's* magazine, he rented a studio in the Flatiron penthouse, which had just been added, an afterthought to the original building plan, just as the restaurant, down in the basement, had been. The penthouse increased the Flatiron's height to twenty-one stories. Doubtless it was Bailey himself who, after his *Munsey's* assignment, approached U.S. Realty and convinced them to construct the penthouse, to be used as artists' space. The top of the Flatiron was heaven for artists, giving unobstructed light and views, and, what is more, easy access to the roof. On a fine day, he could just step outside, to draw or paint. Bailey loved to draw, sitting outside. And, he must have said, you will rent out the spaces immediately, to my colleagues. Bailey was a member of an art collective, the "Carlton Illustrators," which had started in London, and now had a New York branch. The Fuller Company quickly completed the penthouse, and all the members of the Carlton group—F. E. Wiles, Jay Hambidge, Armand Both, Alexander Popini, Remington Schuyler, Carton Moore-Park, Stanley R. David, Louis Fancher, and Bailey—immediately moved into the studios. Each artist had a specialty, and worked independently. Remington Schuyler painted Native Americans ("American Indians") who posed for him in the studio. Louis Fancher produced posters in a strikingly modern style, advertising theater events. He also designed a panel for the smoking room in a theater. Bailey etched his vistas of streets. But the group sometimes together took on a single project, such as on special book editions. Carlton members also produced all kinds of "pulp art" for magazines, like *Munsey's* downstairs.

Harry and Allon's divorce was finalized on May 29, 1905, in Westchester County. The judge handed the papers over to the county clerk, and ordered them sealed. The clerk locked them in a safe. One hundred years later, the document became public record, which I opened and read one freezing December day in 2005 at the Westchester County courthouse. But at the time of their divorce, the newspapers never did get the story on why Allon divorced Harry.

Eight months later, in January 1906, Allon, now twenty-eight, married Tyler Morse, whom she had met the previous winter at Palm Beach, while still married to Harry. Allon's new husband, one year older than she, was the scion of an old and socially prominent Boston family.

"As Mrs. Morse, the daughter of the man who invented the skyscraper may attain the prominence in Boston society which as Mrs. Black she never had opportunity to reach in New York. This was not exactly her fault, in view of the fact that it is only within a season or two that Mr. Black has been able to spare the time from his multifarious business operations to cultivate the pleasant arts of polite society. He is a rattling good fellow, but distinctly a man's man," wrote the snarky Colonel Mann in his weekly gossip-sheet *Town Topics,* one week after Allon's wedding. Evidently, Mann no longer considered Harry Black's affairs off-limits to his publication.

Morse had gone to Harvard, where he had belonged to the student theatrical group known as the Hasty Pudding Club. After graduating, he attended Harvard Law School, but he only practiced law for a short time, in Boston. The young man had no need to earn a living, because he, like his bride, was worth millions. Instead of working, he had traveled widely, to Africa and Abyssinia (i.e., Ethiopia). Besides travel, his main pasttimes were sports, hunting, automobiles, and breeding bulldogs and sheepdogs. The latter hobby he shared with Allon, who had been breeding sheepdogs since her late teens, when she was first married to Harry.

Their wedding, in Allon's Fifty-sixth Street apartment, decorated with floral arrangements for the occasion, was attended only by a few close friends. A string quartet furnished music. After the couple had exchanged vows, their friends showered them with rice as they hurried into a waiting automobile, which whisked them off to Pennsylvania Station. There, they caught a train for Palm Beach.

The couple spent their honeymoon at the Royal Poinciana, the same hotel where Allon and Harry used to stay. "Mrs. Tyler Morse appears to be much livelier than when here before with her former husband, Mr. Harry Black," wrote *Town and Country,* which blandly reported on the comings and goings of high society. "Mrs. Morse is much in evidence, and is very vivacious at the numerous little dinners at which she and Mr. Morse are guests. The latter is about the same age as his wife and enters upon the pleasures of Palm Beach life with quite as much zest."

Allon's choice of venue for her honeymoon did not escape Colonel Mann. It was, he remarked in *Town Topics*, "rather strange." Strange, too, was that Mr. and Mrs. Morse spent the following winter, 1907, at the Savoy Hotel, at Fifth Avenue and Fifty-ninth Street, where Allon and Harry had often stayed when they were still married. From the window of their hotel room, Allon had a clear view of a massive construction going on across Fifth Avenue: the new Plaza Hotel, the latest of Harry Black's seemingly endless ventures.

The Morses left the Savoy in March for Atlantic City. Arriving at the Marlborough Blenheim resort there, Allon had her servants unpack her trunks. She soon realized that her pearl necklace, valued at $100,000— the one that had been seized by customs in 1902 when she and Harry were returning to New York from France—was missing. Allon, frantic, called the Atlantic City police department. A detective—his first name, coincidentally, was Harry—came to her aid. Harry Wilson went immediately to New York. An hour after his arrival there, he called the Morses, to tell them that he had the pearls. Later he told the newspapers that a chambermaid had found the pearls in a bureau drawer soon after the Morses left. She immediately turned them over to the hotel manager, who was holding on to them, waiting for the Morses to return. Why the manager hadn't immediately called the police to report the pearls is anybody's guess.

Wilson returned to Atlantic City with Allon's pearls. She, the newspapers reported, gave Wilson a $1,000 reward.

By 1907, Harry was being seen often in public on the arm of the plump, nondescript-looking Theresa "Tessie" Oelrichs, who had been recently widowed. In her mid-forties, Oelrichs was the same age as Harry, and was a reigning queen of New York and Newport society, along with two other matrons, Mrs. August Belmont and Mrs. Stuyvesant Fish. The three, known as the "Newport triumvirate," had stepped into the shoes of the once all-powerful Mrs. Astor, who was now, in her mid-seventies, slipping into dementia. Mrs. Astor died in 1908.

Tessie Oelrichs's sister, Virginia "Birdie" Fair, was married to a Vanderbilt. The two sisters were the daughters of an innkeeper and an Irish immigrant named Charles Fair, who had made millions silver-mining Nevada's Comstock Lode, and then invested much of his fortune in San Francisco. Tessie's marriage to her late husband, Hermann Oelrichs, wealthy in his own right from inheriting and expanding his father's Baltimore-based shipping business, had been spectacularly miserable. Oelrichs loved sports and hunting, and hated everything that his wife thrived on: the dances, the entertainments, the dinners, and all the other venues frequented by "high society." Eventually Hermann Oelrichs moved to San Francisco, where he took care of his wife's

Tessie Oelrichs, 1904.

financial interests. His wife remained in New York. The couple was never seen together anymore, and society pages periodically talked about a coming divorce. But he instead died in September 1906, on board a ship crossing the Atlantic, traveling as usual without her.

Before they had separated, the Oelrichs built a mansion at 1 East 57 Street, on the corner of Fifth Avenue, opposite the Vanderbilts and the Whitneys, and a Newport "cottage" called Rose Cliff. Their palatial summer home, perched on a cliff overlooking the ocean, was designed by Stanford White after the Grand Trianon in Versailles. Society pages reported in excruciating detail on the lavish parties that Tessie threw there during the "season." The most famous was the "Bal Blanc," in 1904. Huge arrangements of exotic flowers, all in white, decorated the ballroom, and the women were required to dress only in white, and powder their hair. Down below, eleven fake ships constructed specifically for the occasion, their wooden hulls painted white, were anchored in the water.

Black's association with Tessie coincided with a time when he was surely feeling lonely. Not only did he no longer have a wife to come home to, but he was now finding himself something of a pariah in polite society. ("There has been a good deal of sympathy expressed for the erstwhile Mrs. Black in the progress of her domestic affairs, for there is no doubt that her late father and his millions were very helpful to her first husband," wrote Mann.) Nor did Wall Street, after the debacle at U.S. Realty, feel kindly toward Harry Black, either. But Tessie could provide him entrée into the highest echelons of New York society, at a time when he badly needed some new friends.

When Hermann Oelrichs died, the couple had been de facto separated for years. And then she had been humiliated when the papers revealed that Hermann had left her nothing in his will, and to their fifteen-year-old son, Hermann Jr., only a few pieces of jewelry, some guns, and other trifles. The reason, his will stated, was that Tessie was exceedingly wealthy, and would therefore provide for the boy. In fact she was, and far wealthier than Hermann. But of course this was not about money. Tessie had been forced to resort to suing Hermann's brother, to whom

Hermann had left everything. The out-of-court settlement, by which she agreed to give up all other claims, had netted her $100,000, plus Oel-richs's California ranch for Hermann Jr. It had been an ugly affair.

But now, Tessie was, for the first time in years, feeling young again, and it was all thanks to Harry. Everybody was talking about them. Some were saying that the two were in love, and would announce their engagement, as soon as the period of mourning for Tessie's husband was finished, in 1908. "In many ways Harry is just the sort of man Mrs. Oel-richs might be expected to choose for a husband, and no one has doubted that she would wed again," wrote Mann. "Mr. Black is not a society man, and knows nothing of the social politics that Mrs. Oelrichs has learned. . . . Mr. Black, however, seems ambitious to learn, and as the husband of the former Tessie Fair, he will have no end of opportunities."

Tessie refused to confirm or deny the rumors. "It is," she told a reporter, "a matter of perfect indifference to me." Since her husband's death, Tessie had been going everywhere with Harry—to Palm Beach, to the Madison Square Garden automobile show (where *Town and Country*—January 17, 1907—described her as "stunning in her widow's attire. Her big hat had very long, full streamers hanging from under the brim, beneath which were discreet little white rosettes. She picked her way about carefully, and studied every car."). Harry had even accompanied her to the police station, after the arrest of Tessie's chauffeur, who had used her car without her permission to joyride some of his friends around the city. (Harry, the newspapers said, was acting in the capacity of her "advisor.")

If Tessie's goal was to march down the aisle with Harry Black, no matter if she snared him or not, she was setting herself up to get hurt.

In March 1907, a credit crisis caused the stock market to take a plunge. Too many loans had been made by large trust companies to stock and bond speculators, and those investments were now faltering.

Within a few days stock prices had somewhat recovered, but the public remained anxious. Those old enough to remember were now talking about the great panic of 1893. There was as yet no Federal Reserve to turn to; each bank stood on its own. The previous year, the banker Jacob Schiff had warned that if the American monetary system were not fixed, the country would soon experience "a panic . . . compared with which the three which have preceded will be only child's play."

Wall Street turned to its de facto banker, savior, and father figure: J. P. Morgan. He was an old man now, retired from daily business dealings. He was in Europe, buying art for his collection, when he got the news. He cautioned everybody to sit tight. And they did. Nervous businessmen stopped selling, buying, lending, and borrowing. In the midst of all this, Harry Black called U.S. Realty's board to a special meeting. Word of this got out quickly to the street, where everybody assumed that Black had bad news to announce. That very afternoon, the company's stock fell to below fifty; one year previously, it had reached one hundred.

The board met for lunch, at the Waldorf. There, Black announced, against everybody's expectation, that the company was issuing dividend on its stock. By the market's closing time, the news about U.S. Realty had been printed on the ticker tape, and circulated about Wall Street. People were astounded. Traders now jumped in to buy U.S. Realty stock. By the end of the trading day, the price had gone up again, into the nineties.

The men of U.S. Realty celebrated by extending their lunch meeting into dinner. Their guest of honor was Harry Black, whom they hailed for his courage and independence, and his dividend initiative.

During these uncertain times, U.S. Realty's real estate, even with the drop in the company's stock prices, had nonetheless been doing well. Its books for the previous quarter had shown a profit, and its buildings were fully rented. And now, on October 1, 1907, Harry's prize project, the Plaza Hotel, which Allon and Tyler Morse watched going up from their window at the Savoy during the previous winter, opened.

Harry and his partners in this venture, his pal "Bet-a-Million" Gates and Bernhard Beinecke, had picked as their architect Henry Janeway Hardenbergh, famous for his hotels and apartment houses, among them the new Willard in Washington, D.C., and, in New York, the Waldorf-Astoria on Fifth Avenue and Thirty-fourth Street,* and the Dakota apartment house on Central Park West. Hardenbergh's new, massive Plaza, eighteen stories high, occupied an entire city block, and had 753 rooms, with some suites having as many as 17 rooms. Black's intention was that the new Plaza be the absolutely most luxurious hotel in the world, attaining a level of perfection that none other could. It would be the most beautiful, too, although it wasn't the Plaza's aesthetics per se that most excited him. To be sure, he enjoyed beautiful things, for which lately, thanks to Tessie, he was beginning to develop a more refined awareness, but Black appreciated beauty above all as a means to attract only the wealthiest clientele, who would spend their money at the Plaza, and therefore assure him the maximum return on his investment.

Hardenbergh modeled the Plaza after a French chateau, with a mansard roof and glittering, baroque-inspired interiors, and stuffed with décor purchased in France, some custom-made. The dining rooms were decked in chandeliers and mirrors and old-rose brocade; the white, cream, and gold ballroom accommodated 500 people; a lobby filled with green-and-white enamel tables, and sofas, chairs, draperies, and tapestries, all in soft shades of rose and green, and Brèche Violette marble walls and Caen stone floors, extended into the leaded glass–domed tea room, decorated with potted palms, that occupied the hotel's center courtyard. The rear wall of the "Palm Court," as it would come to be known, consisted entirely of mirrors, above which arches sprung, supported by four marble caryatids—statues in the form of classical Greek maidens—which had originally stood in an Italian palazzo. At

* The Waldorf-Astoria was demolished in 1929, to build the Empire State Building.

the northeast corner of the hotel was an oak-paneled restaurant for men only. The Plaza felt like a gorgeous French fantasy world resting on a twentieth-century steel skyscraper frame in New York, a city where anything that mattered always came down to money. As if to underline that fact, the offices of six stock-brokerage houses—one featured a mahogany stock board that had cost $1,500—occupied the west side of the Plaza's main floor, so that businessmen didn't have to travel down to Wall Street to buy or sell.

Into the Plaza had been built every modern convenience and the latest technologies. (Although the hotel was not so modern as to allow women to smoke in its restaurants—a practice which some women, Tessie Oelrichs among them, were now daring to do in public.) Each room had a magnetic clock, attached to a master clock downstairs, so as to make certain that guests always had the correct time. Each floor was equipped with full staff, so as to ensure fast service. If a guest needed anything, they had only to push one of the three electric buttons next the telephone—"bellboy," "maid," or "waiter"—and within moments, a carefully uniformed employee would be at the door. And if you ordered room service, one of thirteen electric dumbwaiters transported your meal so quickly from the hotel's gigantic subterranean kitchen— all glistening white-enamel brick, and presided over by a French chef, Monsieur Laperraque, from his glass-enclosed office—that your food arrived piping hot, even if you were on one of the top floors.

Below the kitchen, an iron staircase descended deeper into the ground, sixty feet below street level, to the subbasement. There, a complex of coal-fired heavy machinery had been installed. Four generators furnished all the electricity required for the Plaza's 17,000 lights, 3 laundries, and such innovations as the ballroom's movable balcony section, which, by pushing a button, could be silently lowered to the dance floor, to be used as a stage. Nine boilers produced hot water for nearly 1,000 bathrooms, and steam for the individual radiators, each with its own thermostat, installed in each guest room. An incinerating plant processed all waste, including dirt and dust sucked in from everywhere in the building by a built-in vacuum cleaning system. Around the periphery of the basement walls, which measured one-seventh of a mile, Black had built a miniature speedway, especially for the use of his nephew, ten-year-old Fuller Chenery. (Although Allon apparently had custody of the child, Harry seems to have been close with him.) Here, little Fuller would be able to safely race the miniature electric motor car that his uncle was having made especially for the boy for Christmas. The car's one-horsepower motor would attain a speed of twelve miles an hour, and was fueled by a battery that would be charged right in the power plant. The toy car would be elegant, with a shiny black body and red running gear, and an expensive black-leather upholstered seat where the child would sit.

The Fuller Company had torn down the old Plaza in 1905, and constructed the new one in just two years. The cost, slated originally at $8 million, had ended up at $12.5 million, with Black, Gates, and Beinecke

Henry Hardenbergh's Plaza Hotel, circa 1907.

making up for the difference out of their own pockets. The night before the hotel's formal opening, on October 1, 1907, the owners had thrown a lavish dinner party. The guest list included some prominent publishing people—among them, Fred Munsey—along with a slew of lucky newspaper reporters, who, after being feted with champagne, oysters, and roast pheasant, obligingly filled the next day's editions with elaborate descriptions of New York's newest hotel, along with lists of which glamorous New Yorkers would be maintaining residences there. Alfred Vanderbilt, son of Cornelius II, was the first to sign the hotel registry, leasing a suite at $10,000 a year. And Gates left his Waldorf-Astoria apartments, to lease a sixteen-room suite at the Plaza for $15,000. (Hearst's *World* claimed the figure was $43,000.)

The morning after the festivities, Gates stood outside, on top of the marble stairway at the hotel's Fifth Avenue entrance, watching as hoards of curious people streamed in and out of the lobby. Parked at the curb was a line of red-and-green taxicabs, their uniformed drivers awaiting passengers. The city had inaugurated these French-made models, outfitted with meters and running on gas, only the day before, coinciding with the Plaza's opening. The city's shabby old taxicab fleet—battery-driven, maddeningly slow, and which, having no meters, made passengers vulnerable to drivers' price-gouging—could now be retired.

And then, Gates noticed a horse pulling a rickety old hansom cab past the gorgeous new cars. There were still plenty of these relics of the old New York on the streets. As the driver pulled up to the curb, the horse cast off its shoe, which caught Gates's eye. The gambler was superstitious by nature. He walked down the stairs, and approached the driver, who was now cursing in frustration over the loss of the shoe, the latest, he was saying, in what seemed an endless round of bad luck.

Gates interrupted him, saying: "I'll give you one hundred dollars for that shoe." The driver, startled, looked at Gates, who then said, "Just buying good luck for the new house." The driver handed him the horseshoe. Gates reached into his pocket, pulled out a $100 bill, and gave it to the cabman. Gates went inside, and offered the token to the Plaza's manager, who hung it in his office. And therefore, Gates said, the Plaza would be one of the most successful hotels in the world. "Because," he said, "I paid one hundred dollars to make it so."

Three weeks after guests had partied the night away at the Plaza's opening night, Wall Street's trust companies began calling in loans that people couldn't pay back, causing the stock market to once again plunge. Depositors lined up to pull out their deposits before the banks failed. The word "panic" began appearing in the newspapers.

J. P. Morgan stepped into the vacuum, and took charge. He gathered together the heads of New York's banks and trust companies, and everybody, including Morgan, coughed up millions of dollars, which they used to prop up the stock market, and make loans to financial institutions. Among the contributers was "Bet-a-Million" Gates. Soon confidence was restored. The stock market recovered.

With the economy in turmoil, business at the Plaza had been terrible during 1907. The hotel had survived. By 1908, it was thriving, and so was the economy. But everybody knew that another panic was inevitable. And with J. P. Morgan now in his seventies, he wasn't going to be around to bail out Wall Street the next time around. Amidst increasing cries for government action, Congress in 1908 established the national monetary commission, to create legislation to rein in the banks.

With the economy rebounding, for the time being the race to erect the tallest skyscraper in the world, which had begun around the beginning of the century, resumed in New York. In 1909, the Metropolitan Life Company won that coveted distinction with its new 700-foot tower at the northeast corner of Madison Square. The engineer for the project was Corydon Purdy, the architect Pierre le Brun, of the firm Napoleon le Brun and Sons. During the 1890s, Napoleon le Brun had designed ornate, Renaissance-inspired buildings for the fire department. The mansard-roofed Home Life Insurance tower, at Broadway and Warren Street, built in 1894, was the work of him and his sons.

The stunning marble-skinned Metropolitan Life Tower was based on the design of a Venetian campanile, its trapezoidal roof topped with a bright golden globe. The new structure soared above the nearby Flatiron, which until now had been the sole skyscraper in the area. Because of its shape, the Flatiron still startled the viewer. But now, dwarfed by the new tower, its impact had been diminished.

For Harry Black as well, the importance of the Flatiron was receding. Early in 1910, Black moved the Fuller Company offices from the building constructed as its headquarters to U.S. Realty's huge, Gothic-inspired Trinity Building downtown, in the financial district. He was now restlessly traveling up and down the East Coast in his private Pullman car, going after new construction contracts. He was especially hungry to be awarded the job that every builder in New York was dying to get: the erection of Frank Woolworth's new skyscraper on lower Broadway, across from City Hall. The five-and-dime-store mogul had chosen Cass Gilbert as the architect, but he couldn't decide on a construction company. Ever since he had begun planning the project in 1908, he had been conducting interviews, some over and over again with the same people, then eliminating names from his list of bidders, only to change his mind and start all over from the beginning.

In March 1911, Black landed in Palm Beach, Florida, where the wealthy liked to party away the winter months. There, he ran into Woolworth and Cass Gilbert. The two men were taking a brief working vacation together, accompanied by Woolworth's daughter and Gilbert's wife, Julia. Although Woolworth had still not chosen a construction company, he had narrowed his choice down to two: the Fuller Company, and its arch-rival, Thompson-Starrett.

Gilbert had worked for Black in 1900 on the Broadway-Chambers Building, right after Black had taken the Fuller Company to New York.

Getting the assignment had been a real prize for the then-young architect, resulting in a Beaux-Arts-inspired building of astounding beauty. It had a classical base-shaft-capital division, with a skin of dark-red brick. The capital was a loggia of terra-cotta in different pastel hues. Rosy-colored granite covered the bottom three floors, or the base. But the experience had not been a happy one for Gilbert. The sheer size and economic power of the company had overwhelmed him, making him, the architect, feel marginalized. But now it was Gilbert, not Black, who held the cards, because Gilbert had Frank Woolworth's ear. So Black, desperate for the Woolworth contract, took himself to the Poinciana Hotel on a hot, humid afternoon, where the Woolworths and the Gilberts were staying. Determined to bypass Gilbert, and get to Woolworth, he tried flirting with Gilbert's adoring wife, Julia. At first, she responded. That is, she pretended to. "Mr. Black naturally is charming to me," Julia would later write about her meeting with Black at the Poinciana. "I am afraid I led him on for I wanted to see him beautifully turned down because he has been untrue to Cass in several instances. He offers to take me to tea at Mrs. Flagler's which I laughingly and flirtatiously (loathsome thought) refuse." Julia had made it her life's work to protect her husband, both from his own propensity for overwork, and those she deemed were trying to work him to death, or in any other ways to take advantage of him. Moreover she found Harry Black particularly distasteful, "a man whose wife divorced him because of intoxication and adultery, quite as illiterate as Mr. Woolworth, quite as keen a business man, but who gritted his teeth and started up the social ladder, determined to get to what he thought was his lot."

No other contemporary reports about Black mention anything about him drinking. Perhaps Julia knew something about him that nobody else did. In any event it didn't take long for Black to realize that he was getting nowhere with Julia. ("From now on my social gymnastics are complicated with business acrobatic performances in the shape of special 'stunts' to keep Mr. Black from having heart-to-heart talks with Mr. Woolworth," she later wrote.) He then tried something else: waylaying the Gilberts together, he invited them to travel back to New York with him in his private Pullman.

Cass and Julia politely refused.

Black had had enough. "With little eyes closed and speaking between clenched teeth," Julia later wrote, "he told Cass Gilbert: 'If the U.S. Realty Construction Co. don't get that contract, I'll do everything in my power to prevent the Woolworth Building from being built.'"

One month later, Woolworth awarded the bid for his skyscraper to the Thompson-Starrett Company. Construction began immediately. And now, having lost the bid to build the world's tallest skyscraper, Harry Black was telling the newspapers that New York was overbuilt. His sour grapes notwithstanding, his statement was the truth, and everybody knew it. After the 1907 panic, speculative building had resumed with a vengeance, resulting in an oversupply of office space.

As the Woolworth Building was being constructed, rents were falling, and lower Broadway was jammed with so many skyscrapers that anybody walking in the streets below felt as if he were in the bottom of a canyon. The question of building height limits, which came up time and time again over the last decade, as New York's skyline kept rising higher and higher, was again in the air.

Feeling restless, Black was making frequent trips to London and Paris, seeking opportunities to expand U.S. Realty's operations abroad. But he did not succeed. Excessive building regulations in Europe's cities made building anything at all, let alone American-style skyscrapers, well-nigh impossible. The result was that Europeans tended to reconstruct, rather than build anew. Moreover even their reconstructions were subject to all kinds of regulations. Black, disappointed, returned to New York, where he didn't know what to do with himself. He stopped seeing Tessie Oelrichs, perhaps because he was feeling the pressure to marry her. Or perhaps he just grew tired of her company. Julia Gilbert disapprovingly remarked: "By means of cutting and trimming, Harry Black has succeeded in rounding off his corners so that he fits in a wobbly kind of way into the social hole. His flirtation with and then-dropping Mrs. Hermann Oelrichs is one of the nicely trimmed-off corners."

In late November 1910, the *Washington Times* society pages reported that Black, while vacationing in Hot Springs, Virginia, invited two sisters from an old Baltimore family, Isabelle and Cecelia May, both in their early twenties, to a large tea that he gave, especially in their honor. The party was held at the resort clubhouse, and on the surface it seemed perfectly respectable. Yet there was something a bit off about it. Harry Black was now forty-eight years old, and, as *Town Topics* had pointed out, a real "man's man." Women all over had their eye on him. And why wouldn't they? He was single and extremely rich.

Black had come from nothing, married the boss's daughter, and turned the Fuller Company of Chicago into a gigantic concern with offices all over the country. He had put together the deals financing some of New York's biggest and tallest structures. He had multiple homes, and more money than he could ever spend.

But now what? U.S. Realty had lost out on the Woolworth Building bid, and at the moment, Black had no big projects in the hopper. He felt at loose ends, and lonely, too. In his current state of mind, hosting a perfectly innocent party for much younger women, like the May sisters, might soothe his troubled soul.

CHAPTER TWELVE

SUR LE FLAT-IRON

*I*N AUGUST 1911, JOHN "Bet-a-Million" Gates died of kidney failure and pneumonia in Paris, where he had fallen ill several months earlier. Black had especially come from London, where he had once again been looking for business opportunities, in time to see his old friend before he died. Black, along with Gates's widow and son, accompanied Gates's body, which was enclosed in a mahogany coffin, aboard the steamship *Kaiser Wilhelm der Grosse* back to New York. There, Gates's body was removed from the gangplank and brought to the Plaza Hotel, where the funeral would take place the following day. All around the city, flags atop buildings were flying at half-mast, to mark the death of one of New York's most colorful financiers. Hundreds of mourners crowded into the Plaza's ballroom on the morning of August 23 to participate in his funeral. Harry Black was one of the pallbearers.

In Gates's last business discussion with his wife, who, with their son, Charlie, would inherit his estate—later, it would be appraised at $38 million—he told her to sell all his stock when he died, but with two

John W. Gates's funeral, August 23, 1911.

exceptions. One was his holdings in his Texas Corporation, the giant railroad company that he had helped build after he had left Wall Street. The other was U.S. Realty.

"Do not sell a share of United States Realty under one hundred," Gates told his wife. "Harry Black is bound to make it worth more than that."

In November 1911, a Basque restauranteur named Louis Bustanoby bought the Flatiron Restaurant, to remodel into a real French café. Bustanoby had come to New York in the 1890s as a teenager, from Pau, a village in the Pyrenees, where his parents had a restaurant. One of his brothers, André, accompanied him. Another brother, Jacques, joined them a few years later, and soon after him, a fourth, Pierre. The four Bustanobys had a grand plan: together, they would open a French restaurant in New York. But first, they would have to learn how the business worked here in America. Like any immigrants, they started at the bottom, waiting tables in various restaurants, and then graduating to be head waiters, even managers at the finest ones, Delmonico's, and the Café Martin (which took over the old Delmonico's space on Fifth and Twenty-sixth in 1899, when the latter moved uptown to the theater district). They saved their money, pooled it, and in 1902, opened their own restaurant, the Café des Beaux-Arts, on Fortieth Street and Sixth Avenue, one block west of the theater district.

In this spot, they brought Paris to New York, the city that fascinated the whole world, where everybody dreamed of coming, and getting rich. But those who had made it here often went to Paris to spend their money on luxuries and pleasures that the New World, with its still-rough edges and strange puritanical ways, did not have. At least, not yet. And the Bustanobys, shrewd businessmen all, understood this, and tapped into this unmet need for European-style nightlife, and, in true American fashion, turned it into a successful business venture. With their new restaurant they created what we now call a "brand." Their Café des Beaux-Arts was a sensation, with its orchestra, French menu, sexy young European waiters, souvenirs handed out on holidays, and the restaurant's trademark liqueur. "Forbidden Fruit" was a delicious blend of grapefruit and cognac, for which André Bustanoby designed, and patented, a distinctive grapefruit-shaped bottle.

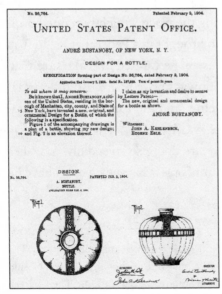

André Bustanoby's patented grapefruit-shaped bottle for "Forbidden Fruit."

And besides all these goodies the Beaux-Arts offered something else, unheard of in New York: dancing between courses, both at lunchtime and dinner, to all the new tunes with the fabulous-sounding names— the turkey trot, the bunny hug, the grizzly bear, the Piccadilly crawl, and, the most scandalous of all, the tango, the subject of indignant clergymen's Sunday sermons all over town. And every night, long after the supper crowds had departed, the place filled up again with theater people after the shows had let out, for the wildly popular *soirées artistiques*. Performers gave impromptu encore performances. Lillian Russell sang "My Evening Star," and Anna Held, "I Just Can't Make My Eyes Behave."

In 1906 the Bustanobys had expanded to Long Island, opening the Château des Beaux-Arts on Northport Bay, on Long Island's "Gold Coast." The luxurious resort had a casino and golf course, and was designed by Stanford White.*

The rivalry that naturally occurs between siblings everywhere eventually turned toxic in the case of the Bustanoby partnership. In 1909, Louis, claiming that Jacques and André were trying to push him out of their partnership, sued. His litigation forced the Café des Beaux-Arts into receivership. The trustee, a man named Augustus Skillin, continued operating the place, which remained profitable, with André as manager. Skillin brought in a Federal judge to inspect the place with him because as trustee, he wanted to make sure that everything going on at the restaurant was above board. Both he and the judge were appalled by the dancing, and the turkey trot, no less. Get rid of it, they told André. André was livid. "Poof with our dancing, and poof with our profits, and we are doing so splendidly, too," he told *The New York Times*. "We give our people what they want, I have been here ten years.

---

* This was one of White's last commissions before Harry Thaw, the very rich and psychologically unstable husband of showgirl Evelyn Nesbit, White's lover, shot the architect at Madison Square Garden in 1906. The Château des Beaux-Arts was demolished in 1957.

I know that without dancing we will be without income." So Skillin allowed the dancing to continue.

The litigation that Louis had brought against his brothers was still in the courts when he purchased the Flatiron Restaurant, in 1911. He set about remodeling it, sparing no expense. He had large electrically powered chimes installed, out of sight, behind the walls. The chimes would be played in tandem with a live orchestra. Louis clearly was not concerned that the surrounding neighborhood was growing progressively seedier. It was still lively by day, as people hurried to and from work in office buildings or *schmatte* factories in the West Twenties. But by night the streets were unpleasantly quiet. Stanford White's Moorish fantasy, Madison Square Garden, had been in decline, especially since U.S. Realty had constructed the Hippodrome twenty blocks uptown in 1905. The Garden still functioned, but was now being used mostly for boxing matches, a form of entertainment that did not draw crowds of the fashionable sort. In fact, the base of the Flatiron had by then turned into a cruising spot for gay men, some of them prostitutes, with their rouged cheeks and eye makeup.

Louis opened his Taverne Louis on February 20, 1912. His case against his brothers was still pending. The electric bells hidden behind the walls worked perfectly, ringing out in unison with the orchestra from time to time. The effect was startling. The opening corresponded to the beginning of the Lent season, and the theme was French carnival, complete with hats for the men, and mirrors and fans for the women. The 400-seat restaurant was filled to capacity with revelers. Clearly, the male prostitutes had not posed a problem. On the contrary, they may have even proven an asset, adding a touch of the louche to Louis's novelty-seeking American club patrons.

And it was that same week that the Bustanoby brothers settled their litigation. After their lawyers worked out a division of their assets, the Café des Beaux-Arts ended up with Louis. His brothers Jacques and André, along with a third Bustanoby, Pierre, would use their settlement to open another restaurant.

Louis now placed ads in the papers, announcing that he, Louis Bustanoby, was the sole proprietor of the Beaux-Arts, along with his new establishment, the Taverne Louis. Every night the Taverne Louis was mobbed with people looking for a good time. Always among the clientele were groups of gay men, who, already knowing the Flatiron as a pick-up spot, now found themselves being warmly welcomed by Louis Bustanoby. Louis was displaying an unheard-of openmindedness at a time when other New York proprietors most certainly did not tolerate a homosexual presence in their clubs.

But the French understood anything having to do with *eros* so much better than their American cousins. To the Beaux-Arts Louis now added yet another novelty: a bar just for women. His timing seemed right, because at the time, society was seeing more and more women going out to lunch or tea, unescorted. But women could not go to bars without male escorts; no respectable place would serve them. Louis's innovation turned this convention on its head, and with a wink, too: at his new women's bar, men were not served unless accompanied by a member of the opposite sex.

At first people regarded the women's bar as freakish. But just like all the Bustanobys' ideas, this one filled a great and obvious void in peoples' lives—in this case, specifically, women's. For the first time, women in New York had a quiet place all their own. At the Beaux-Arts, they could meet, have a drink, and talk to each other in a lovely atmosphere. Best of all, they could do it without their husbands hanging over them, and without, the *Times* noted, "creating any talk."

Louis's women's bar was a great success. It was busiest in the afternoons, when the women shoppers and matinee goers came in. Louis paid close attention to what his clientele liked, and gave it to them. He noticed that women often asked for drinks that matched the color of their eyes, and that they especially asked for Forbidden Fruit. "I serve it to them in little flasks in silken covers, and the combination of the name and the prettiness seems to make a great hit with them," Louis told a *Times* reporter. Louis often added little free touches with his cocktails, such as ripe olives, which served as breath-killers so that a woman's father or husband would not be able to detect that they had been drinking, and perfumed cigarettes with names like Lily-of-the-Valley and Salome.

Jacques, André, and Pierre Bustanoby now upped the ante. With the settlement they had received resulting from their brother's litigation, they opened their new restaurant nearby, on Thirty-ninth between Broadway and Sixth. They called it Bustanoby's. And they, too, sensed the potential financial rewards to be reaped by catering to New York's underserved female clientele. Louis's brilliant idea of dancing-while-you-dined that he'd thought up at his Café des Beaux-Arts had by now spread to other fine restaurants, and now the three other Bustanobys took it one further: they hired sexy young men to dance with the single women. One of the dancing instructors was a raven-haired Italian immigrant named Rudolph Valentino. Women were flocking to Bustanoby's every afternoon, to enjoy their dose of "tea and tango." A Hungarian-born Jewish musician named Sigmund Romberg, who would later become famous as the composer of operettas, led the orchestra.

Louis, looking to go yet again one further over his brothers, went up to Harlem and hired a black musician named Louis Mitchell to play dance tunes in his fancy French restaurants. Mitchell had a fine tenor voice. As a teenager, he had traveled around the country with the Cole and Johnson minstrel show. Now Mitchell had formed his own band, which he called the Southern Symphony Quintette. Mitchell and his band debuted at the Taverne Louis on April 15, 1912, and soon were performing regularly there and at the Café des Beaux-Arts. It was not usual then for an African-American musician to perform at a white nightclub. Mitchell, in addition to singing, also began to play drums, because the crowds coming to hear him had become so big that he couldn't otherwise be heard. Then he came up with the idea of affixing horns and cymbals to his trap drums, so that, in between his banging, he produced all sorts of sounds—steam whistles, bird calls, babies' crying, the sigh of the sea.

Bustanoby ran newspaper ads for his restaurants, to which he now added a large photo of the dashing young Southern Symphony Quintette, all smartly tuxedoed, with the caption: "One of the best colored bands extant. They play, besides ragtime, an extensive repertoire of high-class music." Among Mitchell's admirers was a twenty-four-year-old writer of popular music named Irving Berlin. Despite his youth, this Russian Jewish immigrant was already famous. His tunes "Alexander's Ragtime Band," published the previous year, and "America" were already part of American repertoire.

One night Berlin, after hearing Mitchell perform at the Taverne Louis, urged him to try his luck in London. Mitchell, armed with a let-

An ad for Louis Mitchell's Southern Symphony Quintette, which debuted at the Flatiron Building in 1912. Mitchell is the first on the right.

ter of introduction from Louis Bustanoby, did as Berlin suggested. The British had never heard anything the likes of the Southern Symphony before—one critic described the band as "many black men who bang drums and cymbals and even sound motor horns"—and they were captivated. But war was about to break out all over Europe, which would force Mitchell, along with thousands of Americans, to return home.

Daniel Burnham died on June 1, 1912, of colitis, in Heidelberg, Germany, where he had been vacationing with family. He was sixty-five years old. Long suffering from diabetes and digestive problems, he had worked like a fiend until the end. The architecture firm of D. H. Burnham and Sons—Daniel Jr. and Hubert—was the largest in the world, and had designed hundreds of buildings. Burnham had personally devised master plans for Washington, D.C., Chicago, Manila, and San Francisco after the 1907 earthquake.

Burnham's body was cremated in Germany. The ashes were taken back to Chicago, and interred in Graceland cemetery.

After the Flatiron project, the firm of D. H. Burnham went on to design five more buildings in New York. They were: Wanamaker's and Gimbel's department stores, the Claridge Hotel, and the office buildings Eighty Maiden Lane and the New York Edison.

Daniel Burnham came of age during a time of breathtaking changes in the world, when industry ruled everything, and economies were madly expanding, and none more so than in America. At the time of his death, the world was about to change even more, in ways good and often terrible. And along with everything else, the design of skyscrapers, a form that Burnham had helped invent, would also change.

In September 1914, just days after French and British troops defeated the Germans at the Marne, the steamship *Baltic,* which had left from Liverpool, docked in New York. Among its passengers was Harry Black.

He had spent the previous three months in Europe, where, three weeks after he arrived, in June, a Serbian nationalist assassinated the Archduke Ferdinand and his wife in Sarajevo. By the beginning of August, European nations were declaring war against each other. Black, along with at least 100,000 other Americans, now found himself stranded on the Continent. After being stuck in Austria for three weeks, he and his traveling party were able to drive their car across the border to Italy, and then, through Switzerland, to France. By the time they reached Paris at the end of August, Black estimated that they had been stopped at least 150 times by various military police. The French mobilization was nearly complete, and the city was deserted. The parks had been turned into stockyards, and the shops and hotels closed.

"This war," Black told *The Wall Street Journal* (on September 19, 1914), "will set Europe back at least fifty years, and will to a large extent destroy the financial fabrics of the continental countries." But Europe's losses, he said, could transfer into trade opportunities for the United States.

"I predict an era of great prosperity for the United States in the coming years," he told the *Journal*.

The United States had no intention of getting involved in the European war, which they regarded as a strictly local conflict. In any event, everybody was saying, it would surely be over in mere months. But the Germans responded to their defeat at Marne by digging trenches, seven feet deep and six feet wide, from which they continued to wage war. The Allies then dug in their own trenches. In between the battle lines was muddy, corpse-riddled no-man's-land. Both sides hunkered down in the hellish conditions. Casualties were high, but progress, nil. It was obvious that the fighting, unless greatly escalated, would be endless.

In the meantime, Harry Black's business instincts were proving correct. The war was raising demand for American steel—to be turned into helmets, bullets, hand grenades, machine guns, torpedo boats, destroyers, army trucks, tanks, and airplanes—to new heights. There was especially a high demand for barbed wire, the commodity that the late John Gates had sold in Texas for corralling steer, thereby making him his first fortune. It was now put to a new, war-related use—fencing in the first rows of trenches, which extended along the Western Front, from the English Channel, all the way through Belgium and France, down to the Swiss border.

But this boom in demand had unintended consequences. As the war now consumed all available steel, and other building materials, too, construction in America came to a halt.

Among the thousands of Americans forced suddenly to leave Europe in 1914 as war was breaking out was Louis Mitchell. Back in New York, he joined the orchestra of another supremely talented black musician: James "Big Jim" Reese Europe. "Big Jim," like Mitchell, knew how to benefit from the current dance craze in white America, which had discovered that only black musicians could play the dance tunes that everybody couldn't get enough of. "Big Jim's" orchestra had played Carnegie Hall, and all the society parties in New York. The famous dance team of Irene and Vernon Castle was present at one of those parties, and soon he had an exclusive contract with them.

During November 1914, Mitchell participated in a tour with Europe's orchestra, traveling up and down the East Coast. They played thirty cities in twenty-eight days, and introduced a new dance tune called the fox-trot. In Richmond, Virginia, Mitchell sang the popular tune "It's a Long Way to Tipperary." After the tour had finished, Mitchell, back in New York, started his own band. With them he returned to London, where they played at Ciro's. It was now 1915.

Back in New York, Louis Bustanoby's supper clubs were doing better than ever, and the restaurateur wanted Mitchell back. He wrote to Mitchell in London and begged him to come home. There was, Bustanoby wrote him, no combo on earth who could play like Mitchell's. But Mitchell did not oblige his former patron. He had discovered that even in the middle of a war, the life of an African-American musician was far better in Europe.

Harry Black, still single and much sought out by women, began seeing Tessie Oelrichs again. The two appeared together at the opening of the new, gigantic speedway at Sheepshead Bay, Brooklyn, in the fall of 1915, where, among the 60,000 people who crowded the grandstands, sat New York society, conspicuous and lavishly dressed, as if at an autumn fashion show. Tessie's sister, Birdie Vanderbilt, was there, too, and Mr. and Mrs. Vincent Astor, who shared their box with New York's Mayor Mitchel.

An American, Gil Anderson, received the Astor Cup, breaking the world's speed record in his American-made car. *Town Topics* reported that during the race, Harry and Tessie "made a dash for the back of the grandstand. While they were lost something put Tessie in a good humor, as even the silver roses on her hat looked more than gay when she returned."

That was on Saturday, October 10. The next day, Allon Fuller Morse, the former Mrs. Harry Black, suddenly fell ill with pneumonia. She died twelve hours after the onset, in her and Tyler Morse's Long Island mansion. She was only thirty-seven years old.

Allon's marriage to her second husband was said to have been happy. Unlike Harry, whose neglect of Allon had shamed and pained her, old-money, Bostonian Tyler Morse had no outsized ongoing business ventures to distract him, and was almost always by Allon's side when she appeared in public. His presence had certainly proven an added boon to Allon, who, already the object of much society interest while still Mrs. Harry Black, during the ten years of her marriage to Morse had hastened her ascent up New York's social ladder. Writers of society columns faithfully recorded the couple's comings and goings, complete with lush descriptions of Allon's wardrobe.

The couple had no children. They spent much of their time with their dogs, even hiring a specially trained dog nurse whom they brought over from England to care for their kennel. The Tyler Morses' breeds consistently won prizes in dog shows. The year before she died, Allon's old English sheepdog, Slumber, won first prize as the best dog of all breeds at the annual Westminster Kennel Club dog show. Allon and Tyler filled the rest of their time with auto shows, horse races, and trips to Europe, between winters in Palm Beach, and summers at Morse Lodge, their Westbury, Long Island, mansion.

Allon left half of her estate, which was reported variously worth $4 to $5 million, to her husband, Tyler Morse, and the other half to her sixteen-year-old nephew, Fuller Chenery, who was in boarding school in Massachusetts. The boy had by now taken his grandfather's name, George Allon Fuller. Allon left Harry $250,000, and also made him a co-trustee, along with the New York Trust Company, of her nephew's portion of her estate, until the boy reached twenty-one. A paragraph stipulated that if Tyler Morse remarried, he would lose all interest in Allon's estate. And she left $5,000 to her poor grandmother, Almira Fuller, who had outlived her son, George Fuller, and both her granddaughters as well.

Soon after Allon's death, George Fuller *fil*'s biological father, Horace Chenery, now a Maine banker, turned up at Harry Black's doorstep. Horace had given over his son to be raised by Harry and Allon when then–Fuller Chenery was just an infant, after his mother, Grace, had committed suicide. Horace had then remarried. It is not known if Chenery had any further contact with his son after Harry and Allon adopted him. But now, smelling money, he was seeking to regain guardianship. Chenery sued, but lost. Harry Black would remain his nephew's guardian. And this, the newspapers noted, was in accordance with the boy's wish.

By the time young George Fuller graduated from his Massachusetts prep school in the spring of 1917, Congress had declared war on Germany. The U.S. government seized the moment by immediately instituting the "Wake Up America!" propaganda campaign. Among the artists who now received lucrative commissions to create posters encouraging men to enlist was Louis Fanchon of the Carlton group.

On April 19, the anniversary of Paul Revere's ride through Lexington, arousing men to arms, parades were staged all over the country. In New York, 60,000 people, most of them women and children, marched up Fifth Avenue. The parade started at Washington Square, continuing past the Flatiron, and then the cowcatcher at the northern tip. The United Cigar Store, which occupied the cowcatcher, had now temporarily donated its space to the Navy, to serve as one of the many recruitment centers that were popping up all over the city. Posters urging men to join up decorated the windows, and an American flag had been placed on the roof, transforming the glass-and-cast-iron extension into a miniature fort. As the parade continued up Fifth Avenue, past the Public Library, all the way up to Seventy-second Street, three airplanes flew overhead, from which the aviators dropped thousands of leaflets, urging America's men to take up arms at once, just as they had in 1776. Among the marchers was a detachment of Camp Fire Girls, clothed in khaki bloomers. Some carried a stretcher, on which lay a dummy, the effigy of a dead pacifist. Another girl carried a banner that read: "Dead—He can't enlist, but you can."

Every day, men came to the Flatiron's northern point, where they set up sidewalk stands and hawked Liberty Bonds. By summer, American soldiers were sailing to France. Among them was the musician James Europe, who had enlisted in Harlem's new, all-black regiment, the Fifteenth. Europe's white commanding officer assigned him the job of putting together and leading a brass band, which was soon performing for soldiers and civilians around France.

Europe's pal Louis Mitchell was also in France now. He had recently arrived from London, to play drums in the orchestra of Paris's biggest music hall, the Casino de Paris at 16 Rue de Clichy, at the edge of Montmartre. "He is the only Negro in the orchestra," wrote a visiting reporter from the *Age*, a Harlem-based black newspaper. "The

"WAKE UP
AMERICA!"

A glimpse of the "Wake up America
Day" parade in New York City-
April 19th ——— showing the
famous "cowcatcher" of our
Flatiron Store at B'way. & 5th Ave.
transformed into a mimic fort
This window has been donated
to the Government as a Naval
Recruiting Station.
United Cigar Stores Co.

This "Wake Up America!" poster hung in the window
of the United Cigar Store, in the Flatiron Building.

French idea is for one man to beat the kettle drum while another looks after the bass drum and traps. So when the colored musician presided over all the drums and traps with marvelous dexterity he created a sensation. Each evening his importance is emphasized by the spotlight, a piece of marked attention no other member of the orchestra is accorded." Mitchell was now playing at the Casino every night, where he was being paid an astounding 1,000 francs a week. In between, he and his band, the Seven Spades, gave free concerts to Allied troops in Paris. People were beginning to call this distinct music by a new name: jazz. Afterward Mitchell received letters from soldiers, filled with their gratitude. His music, they wrote, had raised their morale, and helped the war effort. Mitchell was, they wrote, a true American, to be commended for his patriotism.

In America, Mitchell, an African American, would have had to enter and exit his gigs through the back door.

Mitchell's success at the Casino de Paris had theater managers all over Paris offering him contracts. He was front-page news on all the

Parisian newspapers. Paris, one reporter noted, "is wild over America's rapid-fire jazz, and syncopated music, which a colored orchestra best interprets." Mitchell told the reporter that Paris offered a great field for "colored American musicians," and he urged his compatriots to join him.

George Fuller had been accepted into the Harvard Class of 1921. But instead of attending college, he, like thousands of young men swept up in the fervor of war, joined up. He trained for several months in Boston with the 26th "Yankee" division, becoming a member of the 101st Engineers. His unit sailed to France in September 1917, where they and other American divisions received further training, before being sent to join the French soldiers at the front.

As an army engineer, Fuller was not directly in the line of fire. Instead, it was the 101st's responsibility to erect whatever structures were needed to conduct the campaign. The young George was drawing on building skills, perhaps inherited from his grandfather, to help wage this war, the first to employ twentieth-century technology. But, from a technical standpoint, the war was going badly. Nothing was moving, with each side hunkering down in the complex systems of muddy, lice-infested trenches that they had dug, opposite each other, all along the Western Front.

Digging out and maintaining some of the trenches, where soldiers might hunker down in the mud for days, bored, until the next barrage of artillery fire, or bombardment of mustard gas, was now the responsibility of the young George Fuller and his engineer buddies. The 101st put up the miles and miles of barbed wire at the front lines, which marked off the crater-pocked, mined purgatory of no-man's-land. They also excavated shelters and lined them with concrete, constructed field hospitals and barracks, built listening posts and *postes de commandement,* and constructed and repaired roads.

In New York, Harry Black showed his support for the war effort in public, serving on the mayor's committee to greet visiting European officials, and sometimes attending the charity events that rich New

Yorkers were constantly staging. In January 1918, doubtless worrying about his nephew in France, he got on his private Pullman car and headed to Palm Beach. He settled into the Poinciana hotel to wait for the war to end, so that he could resume building in New York. Black liked Florida, where he was now spending a good part of every winter. But he always told his friends that his heart belonged to New York, and that New York was where he felt best.

Harry Black, through his fierce ambition, combined with the heady, unregulated development opportunities in New York, had changed the city's skyline. But with skyscrapers rising higher and higher, blocking out the air and the sun on the sidewalk below, and increasing pressure to regulate building construction, New York had finally passed a zoning law, the nation's first, in 1916. The new regulations restricted heights, and also imposed setbacks from the property lines of the lot, to allow light and air to circulate below—a skyscraper could no longer soar straight up hundreds of feet into the sky in an unbroken line.

What effect the new regulations would have on the shape of New York's next phase of skyscrapers was anybody's guess.

In 1915, the Cubist artist Marcel Duchamp arrived in New York from Paris. A short time later, he was joined by his friend and colleague Albert Gleizes. Both had introduced Americans to modern French art two years earlier, when they, and other contemporaries, including Picasso, had exhibited their work at the International Exhibition of Modern Art at the Lexington Avenue Armory. The show had been a huge success, mobbed every day by outraged Americans, who railed at the strange new forms of art they saw there. They had particular ire for the Cubist canvasses filled with broken, geometric shapes, devoid of depth, which critics derided as "freakish" and "bizarre."

That the place where skyscrapers, the ultimate expression of modernism, had been invented, should be so conservative when it came to art had astounded Duchamp.

"The capitals of the Old World have labored for hundreds of years to find that which constitutes good taste, and one may say that they have found the zenith thereof. But why do people not understand how much of a bore this is?" Duchamp told *The New York Tribune* soon after he returned to New York, in 1915. "If only America would realize that the art of Europe is finished—dead—and that America is the country of the art of the future, instead of trying to base everything she does on European traditions! Look at the skyscrapers! Has Europe anything to show more beautiful than these?"

When Gleizes arrived in New York, Duchamp took his friend to a nightclub in Harlem. The music there was like nothing that Gleizes had ever heard in Europe. That, and everything else about this city— the movement, the noise, the *skyscrapers*—moved him.

Gleizes began to paint scenes of New York: the Brooklyn Bridge, the port at the tip of Manhattan, a vaudeville theater on Broadway.

Albert Gleizes, *Sur le Flat-Iron*.

And then, in 1916, he made an ink-and-gouache drawing of the Flat-iron. Gone were the building's gently curving edges and classical details. Instead, Gleizes's *Sur le Flat-Iron* was all sharp angles and colliding planes. The artist seemed to have taken a hammer and smashed New York's quirky, darling icon into flat, triangular shards, as if mirroring the violent changes that the European war was wreaking on the modern world.

CHAPTER THIRTEEN

THE BIG LANDLORD

$\mathcal{G}$EORGE FULLER RETURNED TO Boston from France with the Yankee division on April 4, 1919. He and over a million American soldiers had been part of the final, painstaking push through the Western Front during the summer and fall of 1918, when the Germans finally agreed to an armistice. Fuller had served his country well. He had graduated from corporal to sergeant after participating in the Château-Thierry and St. Mihiel offensives during the summer of 1918. In the fall, Fuller's superiors had sent him to Engineer Candidates' school in Langres. He had then returned to the field, and attained the rank of lieutenant.

In Boston, Fuller met a young woman named Dorothy Caswell who came from an old Beacon Hill family. The following October the couple married. Among the guests were Fuller's buddies from the 101st Engineers, and his uncle Harry. The bride, *The Boston Globe* reported, wore a veil of "old family lace." The couple afterward departed for a honeymoon in California on Harry's private Pullman car. Fuller was now twenty years old.

When they returned to New York, the couple took an apartment at the Plaza, and settled into a life that reflected the groom's hefty inheritance, which was now his, free and clear. Fuller joined the board of U.S. Realty, but there is no indication that he played an active role in the company. During the cold weather he and Dorothy often joined Harry in Florida. With the passage of the Volstead Act, which criminalized the drinking, manufacturing, and transporting of alcoholic beverages in the United States, Harry was now the main supplier of liquor at the frequent parties he attended in Miami and Palm Beach. He made headlines in 1921, after prohibition agents, obviously acting on a tip, raided his Pullman car, which was parked in Cocoanut Grove, five miles outside Miami. Inside, they found fifty-five cases of assorted and expensive booze. It was the first time a private car had been seized in connection with the Volstead Act; clearly, the Florida authorities were going to make an example of Harry Black, whom they were now charging with an additional crime, of hiding liquor in a shack on property that he owned on Biscayne Bay.

Black was arrested on federal charges, then released, after one of his Pullman porters testified that he had loaded the cases onto the car without Black's permission. The porter was fined $500, which Black paid. Black was then immediately rearrested, this time by state authorities, on the orders of Governor Cary Hardee. The action of the federal authorities, Hardee told the Dade County prosecutor's office, did not relieve him from enforcing Florida's dry laws.

Once again, Black was released, after friends at the First National Bank of Miami posted bond for him.

Black and his bootlegged liquor was now the biggest story in town. Florida preachers blasted Black during their Sunday sermons, among them William Jennings Bryan in the weekly Bible class that he gave for tourists in Royal Palm Park. "The people who come to Miami," Bryan told the crowd, "want law and order enforced." Bryan sent a telegram to Governor Hardee, praising him for his zealous enforcement of Florida's prohibition laws, "regardless of the action of federal officials. Strength to your arms!"

Four days later, testifying in Miami before a jury, Black noted that he had not been aboard his private car when it was seized. He had, he said, no knowledge that liquor had been placed inside. The jury deliberated for five minutes, before acquitting Black of all charges. His fifty-five cases of liquor, however, were to be destroyed. Bottles from the cases had been displayed during the trial. There were wines, whiskeys, and liqueurs; some, wrote a *Miami Herald* reporter, were wrapped in dainty tissue, and looked to have "a Frenchy flavor." This evidence had been uncorked, and their contents even tasted by a few lucky jurors, in order to determine that the liquid inside was, as the prosecution contended, intoxicating.

No doubt feeling gratified at having made Florida's governor look like a fool, Black turned his attention toward business matters. America's economy, post-war, was roaring. In New York, rents were soaring, and everybody was buying and selling properties. But so far, there was little new construction going on. The hot spot for developers now was Florida, where they were rushing to build everything from luxury hotels to boardinghouses. Black was planning to outdo all of them. He would construct the most spectacular resort that the world had ever seen.

That same year, 1922, Paul Starrett, who had worked for Harry Black from the Fuller Company's beginnings, left. He had defected once before, in 1904, to join his brothers at Thompson-Starrett, but had soon returned to the Fuller Company. But this time, he left for good. He and one of his brothers, William, formed their own company—Starrett Brothers. Black took his company president's departure hard. He told Starrett that he would never get business under his family name. In fact, from their beginnings, the Starrett Brothers did just fine, receiving commissions that included National City Bank buildings at Broadway and Canal, another in Brooklyn, and one in Havana.

However, Starrett found that he couldn't get rid of Harry Black. "I was still bound up with him and his strange, baffling personality,"

Starrett later wrote. "He had continuous difficulty with reorganization of the Fuller Company. He frequently came to me to discuss men and methods and to get my advice." Black kept trying to get Starrett to return. After countless turndowns, Black offered to buy out the Starrett Brothers for $3,000,500. But Starrett turned that offer down, too. Finally Black gave up on Starrett.

Black was feeling lonely and abandoned. He tried to cheer himself up by throwing a glittering dinner at his Plaza Hotel in November 1922, to mark the official opening of New York's winter season. Among the guests was Tessie Oelrichs. Apparently, the two were seeing each other again.

Black remained in New York through New Year's. Then, instead of heading down to his usual Florida haunts, he sailed off to Bermuda for a six-week vacation. Accompanying him was the thirty-five-year-old Washington socialite Isabelle May. He had known her since she was a teenager. Twelve years earlier, while on vacation in Hot Springs, he had thrown that tea party for her and her sister Cecelia. Isabelle, now thirty-five, was still single.

In Bermuda, the *Times* reported, Harry and Isabelle were "house guests of Mr. and Mrs. R. S. Reynolds Hitt of Washington at their Winter [sic] home." When they returned, again sailing together, in March, her parents immediately announced their daughter's engagement to Harry Black. He was fifty-nine. By now seven years had passed since Allon's death, and eighteen years since their divorce.

The ceremony took place one week after the engagement notice, in the living room of the Mays' Washington, D.C., home. Only a few family members attended. Isabelle eschewed the traditional white garb, instead wearing, *The Washington Post* reported, "a gown of steel gray canton crepe, with a hat of gray straw trimmed in wheat." Her outfit seemed a strange choice for a new bride, even if she was in her mid-thirties.

Harry's sudden marriage to Isabelle took everybody by surprise, and perhaps no one more than poor Tessie Oelrichs. During the week in between the engagement announcement and the wedding, Tessie suddenly left for Paris, accompanied by her son, Hermann. *Town Topics* wrote: "The rumor of her departure for the other side has been heard for months past, but her determination to sail was really a matter of almost the last moment." Tessie would remain in Paris, at the Ritz, through the summer. By the following year, 1923, newspapers were reporting that she was, in their words, "ill."

In 1923, Isabelle and Harry moved into a new twenty-three-room penthouse on the eighteenth floor of the Plaza. When the weather was fine, they entertained their guests—the roster included Queen Marie of Romania, and the Governor of Bermuda—on the terrace, with its views of Central Park.

Across the street from the Plaza stood the eleven-story Savoy, dating from 1892, an Italian-Renaissance-style gem of Indiana limestone. Harry, gazing out across the street, pictured a larger hotel there. As always, he was thinking "bigger and bigger."

In 1924, Black acquired from the trustees of John Gates's estate all of his old friend's shares in U.S. Realty, which, in combination with stock he already held, gave Black complete control of the company. He also began talking to General Coleman du Pont, former president of the chemicals company. In 1914 Du Pont had sold off his stake in his family corporation. He now headed a huge hotel empire, and Black was interested in a possible merger. If it happened, this would be the largest real estate consolidation in history. It would also be the next obvious step in the career of Harry Black, who had already made real estate history in 1901, when he put together U.S. Realty.

In the meantime, Black announced that the Fuller Company was about to build the largest hotel in the world: the Stevens, in Chicago, by the famous architects Holabird & Roche. The pair had designed the

Monadnock and Tacoma buildings, and many other distinctive structures in that city. The Stevens would have 26 stories and 3,000 rooms. And now Black, realizing that his newest project was going to diminish the stature of his beloved Plaza in New York, thought of the Savoy, just across Fifth Avenue, where, years ago, he and Allon sometimes stayed. A few days later, he approached the Childs Company, owner of the New York restaurant chain that served up food for the working class, and forged a deal to build a new hotel on the Savoy site. It would be called the Savoy-Plaza, and, at thirty-one stories, would outdo his own company's best in Chicago.

Harry Black and Colonel du Pont failed to reach an agreement to combine their companies. With U.S. Realty's two huge new hotel projects on his plate, as well as plans for a new office building on Madison Avenue, Black needed cash. It was time, he decided, to unload some of his old properties. In the spring of 1925, he sold the Hippodrome. Thompson and Dundy's spectacular creation had never been very profitable. Now, the growing popularity of motion pictures was cutting into audiences for all types of live entertainment.

Then Black sold the Breslin Hotel, at Twenty-ninth and Broadway, which the Fuller Company had built in 1904.

In October, Black sold the Flatiron Building.

He had moved the Fuller offices back to the Flatiron from the Trinity Building in 1916, thinking that perhaps bringing the company back to its original location might refresh the neighborhood. But it did not.

In the meantime, back in May, wreckers had descended upon Stanford White's Madison Square Garden, one block east of the Flatiron Building, and three blocks north. They reduced the ornate theater to rubble. For thirty years, the garden had been the scene of circuses, sporting events, and political conventions. Only the tower, and Saint-Gaudens's beautiful statue of Diana, whose nakedness had scandalized the American public when she was first hoisted up, survived, to grace

New York University's campus at University Heights, in the Bronx. A new, much larger Madison Square Garden was now quickly rising at Fiftieth Street and Eighth Avenue, retaining there its former, and no-longer descriptive, name at its new location. Where the old Garden had stood, the Metropolitan Life Insurance Company would erect a new skyscraper, next to the old one.

Black sold the Flatiron to a syndicate headed up by one Lewis Rosenbaum, a Jewish immigrant from Hungary, who added it to commercial properties in other cities—among them the Coca-Cola Building in Kansas City, and the Railway Exchange Building in Seattle—that he had acquired during the previous eight months. Rosenbaum paid a little over $2 million for the Flatiron, which was exactly how much it had cost Harry Black to purchase Eno's Flatiron, and erect the building, twenty-four years earlier.

With a lot of properties changing hands in New York, Rosenbaum likely was planning to use the Flatiron as collateral to acquire more property, which he might perhaps develop. It wouldn't have paid to tear down the building and rebuild on the lot, given its odd shape and location. Nor would Rosenbaum be thinking of putting any money into modernizing the building. Its old birdcage elevators designed by Hecla Iron Works, and original revolving doors at both entrances, with their now-scuffed mahogany panels on the sides, would do nicely for the underwear manufacturers, ambulance-chasing lawyers, the physicist in Room 1704 who wrote for scientific journals, the Mason Box Company, the Collection Company of America, and all the other small tenants who now populated the Flatiron. The basement, where Louis Mitchell had wowed New York in the Taverne Louis with his band in 1912 before going on to conquer Paris, was now empty. Prohibition had forced the Taverne, and all the Bustanoby brothers' gorgeous establishments, out of business. By then, André and Louis had died. Pierre then went into the woolen business. The fourth brother, Jacques, opened another restaurant, in Teterboro, New Jersey.

For now, the Fuller Company would remain in the Flatiron, but

Black had plans to move his offices. He wanted to construct a new sky-scraper for the company, somewhere uptown, and in a more modern style. The world, post the Great War, had drastically changed, and ar-tistic tastes had, too. For inspiration, architects were now looking at the future, not the past. Visionaries like Hugh Ferris, Harvey Wiley Corbett, Raymond Hood, and, most famous of all, Le Corbusier were envisioning cities consisting entirely of mammoth, setbacked skyscrap-ers, surrounded by and connected to elevated highways.

In contrast to these modern visions, the Flatiron's classically inspired demeanor seemed positively quaint. And it was more than twenty years old, which, by the standards of New York, where newness trumps all, made it ancient. In truth, the Flatiron had become irrelevant, or so it seemed, in 1925.

In 1925, Harry Black put together a group of investors who called them-selves "the American British Improvement Company," consisting of a few titled British, whose presence lent the project an air of exclusivity, and two Philadelphia society matrons. Other than them, nobody else was yet contributing to the new endeavor, not even Black. The group purchased 3,600 oceanfront acres just north of Miami that Black, in his many trips through Florida, had noticed, and now wanted to develop. Black announced in December that the new company would build a new Plaza Hotel on this stretch of Florida, to be designed by Cass Gil-bert, who apparently could not bring himself to turn down such a lu-crative commission, even if it did come from Harry Black. The hotel would be part of a resort complex, with Venetian canals, lakes, lagoons, golf courses, swimming pools, a casino with Roman baths, and yacht-ing facilities. It would be called Floranada.

"I want to make the place popular with English society," said the Countess of Lauderdale, a major investor, at a luncheon given in her honor by some of Floranada's stockholders. "Biarritz," she said, refer-ring to the famously chic resort on France's western coast, "is ideal in the summer, but there is no winter bathing, and English travelers will find plenty of bathing all winter at the Florida resort."

Full-page advertisements for Floranada, which had 18,000 lots to sell, now flooded the newspapers in the United States and England. The ads had been created by the ultra-sophisticated firm J. Walter Thompson, whose clients included such giants as Pond's Cold Cream, Corning Glass Works, and the pharmaceutical company Johnson & Johnson. Floranada, would be "a winter resort for American and English society." One ad featured a drawing of a house that the copy stated the former King of Greece "has ordered: a villa with cool rooms overlooking tropical gardens."

The mention of George, the Greek king—he was living in exile in London, after having been forced out of Greece by that country's dictatorship—was misleading. The king wasn't investing anything in the Floranada. Instead, the company was planning to build the villa for him at the company's own expense, in exchange for the use of his name in their ad campaign.

Two months later, Harry Black suddenly pulled out of Floranada, without ever having contributed one cent of his own money. The reason that Black offered for his defection—that he disapproved of the advertising policy, specifically, the mention of the King of Greece—did not convince anybody. To be sure the ads were deceptive, but for Harry Black to insist on such high moral standards in advertising seemed, to say the least, disingenuous. If he was turning his back on the project, he obviously had a change of heart.

Black's withdrawal left the Floranada project with the feel of a sinking ship. Gilbert was understandably furious with Black, as was everybody else involved with the project. Said one of the British investors: "Mr. Black played a scurvy trick on me." Black assured Gilbert that although he had withdrawn, the project was financially sound. Don't worry, Black told the architect. You'll get paid.

The lots did not sell. Six months later, the Florida real estate bubble had burst, and the Floranada project went into bankruptcy. Its investors lost everything, some of whom sued the company. Cass Gilbert also sued, to recover his fee. The architect surely kicked himself for having gotten involved with Harry Black.

Tessie Oelrichs died in November 1926 at Rosecliff, her palatial Newport home, where she had lived as a recluse during the last two years. Her niece Blanche Oelrichs, a poet and actress married for a time to John Barrymore, wrote of her poor aunt: "Gorgeous toilettes, society—a flux of faces in and out of rooms, on beaches, in casinos—absorbed her." Tessie had, Blanche wrote, lost her reason. "I have heard that during those last years when none of us ever saw her, she would wander, a fragile and still incredibly beautiful person, her raven hair with its deep wave gone snow-white, through the rooms of her immense marble copy of the Villa Trianon, reseating her guests"—guests who existed only in Tessie's mind—"over and over again, pressing them to take just another ice, one more glass of champagne!"*

Black did not attend Tessie Oelrich's funeral.

U.S. Realty celebrated the Savoy-Plaza's official opening in September 1927 with a dinner in its Renaissance dining room. Adolph S. Ochs, publisher of *The New York Times* and featured speaker, congratulated Harry Black. Ochs noted that, taken together, the Savoy-Plaza and the Plaza represented "the biggest hotel proposition in the world."

The Savoy-Plaza, designed by the firm McKim, Mead, and White, had thirty-one stories, thereby dwarfing the eighteen-storied Plaza across the street. The new hotel's distinctive trapezoidal roof, crowned

---

* Blanche Oelrichs and John Barrymore had a daughter, Diana Barrymore. Oelrichs wrote under the pseudonym Michael Strange. The quote is from her autobiography, *Who Tells Me True* (New York: Scribner's, 1940).

OPENS OCTOBER 1ST

The

SAVOY-
PLAZA

*Fifth Avenue
at
Central Park*
NEW YORK

Under The Plaza Management
HENRY A. ROST, *General Manager*

A Hotel of Distinction

An advertisement for Harry Black's new Savoy-Plaza.

with twin chimneys, towered over Fifth Avenue. Its exterior had the same creamy-white terra-cotta as the Plaza, which it resembled, yet didn't, not only because the Savoy was, because of the new law, set-backed, but far taller, bigger, and bulkier than its elegant predecessor across the street. So you could say that Harry Black had succeeded in his compulsion to build bigger than anybody else. Even himself.

U.S. Realty's stock was up, and climbing. The company was in the black, with plenty of cash on hand. Except for the war years, its share-holders always received dividends, by now as high as 10 percent. "Harry S. Black is well known on the Street as the world's greatest landlord," *The Wall Street Journal* had written in an article about him in 1926. "He believes in doing everything in a big way. Big dividends to stockholders is his slogan, when sitting in at directors' meetings of the various corporations of which he is a director."

In 1928, as America's economy boomed, New York was once again constructing skyscrapers. Black went on a personal buying spree. It is not known if Isabelle participated. First he purchased a fifty-seven-acre Dutch Colonial house perched on Long Island Sound from his nephew. George Fuller had built the estate five years earlier, but was now planning to move to Southampton. Black called his new country estate "Allondale." Soon after he bought a new yacht, which he called *The Allon.* Finally he bought yet another summer retreat. This last one, Clarendon Court, a Palladian-style oceanfront mansion, was in Newport.*

In the meantime, U.S. Realty purchased a parcel of land occupied by a Presbyterian church at Madison Avenue and Fifty-seventh Street. On it, the Fuller Company announced, it would construct a new limestone, granite, and slate skyscraper, forty stories high. A drawing by its architects, Walker and Gillette, showed a strikingly modern design, all sharp angles and setbacks, in the new style called "art deco," which had its beginnings in Paris, at the 1925 Exposition Internationale des Arts Décoratifs et Industriels Modernes.

Walker and Gillette explained that this would be the first multipurpose skyscraper in the city, with offices on the top floors, art galleries on the middle floors, and, on the first six floors, *vertical stores,* where retail tenants could rent corresponding space on successive floors.

The new skyscraper would house the Fuller Company offices, now in the old Flatiron. In honor of George Fuller, whose daring and original engineering ideas had made skyscrapers possible, the new structure would be called the Fuller Building, the Flatiron's original name, which the public had rejected. But this time, surely, the name would stick, because the new Fuller Building's lot had a conventional shape (square) and location (facing Madison Avenue), instead of a skinny right triangle in the center of an intersection.

As the craze for modernism took hold of New York, the old, shabby

---

* Clarendon Court later belonged to the heiress Sunny von Bulow. It was there that Claus von Bulow was accused, and later acquitted, of murdering her.

Flatiron was receding in the city's consciousness. In November 1927, *The New Yorker* in its "Talk of the Town" section wrote: "Coming up Fifth Avenue on the bus, we were disturbed to see an elderly out-of-town couple in front of us grow ecstatic at the sight of the Flatiron Building. 'See!' They exclaimed to their poor, innocent children, 'there it is, looking just like its pictures.' Knowing that the Flatiron Building ceased being worth looking at more than ten years ago, we could not contain ourselves. 'Please!' we said. 'If you must lead your children astray, do it in the home and not on Fifth Avenue.'"

Early in 1929, Black came up with a new financial plan: investors would buy stocks in construction projects, thereby supplying the necessary cash. This marked a radical departure from previous practices in the real estate business, which traditionally relied on mortgages, or, sometimes, the issuance of bonds, to supply the means for builders to build. But bank credit was now tight for the construction business. And bonds

The Fuller Building, 2009.

were a less attractive investment than stocks. Bonds offered at best merely interest on the outlay. Whereas stocks appreciated, especially in the current economic conditions. The whole world was now getting rich, buying shares in all kinds of companies. It made sense, now, to offer shares of real estate.

Wall Street liked the idea. Black collected some backers, and set to work, setting into motion a new corporation to issue the stock.

In September 1929, as the Dow Jones Industrial Average reached an all-time high, the Fuller Company moved out of the Flatiron Building for the last time, into its beautiful, teakwood-trimmed new offices in the Fuller Building. The structure had been completed in nine months, six months ahead of schedule.

One month later, even blue chip stocks were tanking, and Wall Street was sitting on its hands. It looked like Black's new financing plan was going to have to wait, at least until the market recovered. In the meantime, Black invited Paul Starrett for lunch at the Manhattan Club, on October 19. Ever since Starrett's departure from the Fuller Company in 1922, Black had never stopped trying to woo him back. Every time Starrett refused, Black sweetened his offer. "I was amazed at Black in this interview," Starrett later recalled. "He was in his sixties, but he abounded with youth, his eyes sparkled, his smile and laugh had all their old magic. 'We'll get together again, Paul, and we'll beat the world,' he said. 'Come on, Paul, come back and join me again!'"

Starrett told Black that he would think about it over the weekend. The two men agreed to have lunch again the following Monday.

After his meeting with Starrett, Black returned to his suite at the Plaza Hotel. In the evening, his wife Isabelle went out to dinner with friends, leaving him with his valet. She had hired a nurse several weeks ago to look after her husband, because, as the papers the next day discretely put it, Black had been "ailing, but not confined to his apartment." The nurse was not there when Isabelle left the Plaza, but was due back soon.

Black now told his valet that he had dinner plans for the evening, and was going to take a bath. He went into a bathroom, and locked the door. Soon after, the nurse returned to the apartment. She asked the valet where Mr. Black was.

"He's in the bathroom," the valet replied, and then the two heard strange noises coming from behind the door. They knocked, and forced it open.

They found Black unconscious in the bathtub, with the faucet left on, and water running over the sides. His head was partly submerged in the water. They carried him to his bed, and called the hotel physician, Dr. George Lee, who called not an ambulance but the Consolidated Gas Company. Dr. Lee told the gas company to send over an emergency medical crew. The crew rushed to the Plaza, and placed Black, still unconscious, on the floor. For eight hours, they worked on him with oxygen tanks and an inhalator. Finally, Black regained consciousness. Afterward he remained in his Plaza penthouse, recovering. He had suffered no brain damage. The papers the next day described the financier's mishap as an accident, brought on by an attack of indigestion.

Five days later, the stock market collapsed.

After spending a few months recovering in Europe, Harry Black returned to New York. By the winter of 1930, the market had recovered somewhat, but it was unstable. It was obvious that Black's ambitious plan to finance real estate projects with stocks was never going to happen. The effects of last October's crash, which had initially impacted mainly the stockholders who were suddenly wiped out, were now being felt all over. Businesses and banks were failing, and people were scared. But Black told everybody that he was optimistic. Real estate, in particular, he predicted, would recover.

"After what Wall Street business calls a panic, securities climb back slowly, cautiously. There has never been a real estate crisis that has not scored much quicker upward reaction. The holders-on get their 'turn' sharp and quick," he told *The Wall Street Journal*.

During the spring of 1930, the stock market once more began to fall. President Hoover assured the nation that prosperity would soon return.

The market fell even lower. By July, U.S. Realty stock, which had been trading at $75 a share during the winter, had fallen to $54.

"Signs of trouble do not have to be searched for," Harry Black told *The Wall Street Journal*. "They are all about." But he insisted that he wasn't worried. "Real estate ownership, with which I have most familiarity, will I figure be the last of the great interests to feel the contraction," he told the paper.

Real estate, he said, was different from other forms of capital. "Once a man owns a piece of real estate, an affiliation—it may not be actual affection but something very near it—grows and fastens into his consciousness which comes close to making him feel that it is somehow part of himself."

He added: "I know I own pieces of property that I couldn't let go any more than I would for a profit dismiss a near dear relative."

On a hot, muggy Friday night, in July 1930, one week after Black's interview with *The Wall Street Journal,* he and an old friend, the painter Robert Van Boskerck, seventy-five, drove together to Long Island from the city, where the two men would spend the weekend at Harry's country estate, Allondale. Isabelle was away, on a two-month tour of Ireland. After arriving, the friends dined together, and retired.

The following morning, Harry Black woke up in his bedroom around eight o'clock. After walking around for a bit, he went back to bed. Then he rose again a little before ten, took a .38-caliber revolver, and fired it into the open fireplace. The bullet grazed the brick, before ricocheting back onto the floor. Satisfied that the gun was working properly, he went back into his bed, placed the muzzle against his scalp line, just above his right ear, and fired again. The bullet penetrated his brain, and emerged three inches above his left ear, carrying with it bits of brain tissue. Later, police found the bullet, embedded in the upholstered headboard.

Black's valet found him soon afterward, in his bed, propped up on pillows. His head sagged forward onto his broad chest. Black's hand was still holding the revolver. Incredibly, he was still alive. He was rushed to the hospital, where he died ten hours later, without ever regaining consciousness. He was sixty-eight years old.

The news about Harry Black headlined the next day's papers all around the country. Some who knew him, among them Paul Starrett, were shocked. Black, like everybody else, had been hurt by the crash. But he had not, like some, lost everything. Far from it. U.S. Realty, despite the drop in its stock price, was holding its own. And, friends said, he had seemed in good spirits.

Paul Starrett was among those caught off guard by Black's suicide. But other friends, having recognized his vulnerabilities, were not surprised. One told a newspaper reporter that Black had no hobbies "to make the prospect of further life pleasant. Harry Black did not play cards or indulge in any other sport. He spent five days a week at the office." Another friend remarked: "There is no puzzle about it. Black had betrayed and lost every friend he had. What else could he do but kill himself?"

But Starrett did not agree. To him, Harry Black remained a dear friend, for whom he felt, in his words, genuine affection.

Harry Black's skyscraper trust had seemed like a brilliant idea at the time. But it never rewarded him and his investors in the way they had expected. Perhaps this is because real estate, just as Harry Black once said, is different from other forms of capital.

When President Theodore Roosevelt went after the big trusts in the first years of the twentieth century, he did not include Harry Black's.

Not Black, nor Harry Helmsley, nor Donald Trump, has ever been able to corner and control New York's real estate market, in the way that the Dukes controlled tobacco, or the Fricks the railroads, or Carnegie steel. No matter how much of New York the major players own today, much of the city's properties still remains in the hands of small owners. Many of them are second and third generation, the descendants of immigrants like my grandfather, Abraham Braun, who worked every day of their lives, saved every penny, and bought as much property as they could afford.

Harry Black, who started out knowing nothing about construction and even less about architecture, had a genius for making deals. With this he transformed New York from a city of wood-frame houses and dull brownstones into one of grand Beaux-Arts buildings and steel-framed skyscrapers.

EPILOGUE

An appraisal of Harry Black's personal assets after his death revealed that half of his wealth had evaporated in the aftermath of the 1929 crash. Still, he left a substantial estate, valued at $6 million. Half went to his widow, the other half to his nephew and only heir. But George Fuller, who had fought as a young man in France, and, unlike so many other American soldiers, survived, outlived his uncle by only thirteen months. Fuller died in his sleep in September 1931, from heart disease. He was only thirty-two. At the time of his death, Fuller was married to his second wife. He, like his Uncle Harry, had no children. The money that Fuller had inherited from Black went into a charitable trust that Black had set up before he died.

Harry Black was buried in an idyllic cemetery located in appropriately named Valhalla, New York, in upper Westchester County. A twelve-foot-high gray granite stele, in simple and consciously art-deco style, marks the plot, which, in characteristic Harry Black fashion, is bigger than all his neighbors'. A simple marker sits on top of Black's grave.

Another marker, located at the edge of the plot, and a good fifteen feet from Black's, reads: GEORGE ALLON FULLER JR.

Why uncle and nephew were buried so far away from each other can only be guessed at. Whatever the intention, the stretch of empty space in the plot gives it an air of terrible loneliness and poignancy. It is as if Black and Fuller are longing for progeny to one day lie at rest with them in this beautiful spot.

Isabelle May Black, who was forty years old when her husband committed suicide, never remarried. Within a few months of Harry's death, she sold Allondale, and bought a home in Southampton. She was devoted to her sister's three daughters, hosting parties for each of them when they made their debuts to society in the 1930s. Isabelle died in 1961.

New York soon forgot the man who forged the deals to build some of New York's grandest structures—the Trinity Building, Macy's, the Plaza Hotel, the old New York Times Building, its exterior later covered over with advertisements and encircled with an electronic news ticker tape that runs twenty-four hours a day—and, of course, the Flatiron. These monuments are what remain of Harry Black. They embody the very soul of New York, and all who love the city owe him a great debt. With these buildings, he left a far greater legacy than most people could claim.

But Black had no descendants to remember him, and so he remains elusive. If there were any letters that he might have written, and photos that were taken of him, and diaries he perhaps kept, they have vanished. Maybe some day they will turn up in an attic. I did locate a great-niece of Isabelle's who remembered her great-aunt's "big old house in the Hamptons." She also recalled hearing stories about Harry, including one about him once playing a bit part in a movie. He appeared, she told me, wearing only a pair of silk briefs. What a great tidbit! This certainly sounds like something that Harry Black would have done. But I couldn't verify it. I couldn't find any mention of it in the newspapers, which, together with Paul Starrett's autobiography, constituted my main sources for Harry Black.

Black's will also stipulated setting up a charitable trust "for the relief of unfortunate men, women, and children, who are either sick or physically disabled," to be called the "Harry S. Black and Allon Fuller Fund." That, and his naming both the lovely summer home where he later died, and his yacht, after Allon, suggests that he never got over the loss of her. All of which must have cut Isabelle deeply, adding to the pain he had already inflicted upon her by killing himself, and, to boot, waiting to do the deed when she was traveling abroad.

Of course Harry had mistreated not only Isabelle, but all the women in his life: Allon, of course, and Lucy Kennard, who had nursed his mother-in-law and afterward had been taken advantage of by him, and poor Tessie Oelrichs, and doubtless others, too, whose names we do not know. Whatever miscellaneous facts that I pieced together about Isabelle and Harry's marriage led me to the inescapable conclusion that it was an unhappy one. And all the while, Isabelle spent more and more time traveling and socializing, apart from her husband. At the time of Harry's suicide, they had been married for eight years. By then the couple seemed estranged, and perhaps thinking of divorcing.

What an enigmatic figure Harry Black was. And how tragic. No matter that he put together the biggest real estate deals ever, which enabled him to build some of New York's tallest skyscrapers, and the world's largest, most luxurious hotels—he wanted still more. But of what, he didn't know. His lack of self-knowledge was Harry Black's weak spot, and, as with many a powerful man, drove him to success and then it did him in.

Allon's second husband, Tyler Morse, never remarried. He died in 1933, at age fifty-nine, of cirrhosis of the liver. Obviously, Morse had been an alcoholic. And, despite his great wealth, which came both from his own family and Allon, Morse seems to have had trouble living within his means. In 1931, George Fuller, Allon's nephew, had willed to Morse all the sporting prints, pictures, rifles, and pistols that the latter had given to Fuller. And in addition, Fuller's will released Morse of all debts.

Frederick Dinkelberg, who designed the Flatiron, and soon after some of Chicago's most distinctive buildings, among them the Railway Exchange and the Heyworth, died in that city in 1935, at age seventy-four. His work as an architect for the firm of Daniel Burnham had earned him a fortune, which he invested in utilities stocks, all of which went bust in the '29 crash. He and his wife, Emily Dunn Dinkelberg, had to sell their beautiful Evanston home. At the time of his death, they were on the relief rolls, living in a tiny apartment on Kendall Street, in Chicago. Dinkelberg died in his sleep, after he and his wife shared a coffee cake that she had baked to celebrate their fiftieth wedding anniversary.

As Emily had no money to pay for a funeral or burial, some of Dinkelberg's colleagues at the American Institute of Architects bore the cost. The couple had no children. Dinkelberg's name was soon forgotten, except to the occasional architectural historian. Hopefully Dinkelberg will now receive his long-overlooked due as the designer of the Flatiron.

During the fifteen years following the building of the Flatiron, Corydon Purdy continued to design large and complex structures in New York and elsewhere—office buildings, department stores, banks, hotels, newspaper buildings, and railroad stations, including Union Station in Toronto. The firm of Purdy & Henderson had offices in Boston, Montreal, London, Paris, and Havana. As the company expanded, rivalries developed, and the atmosphere grew poisonous. Finally, in 1917, young members pushed Purdy out of the firm that he had founded, and with little compensation. Purdy never worked again as an engineer. He bought a farm in Monroe, New York, and moved there with his wife and only child, a son. He raised chickens, and planted orchards. But he could not make it pay.

Then the Depression came. During those bleak years, his grandson, Corydon Purdy III, who was born in 1928 and raised by his grandparents, remembers them "wringing their hands, as their bank account decreased. We became poorer and poorer. We had a radio, but not many clothes. And most of what we did have was patched." Finally, the bank foreclosed on the farm. Purdy Senior moved his family to Florida, where he built a modest home with the little money left to him. He remained there until his death, at age eighty-five. His son, Corydon Purdy II, married four times. He died broke, leaving his son, Purdy III, nothing but the trailer he had lived in with his fourth wife.

The enigmatic, successful, and much-despised publisher Frank Munsey, who occupied the office with the fabulous views at the Flatiron's northern tip, on the eighteenth floor, missed the Great Depression by dying of peritonitis in 1925. He was seventy-two years old. Munsey left no heirs except for a sister and her daughters. The bulk of his estate, valued at $40 million, went to the Metropolitan Museum of Art.

After Munsey's death, his *Argosy* magazine was bought by William T. Dewart, the publisher of *The Sun*. He continued to publish *Argosy* in the Flatiron until 1933, when he moved the magazine to offices uptown (205 East 42 Street). *Argosy*, advertised as "good red-blooded fiction for the millions," much of it the work of famous writers before they became famous—Upton Sinclair and Cornell Woolrich, for example—occupied a special and very lucrative niche: a cut above all the other pulps, but not quite in the league of *Collier's* and the *Saturday Evening Post*. It published romance, adventure, fantasy, and a new, up-to-now fringy genre that was now breaking into the mainstream. It was called science fiction. *Argosy* published its last issue in 1978, by which time it had morphed into a kind of working-class *Esquire*, targeting men only.

Before the Depression ruined the men who had built the Flatiron in some way or another, Prohibition had shut down the Taverne Louis, along with all the Bustanoby brothers' restaurants, and the rest of New York's legitimate nightclub scene. During those years that we affectionately call the Roaring Twenties, Louis Mitchell, who in 1912 had wowed the crowds at Louis Bustanoby's New York night spots, remained in Paris. There, he found success beyond his wildest dreams.

He continued playing at the Casino de Paris, where he and his seven-member band, the Jazz Kings, often accompanied the top-billed stars Mistinguett and her protégé, Maurice Chevalier. The French record company Pathé cut a record with Mitchell in 1921, probably that famous label's first jazz recording (it does not survive). By the mid-1920s Mitchell opened his own nightclub, Le Grand Duc, in Montmartre, where he and his Kings played such hits as "Ain't We Got Fun" and "When Buddha Smiles." Then he opened another club, the Music Box. Every night the crowds flocked to hear Mitchell and his Kings, and other black American artists, too, who, encouraged by Mitchell, were now coming to Paris and finding work, often through his connections. With Montmartre now a hopping jazz scene, Mitchell opened up another place, around the corner from the Casino, at 35 Rue Pigalle, in a space hardly big enough to accommodate a postage-stamp-sized dance floor and a piano. Besides *le jazz,* the new place, Mitchell's Quick Lunch, offered something exotic and unheard-of in Paris: an American lunch counter, which served fried chicken, ham and eggs, flapjacks, grits, and *café américain* all night. Mitchell's Quick Lunch became *the* place to go after a night of boozy clubbing, mobbed every night with everybody from the neighborhood prostitutes in Pigalle to homesick Americans, the King of Romania, and the Prince of Wales, who was a regular customer. Eventually Mitchell had to move his Quick Lunch to larger quarters.

Mitchell's Parisian clubs made him a millionaire. He moved with his elegant wife, Antoinette, and their son, Jack, to a big house with a walled garden in the Parisian suburb of St. Cloud. Their home, the Villa Jacques, became *un vrai salon,* where white Parisian artists and intellectuals, now fascinated with all things African-American, mingled with ex-pat musicians from Harlem. Some of the artists who had gotten their first break in Paris with Mitchell later became famous, such as Bricktop, who later opened her own club on Rue Pigalle.

But Mitchell, the granddaddy of them all, who had brought the first jazz band to Paris, was forgotten. He returned to the States in 1931, ruined not so much by the Depression, which was now spreading

Louis Mitchell and his Jazz Kings at the Casino de Paris.

across the Atlantic and into Europe, as the good life that he had enjoyed in Paris during *les années folles*. All the money he earned had given him license to gamble it away on his weakness: racehorses.

The Mitchells went first to New York, where he, along with the Bustanoby restaurants, had faded from the city's collective memory. Mitchell tried, and failed, to persuade investors to back him in a nightclub venture. After spending a few humiliating years eking out a living by escorting white groups around Harlem night spots, he, his wife, and son moved to Washington, D.C., where Antoinette's father, Walter Brooks, was a well-known Baptist minister. There, Mitchell found work selling Miller High Life out of a red company truck. The nation's capital was still strictly segregated, and Mitchell, the Miller Company proudly announced, was the first salesman they had ever hired who was a "Negro," as one then said.

Antoinette, who had once designed costumes for the lavish shows at the Casino de Paris, and hosted *tout Paris* in her St. Cloud villa, opened a dress shop on Y Street. Mitchell died of heart disease in 1957. He was seventy-one years old. His only child, Jack, fought in World War II, and earned the Purple Heart. Jack Mitchell had no children. He died in 1972, two years before his mother.

As the Depression dragged on, New York's skyscrapers were going begging for tenants. "Megalopolis seems to have run its course," *The New York Times* wrote during the 1930s. "It has built too high for profit." During those bleak years, vacancies mounted to one-quarter of the Flatiron. Its beautiful terra-cotta skin, untouched since the building's erection in 1902, grew grimier. In 1933, the syndicate headed by Lewis Rosenbaum, who had bought it from the Fuller Company, defaulted on the mortgage. The building ended up on the auction block. There, it reverted to the lender, Equitable Life Assurance Company. (The penthouse, where the artists of the Carlton group had invented poster art, was now a commercial art school. David Kyle, a science-fiction writer, remembers hanging out on the roof on May 6, 1937, watching the dirigible called the *Hindenburg* floating across Manhattan. Later that evening, the Hindenburg blew up.)

In the early 1940s, with available office space in Manhattan still outstripping demand, but economic activity somewhat improving, Equitable decided to take a step toward modernizing the Flatiron as a way to attract tenants. They replaced the original birdcage elevators designed by Hecla Iron Works with enclosed rubber-tiled cabs. That also necessitated tearing out the lobby's open grillwork fronts, and, as the *Times* described, "large ornate elevator dials." In their place were installed white marble, floor-to-ceiling panels, "with neat bronze numerals set flush with the marble." The improvements resulted in an immediate increase in new leases. By the mid-Forties the Flatiron had no vacancies. Its tenants were small businesses, many of them—Allied Importers Association, toys; Consolidated Clothiers, men's wear buyers—connected with the clothing factories and toy-and-novelty salesrooms now proliferating in the surrounding area. Anthony Nizzardini supplied fezzes, medals, and swords to the Masons, whose temple was just one block west, on Twenty-third Street. The glass-and-iron-enclosed retail space at the crossroads of Broadway and Fifth that had once housed the United Cigar Store was now a Walgreens. Every day at lunch hour, workers from the Flatiron streamed across Fifth Avenue to Eisenberg's Sandwich Shop or over to Twenty-third Street, to the Chock full o'Nuts coffee shop. A lively neighborhood, and decidedly unglamorous.

In 1946, a group of investors that included Harry Helmsley, then thirty-six, and my grandfather, Abraham Braun, who had a button factory a few blocks down off Fifth Avenue, on Seventeenth Street, finally took the Flatiron off Equitable's hands. As part of the deal between the partners, who called themselves Flatiron Associates, Helmsley's own real estate firm, Dwight-Helmsley, would manage the building. Helmsley now moved his offices to the Flatiron. And he went on to forge dozens of ever more complicated deals, ultimately acquiring hundreds of properties, from old industrial lofts in the garment district to the Empire State Building. Often Helmsley personally had only a small percentage of a given property, but always, a sine qua non of any deal he'd put together was that his firm—renamed Helmsley-Spear in the Fifties after merging it with another real estate operation, Spear & Company—would act as managing agent.

During the 1950s and Sixties, Helmsley became exceedingly wealthy by buying, leasing, and managing properties of all sizes. He moved the Helmsley-Spear offices from the Flatiron during the 1950s to the Lincoln Building, then to the Empire State Building. People in the real estate industry respected him, even loved him, for his sense of honor—once he shook hands on a deal, they said, he never reneged—and his business genius. His tenants, however, knew another side of him, and it was not a nice one. Helmsley-Spear oversaw hundreds of properties, and those that Harry or his major investors did not care about were often neglected. He developed a reputation for milking his buildings.

Helmsley did build some new structures—the office building One

Penn Plaza, for example, and, later, a string of hotels—but he was not by nature a developer in the way that, say, Donald Trump is, arguably the successor to Helmsley's title as the great New York real estate *macher* of his time. Rather, Helmsley held on to what he bought, through the inevitable ups and downs of New York's real estate cycles. This was not because he loved the buildings for themselves—aesthetics did not matter to Harry Helmsley—but because he was conservative, and saw no need to tear down the old buildings that he owned. That was something developers did without a second thought during the Fifties and into the mid-Sixties, a time when many irreplaceable structures—among them Penn Station, built by the Fuller Company, and the Singer Building—were torn down, and replaced by buildings notable only for their blandness, in the so-called "international style." All in the name of progress, which in those heady post-war years, meant in effect wiping out the dirty old city.

"Having had so many occasions to mourn the loss of a precious local landmark, we take particular pleasure in writing about a landmark that was completed shortly after the turn of the nineteenth century and shows every sign of surviving the turn of the twentieth century," wrote *The New Yorker* in 1954. "We refer to that noble, if bizarre-looking, old pile of steel and stone known as the Flatiron Building, which still dominates the southern side of Madison Square."

When New York finally created a Landmarks Commission in 1965, one of its first acts was to confer that now-sacrosanct status on the Flatiron. During the years when the building was vulnerable, doubtless Helmsley's propensity to hold on to his properties saved it from the wrecking ball. That, and its strange location. Because what else could you build on a lot shaped like a stingy piece of pie, in the middle of an intersection?

Helmsley-Spear continued to manage the Flatiron until 1997. During those years, my family held on to my grandfather's piece of the building. The experience was a profoundly unhappy one. The building had an unusual and unwieldy ownership arrangement, a "tenancy-in-common," rather than a partnership, which is usual in a piece of commercial real estate. A tenancy-in-common in effect means that all the partners have to unanimously agree when anything has to be done. Why the attorney for the sale, who was also one of the other three investors, wrote the original agreement this way in 1946 is a puzzle. In any case it was a sure recipe for stasis. With all partners having equal veto power, repairs and improvements happened slowly, if at all. This was especially true after the building received landmark status, which makes any exterior improvement a hugely expensive nightmare of red tape for any landlord. From time to time, Flatiron Associates considered getting rid of the old hydraulic elevators—by the 1950s, they were already a relic—but decided not to, doubtless on the grounds that, seeing as the Flatiron was always fully rented, they had no incentive to incur the huge cost of replacing them.

When they first purchased the property in 1946, the owners did make a few cosmetic changes. They had the old-fashioned vaulted ceiling in the lobby "dropped," as 1950s style dictated, which took away the previous grandeur of the space. And in 1952, they got rid of both of the original entrances, one on the Fifth Avenue side, the other on Broadway, along with the mahogany panels that flanked them. (This was twelve years before the creation of the Landmarks Commission, which would never have approved the nondescript modern steel-and-glass revolving doors that were installed as replacements, and still exist today.)

After Helmsley moved his company's office uptown in the mid-Fifties, he ceased paying any attention to the Flatiron. To him it had become just one more old building in his huge empire, which by the early 1980s had expanded dramatically into the hotel business, and way beyond New York, to all over the country. The catalyst to Act Two of Helmsley's career was his wife, the brassy Leona Mindy Rosenbaum, later known as "the Queen of Mean," whom he married in 1972, after divorcing his wife of thirty-four years, the understated Eve

Sherpick Green. Leona transformed the up-to-then staid Harry Helmsley into a New York party animal. She also destroyed his relationships with his longtime business partners, and, along the way, his good name.

In the meantime, the clothing and toy manufacturing that had sustained the neighborhood was moving overseas, leaving empty the old industrial buildings that had housed them along the side streets west of Fifth Avenue. During the Sixties, photographers and the retail businesses that supplied their materials, attracted by the cheap rents, moved into the lofts, and the businesses that supplied them occupied the retail spaces. "The photo district," as people now called the area, was developing a distinctly gritty feel. In 1964, the traffic department proposed building a municipal parking garage under Madison Square Park that you would enter via a ramp. New Yorkers, having by then learned to organize against the piecemeal destruction of their city by private developers and Robert Moses's outsized urban renewal projects, said "no way." Community leaders pointed out that excavating beneath the park would cause damage to it, in particular to the trees, many of them dating back hundreds of years. Several years later, city officials abandoned the plan. Still, the area ended up with a whole lot of new parking spaces anyway, at the corner of Twenty-second and Broadway, right across from the Flatiron. This happened not by design, but as the result of tragedy: On an October night in 1966, a fire broke out in one of the three old low-rise buildings that stood on the site. Twelve fire fighters died extinguishing the blaze; afterward, the owners demolished the ruins and built a parking lot.

In the mid-Seventies, developers announced plans to replace the parking lot with an apartment tower. This seemed quite a daring move, coming in the middle of a worldwide economic recession, and one of the worst times ever in the annals of New York real estate. Companies were threatening to flee to New Jersey, hundreds of small landlords were abandoning their properties to the city, and people obsessed about crime. And yet, the real estate people were onto something: now, for the first time in a hundred years, the Flatiron area was attracting residential dwellers, of the urban pioneer sort, who were renting the old industrial lofts for a song. The downside was that there was not even a deli to buy a carton of milk. At night, the streets were deserted and dangerous. The brave souls who ventured out were often mugged. As for Madison Park, it was now the turf of drug dealers.

The apartment tower wasn't built until the early Eighties, a thirty-story-high affront to aesthetics, but with great views all around. Those lucky enough to have terraces facing west were eating dinner on summer evenings looking directly at the Flatiron.

By then, things were turning around.

Few of the companies that had threatened to leave New York during the Seventies actually did. And of those who did, some even came back. Location, businesses realized, mattered after all. New York had long ceased being a manufacturing center, but not of human capital, even in the worst of times. And to generate human capital, you still needed a place, with familiar, beloved spaces, that had associations, present and past, where you could have lunch, and schmooze.

New York real estate was beginning to recover. Apartment houses were turning co-op. And publishing companies were moving to the Flatiron area, where rents were far cheaper than their traditional midtown locations, and the architecture more interesting. St. Martin's Press, which had been renting an office in the Flatiron since 1969, began leasing more space, and then more. By the early Nineties, the company occupied half of the building.

In the meantime, the Flatiron Building manager, who was also a minority partner, unilaterally embarked upon the enormous and badly needed task of cleaning and restoring the exterior. For this he garnered praise all around, and why not? Fifty years had passed since the building was last cleaned. Graffiti marred the limestone base, and layers of soot obscured the beautiful terra-cotta. And New York was in the midst of a restoration craze. Was he not performing a public service, beautifying a landmark, at the owners' expense?

But there was a dark side. Doing business with contractors in New York offers fabulous opportunities for kickback. And the Flatiron project had zero oversight from the managing-agent, Helmsley-Spear. There, chaos reigned. Leona Helmsley was in jail for tax evasion, and Harry had Alzheimer's disease, which had saved him from being tried along with her in 1989. The result was a feeding frenzy at hundreds of properties that Helmsley-Spear oversaw.

The Flatiron, my family now discovered when we, suspicious, began investigating the restoration project, was one of the troughs.

In 1997, a group of partners—among them my family—representing 52 percent of the Flatiron sold its collective portion to a group of investors from the large real estate firm Newmark Knight-Frank. That same year, Harry Helmsley died. Leona, who inherited her husband's entire $5-billion estate—as his spouse, she paid no inheritance taxes—immediately began divesting herself of real estate holdings. One of the first properties she shed was the Flatiron.

By then, it seemed as if the value of New York real estate would never stop climbing. The Flatiron District, as brokers now called it, was no longer in transition, but glamorous. Newmark soon took over management of the Flatiron from the decaying firm of Helmsley-Spear, where Leona was now embroiled in a bitter fight with her late husband's longtime partners. The new owners were proud of their new icon. They jumped in, cleaned off the graffiti, and continued restoring the terra-cotta.

And, to the enormous relief of their tenants, Newmark replaced the old hydraulic elevators. Tenants today love telling their elevator-related war stories. Rob Renzler of Macmillan reminisced: "They felt like what I imagine a trans-Atlantic crossing in the bowels of a tramp steamer circa 1906 might have felt like, hot and heaving, with a hint of, 'will I make it to my destination alive.'" Sometimes a cab stopped between floors. But by the time you reached the top floors of the building, it might suddenly gain speed, and zoom up to the top of the shaft. Otherwise they were so slow. During busy times, you might wait twenty, thirty minutes to get on. Especially in the mornings, when sometimes the elevator lines snaked outside the Flatiron, and around the corner, to Twenty-third Street.

These scenarios are now memories. If nobody talks about them, they will disappear. That is, until somebody finds them again. Such as happened recently, in the basement, where, once upon a time, a restaurant served up ice cream sculpted in the shape of the Flatiron. There, workers accidentally came upon a staircase, long enclosed within a wall, and, until now, forgotten.

Today, the wind still picks up speed around the base of the Flatiron. But the taller structures that have gradually surrounded it have drasti-

The Flatiron Building, 2009.

cally reduced the impact. People don't get knocked off their feet any-more when they walk by the Flatiron on a windy day. Instead, perhaps napkins get blown off the tables where people now sit on the Broadway side when the weather is fine, enjoying their coffee in a space once filled with nothing but traffic.

On any day, dozens of people are standing in front of the Flatiron, admiring its gorgeously refurbished façade, complete with a newly sculpted angel on the roof, a replica of the original, which was, to the dismay of preservationists, inadvertently demolished during the 1990s' restoration. Some visitors are sitting at easels, painting or sketching its image, and others are taking pictures of it—with everything from cell-phones to cameras mounted on tripods. Across Broadway, in Madison Square Park, a jewel now restored to its former splendor, others sit on benches, and marvel at the fine view of the building. The Flatiron is a monument, which everybody, all over the world, recognizes.

As the photographer Alfred Stieglitz told his father more than one hundred years ago, what the Parthenon was to Athens, the Flatiron is to New York. And now, because it is an official landmark, it is pro-tected. It is here to stay.

NOTES

CHAPTER ONE: GEORGE ALLON FULLER

On George A. Fuller: Quote by Peabody in W. Cornell Appleton, Peabody's last chief designer, in a 1968 interview, in *Journal of the Society of Architectural Historians*, 32, no. 2, May 1973. Description of Fuller in A. Schwinfurth, *American Architect*, November 11, 1931. For Fuller's early buildings in New York: Robert Stern et al., *New York 1900* (New York: Rizzoli, 1995), 227 (Union League Club); *American Architect and Building News (AABN)*, April 26, 1879, and April 16, 1881; Stern et al., *New York 1900*, 227; New York City Landmark Designation Report, Fuller Building. On the United Bank Building: Moses King, *King's Handbook of New York City, 1892* (Boston: Moses King, publisher), 673.

On cast-iron fronts and early skyscrapers: Sarah Bradford Landau and Carl W. Condit, *Rise of the New York Skyscraper* (New Haven, CT: Yale University Press, 1996), 77–79, 87, 197; *A History of Real Estate Building, and Architecture, in New York*, by the editors of the *Real Estate Record and Builders Guide (RERAG)*, 1898; Condit, *American Building*, 1968, 77ff.; *Phrenological Journal and Science of Health*, 1874.

The Brooklyn Bridge: Ric Burns et al., *New York: An Illustrated History* (New York: Knopf, 1999), 170; David McCullough, *The Great Bridge* (New York: Simon & Schuster, 2001); passim *New York Times*, September 11, 1877; the *Phrenological Journal*, August 8, 1883; *Appleton's Journal*, January 1878; Edward Godfrey, *Steel Designing* (Chicago: Robert W. Hunt 1913), 30–32.

Quotes by Louis Sullivan from his 1924 book, *The Autobiography of an Idea*, American Institute of Architects, 1924, reprint (New York: Dover, 1956), 200.

Chicago had far fewer building regulations, etc.: RERAG, *A History of Real Estate*.

There Jenney had trained, etc.: Carl Condit, *The Chicago School of Architecture* (Chicago: The University of Chicago, 1964), 116.

Architectural firms handled every aspect, etc.: New York City Landmarks Designation Report (NYCLDR) for the Potter Building; *Architectural Forum*, April 1961, 112; Corydon Purdy, "The Relation of the Engineer to the Architect," *AABN*, February 11, 1905, 43.

The facts about the Fuller Company and construction in Chicago: Carl Condit, *Chicago School*, 51, 60; NYCLDR for the Fuller Building; *Chicago Tribune*, May 26, 1891, June 25, 1891; Donald Miller, *City of the Century* (New York: Simon & Schuster, 1996), 345; *Atlanta Constitution*, February 6, 1891.

"Some as high as sixteen stories, etc": Henry Ericsson, *Sixty Years a Builder* (Chicago: A. Kroch & Son, 1942), 106. On the new "Chicago style" architecture, see Thomas E. Tallmadge, *The Origin of the Skyscraper* (Chicago: Alderbrink Press), 1939 (he connects it to the "Romanesque revival" that started with Richardson's Trinity Church in Boston).

". . . sixteen stories . . . the world record for building height": *Building and Engineering Journal* (London), December 11, 1891.

For New York's revised building code and curtain walls, see Donald Friedman, *Historical Building Construction*, 115; William Birkmire, *Skeleton Construction in Buildings* (New York: J. Wiley, 1893); Thomas Misa, *A Nation of Steel* (Baltimore: Johns Hopkins University Press, 1995), 68–69; Landau and Condit, *The Rise of the New York Skyscraper*, 173.

CHAPTER TWO: ENO'S FLATIRON

On Beaux-Arts, see David Lowe, *Beaux Arts New York* (New York: Whitney Library of Design, 1998). (On the Statue of Liberty, see p. 23.)

The quote about Chicago as a "purposeless Hell" is from *RERAG*, October 8, 1892. Facts about the 1893 Exposition from Donald Miller, *City of the Century*, 381; Richard Plunz, *A History of Housing in New York City* (New York: Columbia University Press, 1990), 39–40; *Chicago Tribune*, March 20, 1891; *AAABN*, October 14, 1893. Edith Wharton's description of the Fifth Avenue Hotel in her story "New Year's Day," in *Old New York: Four Novellas* (New York: Scribner, 1924), 240.

Description of Madison Square Garden: *New York Times*, May 27, 1892, May 18, 1892; Miriam Berman, *Madison Square* (Salt Lake City: Gibbs Smith, 2001), 73–78.

Detail about the magic lantern show from the *Chicago Tribune*, February 6, 1876. Facts about Amos Eno and his family from his obituary, *New York Times*, January 3, 1914, and other newspaper articles. On the elevator at his Fifth Avenue Hotel: *New York Times*, January 23, 1860, cited in Landau and Condit, *Rise of the New York Skyscraper*. The construction date (1855) for the old St. Germain Hotel, which Eno demolished to build the Cumberland, is mentioned in Frederick S. Lightfoot, editor, *Nineteenth Century New York in Rare Photographic Views* (New York: Dover Books, 1981). For the construction date of the Cumberland: Lightfoot, and *New York Herald*, June 2, 1901.

The Newhouses announced, etc.: *New York Times*, November 27, 1900; March 3, 1901; March 30, 1901; *RERAG*, December 14, 1901. For the sale of the Flatiron to the city: Eugene Rachlis and John Marquese, *The Landlords* (New York: Random House, 1963). George A. Fuller's obituary, *New York Times*, December 15, 1900.

Fuller Company construction projects: *New York Times*, March 30, 1901; December 16, 1900; *Chicago Tribune*, August 26, 1900. Details about Harry and Allon Black: *Chicago Tribune*, October 14 and 21, 1894; *World*, October 30, 1901.

". . . so rapidly that the existing structures were deemed worthless . . .": Landau and Condit, 236 ff.

"... the most densely populated area on earth": Plunz, *A History of Housing in New York City*, 37.

"the Ghetto": *RERAG*, December 15, 1900.

On the 1901 Tenement law: *Chicago Tribune*, May 23, 1901; Plunz, *A History of Housing in New York City*, 47–48.

Sale of the flatiron to Cumberland: *RERAG*, December 14, 1901; *Times*, May 10, 1901.

On retail's uptown movement: M. Christine Boyer, *Manhattan Manners Architecture and Style, 1850–1900* (New York: Rizzoli, 1985), and Robert Stern et al., *New York 1900* (New York: Rizzoli, 1995).

CHAPTER THREE: CHICAGO'S GIFT

The plan of Washington, D.C.: Charles Moore, *Daniel H. Burnham*, reprint of 1921 edition New York: Houghton-Mifflin, 132ff; Thomas S. Hines, *Burnham of Chicago* (Chicago: University of Chicago Press, 1974).

Facts about Burnham: Letters and diaries in Burnham Papers, Chicago Art Institute Library; Paul Starrett, *Changing the Skyline* (New York: McGraw-Hill, 1938); Hines, *Burnham of Chicago*, 21, 234, 236, 254; Moore, *Daniel H. Burnham*, 200; *Times*, March 26, 1893 (description of his fete at Madison Square Garden).

The Sun quote: Reprinted in the *Hartford Courant*, October 31, 1901.

On Frick and Black: Hines, *Burnham of Chicago*, 301.

The original Flatiron blueprint, according to John Zukowsky and Pauline Saliga, "Late Works by Burnham and Sullivan," in the *Art Institute of Chicago Bulletin* (Fall 1984), was filed with the New York City Buildings Department. It is no longer there.

On Atwood: Moore, *Daniel H. Burnham*, 85; Daniel Burnham, interview with Charles Moore, Burnham Papers.

On Dinkelberg: *Chicago Architectural Journal*, 1985; obituary, *Chicago Tribune*, February 11, 1935; September 12, *AABN*, 1891.

"... Burnham had spent most nights in a shanty. ...": Moore interview, Burnham papers.

"Black accepted Burnham's gridiron design": Burnham's daybook, March 5 and 6, 1901, Burnham papers.

Facts and figures about office buildings in 1901: Landau and Condit, *The Rise of the New York Skyscraper*, 252, 280, 430–1.

On Thompson-Starrett: Starrett, *Changing the Skyline*, 86; *Wall Street Journal*, November 20, 1903.

Quote by Burnham: Cited in Starrett's obituary, *New York Times*, July 6, 1957.

Facts about the Flatiron construction: *AABN*, August 1902.

On Sam Parks: Jim Rasenberger, *High Steel: The Daring Men Who Built the World's Greatest Skyline* (New York: HarperCollins, 2004), 50, 86ff; Franklin Clarkin, "The Life of the Walking Delegate," *Century Magazine*, December 1903; Cromwell Childe, "The Structural Workers," *Frank Leslie's Popular Monthly*, July 1901.

Colonel Proskey: *New York Times*, May 17, 1929, and June 6, 1901; *Chicago Tribune*, May 19 and 27, 1901.

". . . at Coney Island beach.": *Los Angeles Times*, July 21, 1901.

CHAPTER FOUR: PREPARING TO BUILD

Description of construction on Broadway and Herald Square: *Brooklyn Eagle*, September 21, 1902.

Description of Broadway: *World's Work*, November 1901; *Brooklyn Eagle*, June 2, 1901.

Purchase of the block south of the Macy's site: *Brooklyn Eagle*, June 2, 1901.

Descriptions of New York in the summer: *Century* magazine, August 1901; *New York Times*, July 4, 1901; *Los Angeles Times*, July 2, 1901; *The Sun*, July 2, 1901.

For the Spate chair story: *New York Times*, *The Sun*, *Brooklyn Eagle*, *New York Tribune*, *New York Evening Journal*, *New York Morning Journal*, and *Washington Post*. For Oscar Spate in Pittsburgh: *New York Times*, December 12, 1907.

Facts about the Flatiron construction: The Flatiron Building docket in the New York City Municipal Archives (contains the original building application); letters from Daniel Burnham to Harry Black, Corydon Purdy, in Burnham Papers, Art Institute of Chicago; *America at Work* by John Foster Fraser (London: Cassell & Company, 1903); *Engineering Record*, March 29, 1902; *AABN*, August 1902; *RERAG*, June 7, 1902; *Construction of the Modern Skyscraper* by Thomas Nolan, in *University of Pennsylvania Public Lectures*, vol. 3, 1913. On the fire code: *New York Times*, September 7 1899, *RERAG*, *A History of Real Estate in New York, 1893*, and *1898*. On terra-cotta: Susan Tunick, *Terra-Cotta Skyline* (Princeton, NJ: Princeton Architectural Press, 1997); letters from Daniel Burnham to the Fuller Company, Burnham papers; *The Staten Island Historian*, April–June 1974; folder on Atlantic Terra Cotta at the Staten Island Historical Society, Tottenville; *New York Times*, April 28, 1912, Dec. 9, 1906; *Brooklyn Eagle*, January 17, 1897; Walter Greer, *Terra Cotta in Architecture* (New York: Gaylay Co., 1891); Heinrich Ries and Henry Leighton, *The History of the Clay-Working Industry in the United States* (New York: John Wiley & Sons), 1909.

Harry Black's auto racing in Saratoga: *The Sun.*

The facts about Starrett, Macy's, and Starrett's relationship with Black: Starrett, *Changing the Skyline.*

On excavation of skyscraper foundations: Landau and Condit, *Rise of the New York Skyscraper*, 24–25; Condit, review of *Why Buildings Stand Up*, October 1981; Federal Writers Project, *New York Panorama.*

Details about the McKinley assassination: From the *New York Times*, September 7–14, 1901.

CHAPTER FIVE: BIGGER AND BIGGER

"He told an American reporter . . .": *Bridgemen's*, November 1901.

Allon's pearl necklace: *The Sun.* October 30, 1901; *World*, October 29 and 30, 1901.

On Paris: *RERAG*, April 19, 1902; June 3, 1904 (Ritz).

On Broadway-Chambers model: *Scientific American,* May 12, and October 13, 1900.

Information about the Flatiron excavation from *AABN,* August 1902, *RERAG,* August 17, 1902 (about the subway line), and conversations with engineer Stephen Cohan. Information about building activity during 1901: *Bridgemen's,* December 1901 (Fuller projects), *New York Times,* August 11, 1901. About men working overtime: *Bridgemen's,* July 1902.

On the Thompson-Starrett building on William Street: *New York Times,* April 29, 1902.

Information about the ironworkers and Sam Parks: "The Structural Workers," by Cromwell Child, in *Frank Leslie's,* July 1901; *Century,* December 1903, *Bridgemen's,* December 1901, February and July 1902, "The Walking Delegate: the Trust's New Tool" by Ray Stannard Baker in *McClure's,* November 1903; *Brooklyn Eagle,* May 2, 1902; *New York Tribune,* June 9, 1903; *The Sun,* June 10, 1903; *New York Times,* September 6, 1903; Jim Rasenberger, *High Steel* (New York, HarperCollins, 2004).

Details about the Flatiron construction: *Frank Leslie's,* July 1901; *Engineering Record,* March 29, 1902, Vol. 45, no. 3; *Bridgemen's,* December 1901, February 1902; *RERAG,* June 7, 1902, "Cowboys of the Skies," by Ernest Poole, in *Everyman's Magazine,* November 1908, *Times,* October 18, 1903; *Tribune,* June 29, 1902.

Details about the February 1902 blizzard from the *New York Times,* February 18, 1902.

For J. P. Morgan and Theodore Roosevelt, see Joseph Bucklin Bishop, ed., *Theodore Roosevelt and His Time: Shown in His Own Letters* (New York, Scribner's, 1920). On Fuller Company stocks, see also *RERAG,* April 26, 1902.

A list of all the vehicles that crossed Herald Square appears in a letter to the editor of the *New York Times,* November 8, 1903.

Other descriptions of reactions to the Flatiron as it was being built are in the *Boston Globe,* July 13, 1902, and the *New York Tribune,* June 29, 1902.

On the Flatiron extension: New York City Archives, Flatiron docket, amendment to building application, dated June 18, 1902. "A typical Burnham, etc".: See Royal Cortissof, "An American Architect," *The Outlook*, July 27, 1907. The letter from DHB to HSB, dated May 2, 1902, is in the Burnham collection.

CHAPTER SIX: THE SKYSCRAPER TRUST

On Saratoga in the summer: *Philadelphia Inquirer*, August 18, 1902.

Description of summer in New York: Mrs. Schuyler Van Rensselaer, "Midsummer in New York," *Century*, August 1901; *New York Times*, July 31, 1902.

On New Jersey and its incorporation laws: John Micklethwait and Adrian Wooldridge, *The Company, A Short History of a Revolutionary Idea* (New York: Modern Library, 2003).

On U.S. Realty: *Times*, August 1, 1902; Arthur Dewing, "Corporate Promotions and Reorganizations," *Harvard Economic Studies*, vol. 10, 1914, in which he quotes *Commercial and Financial Chronicle*, 15, 294. Quote by Harry Black on p. 4 reprinted in John Moody, *The Truth About Trusts* (New York: Moody Publications, 1904). On real estate speculation at the time: *New York Times*, February 7, 1904; *RERAG*, January 4 and March 15, 1902, October 8, 1904, and July 20, 1901. On Black's not being elected president of his own company: *Wall Street Journal*, August 5, 1902.

On "Bet-a-Million" Gates and Saratoga: *Philadelphia Inquirer*, July 30, August 18, 1902; *Cosmopolitan Magazine*, September 1902: Robert Irving Warshow, *Bet-A-Million* (New York: Greenberg, 1932); Lloyd Wendt and Herman Kogan, *Bet-A-Million! The Story of John W. Gates* (Indianapolis: Bobbs-Merrill, 1948). Starrett, *Changing the Skyline: New York Times*, May 5, 1907, Hugh Brady, *Such Was Saratoga* (New York: Doubleday, 1940).

On Grand Duke Boris: *New York Times, Tribune*, August 30, 1902.

On trains at Grand Central at the end of August: *New York Times*, August 31, 1902.

On the critics' reaction to the Flatiron: Partridge's quote cited in the *New Yorker*, August 12, 1939. On Montgomery Schuyler: William Thorn, *Montgomery Schuyler*, dissertation, University of Minnesota, 1976. *Evening Post* quotation is from *RERAG*, March 15, 1902.

CHAPTER SEVEN: THE FLATIRON OPENS FOR BUSINESS

On the first moving pictures: James Sanders, *Celluloid Skyline* (New York: Alfred A. Knopf, 2003); James Sanders and Ric Burns, *New York: An Illustrated History* (New York: Alfred A. Knopf, 1999); Library of Congress, site on Thomas Edison, and Rutgers University, Edison Papers; *New York Times*, April 25, 1926; *Everybody's Magazine,* cited in the *Washington Post,* April 29, 1900; *New York Times,* July 28, 1901. On the use of the word "movies": Irving Lewis Allen, *The City in Slang* (New York: Oxford University Press, 1993) (according to Lewis, the term was in use by 1906); *New York Times,* April 25, 1926. Description of the movies at Coney Island: *Tribune,* August 18, 1901. On the cost of each kinetoscope machine: Andre Millard, *Edison and the Business of Innovation* (Baltimore: Johns Hopkins University Press, 1990); Paul Spehr, "Unaltered to Date: Developing 35mm Film," in John Fullerton and Astrid Söderburg Widding, editors, *Moving Images: From Edison to Webcam* (New Barnet, U.K., John Libbey & Co., 2000).

On Frank Munsey: *New Yorker,* August 12, 1939; George Britt, *Forty Years, Forty Millions: The Career of Frank Munsey* (New York, Farrar & Rinehart, 1935); "Mr. Frank A. Munsey, Author and Publisher," *Town and Country,* September 8, 1906; Frank Luther Mott, *History of American Magazines* (Cambridge, MA: Harvard University Press, 1938), 611.

On sheet music: Nancy Groce, *New York: Songs of the City* (New York: Watson-Guptill, 2003).

Information about Flatiron tenants: *New York Times,* March 31, 1904; *World,* March 30, 1904; *Tribune,* September 12, 1904, July 12, 1908, June 8, 1902; Joseph Oliver Dahl, *Selling Public Hospitality* (New York: Harper & Brothers, 1929); *The Sun,* May 21, 1903; Sara Wermiel, *The Fireproof Building* (Baltimore: Johns Hopkins University Press, 2000).

On Macy's move uptown: *New York Times,* November 2, 1902.

On the old Trinity Building: *New York Times,* November 23, 1902; John Taurenac, *Elegant New York* (New York: Abbeville Press, 1985).

Description of Croker and the Flatiron standpipe test: *New York Times,* November 17, 1902.

CHAPTER EIGHT: 23 SKIDDOO

On the Flatiron winds: *Chicago Tribune,* November 29, 1902; *Washington Post,* January 30, 1903; *World,* March 12, 1903; *Tribune,* January 23, 1903, *Sun,* December 27, 1903; *New York Times,* February 6, 1903; *Fort Worth Telegram,* May 20, 1904.

The quotes by Stieglitz are in Dorothy Norman, *Alfred Stieglitz: An American Seer* (New York: Random House, 1973), 45.

The quote comparing the Flatiron to a wedge of strawberry shortcake is from the *New York Times,* July 10, 1902. Same date for the other *Times* quotes. The quote from *RERAG* appeared September 6, 1902.

CHAPTER NINE: WATER AND WIND

On Thompson-Starrett: *New York Times,* January 2, January 4, 1903; *Wall Street Journal,* November 20, 1903; Starrett, *Changing the Skyline.*

On Sam Parks and William Travers Jerome: *New York Times,* April 8, 1903; *Tribune,* June 9, 1903; *Harper's,* October 17, 1903, January 23, 1904. Rasenberger, *High Steel.*

On U.S. Realty's problems and Black's machinations: *New York Times,* October 23, 1903; Dewing; Starrett; *Tribune,* January 15, 1904.

CHAPTER TEN: ALLON

The details about Harry Black's indiscretions are recorded in the divorce papers filed by Allon's lawyers in April 1905, in the Westchester County Supreme Court. Other sources documenting their divorce: *World,* March 24, 1905.

On the goings-on at U.S. Realty and Starrett's attempted departure: *New York Times,* March 19, 1905; Starrett, *Changing the Skyline,* 124–130; *RERAG,* April 30, 1904.

On Thompson and Dundy, and the Hippodrome: Starrett, *Changing the Skyline*; William Wood Register Jr., "New York's Gigantic Toy," in William Taylor, editor, *Inventing Times Square* (Baltimore: Johns Hopkins Press, 1996); *New York Times*, July 3, 1904; *Herald*, January 1, 1905; "Frederick Thompson's Tribute to Toys," in *Playthings*, July 7, 1909 (cited in Taylor).

CHAPTER ELEVEN: UPTOWN

On the New York Times Building: *New York Times*, January 1, 1905; January 2008 conversation with Corydon Purdy III, grandson of the engineer.

On the Carlton group: *Town and Country*, August 9, 1911.

On Tessie Oelrichs: Eric Homberger, *Mrs. Astor's New York* (New Haven, CT: Yale University Press, 2002); Michael Strange, *Who Tells Me True* (New York: Scribner's, 1940); *Times*, September 8, 1905, March 4, 1907; *Chicago Tribune*, August 1, 1915; obituary, *New York Times*, *Atlanta Constitution*, November 23, 24, 1926; *Town and Country*, January 19, 1907.

On the 1907 panic: Ron Chernow, *The House of Morgan* (New York: Simon & Schuster, 1991); Edmund Morris, *Theodore Rex* (New York: Random House, 2001); Jean Strouse, *Morgan: American Financier* (New York: Random House, 1999) The anecdote about Harry Black's dividend initiative is from the *Wall Street Journal*, July 23, 1930.

On the Plaza: *New York Times*, September 29, 1907; *Tribune*, October 7, 1907. On Fuller Chenery's toy car: *Los Angeles Times*, December 29, 1907. The story about Gates and the horseshoe is from the *World*, October 1, 1907.

On the Broadway-Chambers Building: Gail Fenske, *The Skyscraper and the City* (Chicago: University of Chicago Press, 2008), 101–105.

On the Woolworth Building: Fenske; Cass Gilbert papers, New York Historical Society, Box 528, Folder 1 (letter to F. W. Woolworth from Paul Starrett). Cass Gilbert papers, Library of Congress, Box 17, "An experience," by Julia Finch Gilbert (a description of her encounter with Harry Black in Palm Beach, March 1911).

Notes

On overbuilding: *RERAG*, July 29, 1911; Fenske, *The Skyscraper and the City*, 224; *New York Times*, June 25, 1911.

On Black in Europe: *Wall Street Journal*, September 3, 1910.

CHAPTER TWELVE: SUR LE FLAT-IRON

On Gates's death and funeral: *New York Times*, August 23, 1911; *Wall Street Journal*, September 1, 1911, and July 23, 1930.

On the Bustanoby brothers and the Taverne Louis: *New York Times*, January 30, 1912, and February 21, 1912. On Bustanobys: *New Yorker*, October 19, 1935, in an article *"Music with Meals."* Jacques's obituary in *The American Weekly*, May 10, 1942, and the *New York Times*, March 24, 1942, and the *New York Mirror*, May 10, 1942. The Café des Beaux-Arts: Mic Batterberry, *On the Town in New York* (New York: Taylor & Francis, 1998); *New York Times*, October 12, 1913. On the Flatiron as a gay cruising spot: Joseph Noel, *Footloose in Arcadia* (New York: Carrick & Evans, 1940). (Noel was a journalist, and friend to Jack London; his book describes their meanderings together through New York in 1912.)

On Louis Mitchell: Obituary, *The Evening Star* (Washington D.C.) September 12, 1957; *Washington Post and Amsterdam News*, September 13, 1957; Robert Goffin, *Nouvelle Histoire du Jazz, du Congo au Bebop* (Brussels: L'Écran du Monde, 1948); Library of Congress, Kendrick-Brooks family papers, Boxes 22-26, papers of Antoinette Brooks Mitchell, which contain newspaper clips, photos, letters, and various other memorabilia.

On James Reese Europe: Bill Harris, *The Hellfighters of Harlem* (New York: Carroll & Graf, 2002).

On Allon's dogs: *Desert Evening News* (Salt Lake City), July 16, 1910. On her death: *Town Topics* and *Boston Globe*, October 12 and 19, 1915; *New York Times* and *Washington Post*, October 15, 1915. On Chenery's lawsuit: *Boston Globe*, November 12, 1915; *Times*, December 9, 1915.

"Wake Up, America" parade: *New York Times*, April 20, 1917. Liberty bonds: *New Yorker*, August 12, 1939.

On Fuller's tour in Europe: Frank Palmer Sibley, *With the Yankee Division in France* (Boston: Little, Brown, 1919); yearbook from his prep school; obituary, *New York Times*, September 9, 1931.

Gleizes: the anecdote about the Harlem nightclub is recounted in Christien Briend, *Le Cubisme en Majeste* (Lyon: Musée des Beaux-Arts, 2001).

CHAPTER THIRTEEN: THE BIG LANDLORD

Harry Black's bootlegging: *Tribune*, March 21, 1921; *Miami Herald*, March 25, May 5, and June 4, 1921; *New York Times*, March 18, 21, 24, 25, and June 4, 1921.

On the 1916 zoning law: *Tribune*, December 28, 1919.

On the old Savoy Hotel: Moses King, *King's Handbook of New York City*, 1892.

On Harry's marriage to Isabelle May: *New York Times*, *Washington Post*, and *Town Topics*, March 22 and 30, 1922.

Harry Black's acquisition of Gates's shares: *Wall Street Journal*, November 26, 1924. Black's dealings with DuPont: *New York Times*, May 25, 1925. His purchase of the Savoy: *New York Times*, May 4, 1924.

Sale of the Flatiron: *New York Times*, March 11, 1925; *New Yorker*, November 13, 1954; August 12, 1939. On Lewis Rosenbaum: Obituary, *New York Times*, January 10, 1956.

On the Floranada: Cass Gilbert papers, New York Historical Society, Box 113, Folders 3, 6; *New York Times*, December 12, 1925; June 5 and September 22, 1926.

The Savoy-Plaza's opening: *New York Times*, March 21, 1926.

On the Fuller Building: *New York Times*, December 2, 1928; New York City Landmarks Report. My discussion of modernism is partly based on a series of lectures by Carol Willis, director, Skyscraper Museum, New York, November 2007–January 2008.

Black's 1929 stock plan: *New York Times*, February 6 and March 3, 1929.

Black's suicide attempt at the Plaza: *New York Times*, October 20, 1929.

Black's suicide on Long Island: *Herald Tribune, Times, Long Islander*, and *Atlanta Constitution*, July 20, 1930.

EPILOGUE

On Harry Black's estate: *New York Times*, July 8, 1931.

On Tyler Morse's death: *New York Times*, October 10, 1933.

On George Fuller's (formerly Fuller Chenery) death and will: *New York Times*, September 9 and 10, 1931; November 29, 1932.

On Frederick Dinkelberg's death: *Chicago Tribune*, February 11 and 14, 1935. The facts about Corydon Purdy's later years were told to me by his grandson, Corydon Purdy III, in 2008.

On Frank Munsey's death and estate: *New York Times*, December 23, 24, and 26, 1925; February 21 and May 23, 1927.

On Louis Mitchell in Paris: articles in the *Amsterdam News*, 1930–1940; Goffin, *Nouvelle Histoire du Jazz*: Library of Congress, Kendrick-Brooks family papers, Boxes 22–26, papers of Antoinette Brooks Mitchell, which contain newspaper clips (including Mitchell's obituary: *The Evening Star*, Washington, D.C., September 12, 1957, and a story in the *Paris Times*, February 18, 1927, about Mitchell's "Quick Lunch" in Montmartre); photos, letters, and various other memorabilia.

David Kyle shared his recollections of the *Hindenburg* with me during a telephone conversation in June 2009.

Sale of the Flatiron in 1933: *New York Times*, March 2, June 25, July 1, and 2, 1933. Sale in 1945: *New York Times*, October 26, 1945. On modernization during the 1940s: *New York Times*, May 4, 1941; in 1953, *New York Times*, May 24.

On the proposed parking garage under Madison Square: "The Case for Madison Square," in *The Green*, a newsletter published by the Madison Square Park Association, February 1964.

INDEX

Index

Index

Index

Index

Index

Volstead Act, 240
von Bulow, Claus and Sonny, 250n

Waldorf Hotel (NYC), 18
Waldorf-Astoria Hotel (NYC), 55, 106, 118,
   208–13, 209
Walker, A. Stewart, 250
Walker and Gillette, 250
Wall Street Journal, 103–4, 170, 249, 254
Wallace, James G., 80
Walter, Herbert, 152–53
Walters, William, 94
Wanamaker's department store (NYC), 72,
   227
Washington D.C. renewal, 43–45
Washington Post, 151–52, 242
Weisz, Andor, *xix*
Wendell, George, 58
Western Specialty Manufacturing Company,
   139

Western Union Building (NYC), 2–3
Wharton, Edith, 23, 24
White, Stanford, 5, 18, 19, 23, 97, 104, 199,
   206, 222, 222n, 244, 248
White, Elizabeth, 152
White City. *See* Columbian Exposition
Whitehead & Hoag Company, 141, 146
Wiles, F. E., 202
Willard Hotel (Washington, D.C.), 36, 54,
   209
Wilson, Harry, 204
Wilson's drugstore (NYC), 63
Woolrich, Cornell, 261
Woolworth, Frank, 214–16
Woolworth Building (NYC), 214–16
World War I, 227–29, 229–30, 231–34, 234–35
   propaganda campaign, 232
World's Work publication, 62

Young Men's Christian Association, 28

298